Knight
before the game
1992–1993

Arthur A. Angotti

Knight
Before The Game
1992–1993

Library of Congress Cataloging in Publication Data
2003113455
Angotti, Arthur
Knight Before the Game 1992–1993
1. Knight, Robert Montgomery   2. Basketball—United States—History

ISBN 0-9746376-0-2

Printed in the United States of America

First Edition

To the memory of Judy Rogers.

CONTENTS

Author's Note	*ix*
Acknowledgments	*xi*
Introduction	*xv*

I. Preseason NIT — *1*

"How much better mentally are we going to be?"

Murray State	*3*
Tulane	*7*
At Florida State	*10*
At Seton Hall	*14*
Talk Show—November 30	*18*

II. The December Schedule — *23*

". . . not a particularly good non-conference season."

Kansas	*25*
Talk Show—December 7	*30*
At Notre Dame	*36*
Austin Peay	*39*
Western Michigan	*43*
Talk Show—December 14	*46*
Cincinnati	*53*
Talk Show—December 21	*57*
St. John's	*65*
Butler	*68*
At Colorado	*72*
At Kentucky	*76*
Talk Show—January 4	*80*

III. Big Ten—First Encounters

"We've got to win this game defensively."

III. **Big Ten—First Encounters** 85

Iowa 87
Penn State 92
Talk Show—January 11 96
At Michigan 104
At Illinois 108
Talk Show—January 18 112
At Purdue 121
Ohio State 126
Talk Show—January 25 130
Minnesota 137
At Northwestern 141

IV. **Ivan Renko** 145

IV. Ivan Renko

". . . a real counter to the idea of only 13 scholarships."

Talk Show—February 1 147

V. **Big Ten—Rematch Games** 155

V. Big Ten—Rematch Games

"Exercise patience."

At Iowa 157
Talk Show—February 8 161
At Penn State 170
Michigan 175
Talk Show—February 15 179
Illinois 187
Purdue 191
Talk Show—February 22 195
At Ohio State 202
At Minnesota 207
Talk Show—March 1 211
Northwestern 220
Talk Show—March 8 225

VI. A Big Ten Championship for Senior Night   *233*

"Our first objective is always to win the Big Ten."

Michigan State   *235*
At Wisconsin   *240*
Talk Show—March 15   *245*

VII. NCAA Tournament   *253*

"Victory favors the team making the fewest mistakes."

Wright State   *255*
    1st Round
Xavier   *260*
    2nd Round
Louisville   *264*
    Midwest Regional
Kansas   *268*
    Regional Championship

VIII. Season Recap   *273*

"A singularly unique season."

IX. After Indiana Basketball   *279*

"The most important thing. . . ."

X. The Bob Knight Record   *283*

"Basketball is my business."

About the Author   *287*

AUTHOR'S NOTE

During the summer of 1992, I assumed the contract for the Indiana University sports radio broadcasts on behalf of University Sports Radio Network, Inc. I immediately contracted directly with Coach Knight for the rights to his radio programs, the *"Bob Knight Pre-game Show"* and the *"Bob Knight Talk Show"* because they were not part of the University's contract.

Much to my surprise, Coach Knight's earlier broadcasts had not been archived. I began to tape the programs and later had them transcribed. My hearing was damaged while I was in Vietnam, and I could not follow the content from the tapes.

The material that Bob Knight covered in the programs was interesting, informative and entertaining. I knew that Coach Knight was a very successful basketball coach, but I had no idea how carefully he analyzed each opponent and how interesting his views were on basketball in general. This was Bob Knight in his own words, and the material was excellent.

The *"Pre-game Show"* was recorded before each Indiana basketball game, usually after Coach Knight completed his "walk through" which was the team's final preparation for a game. The pre-game interviews were often conducted at courtside when Indiana played at home or at the team hotel when Indiana was on the road. These pre-game interviews included an analysis of the team Indiana faced that day, an overview of Indiana's previous game and areas of special interest to Coach Knight. The interview was then broadcast immediately prior to each game.

The *"Bob Knight Talk Show,"* which was broadcast on Monday evenings during the regular season, was originated live from Coach Knight's private locker room when he was in Bloomington. The shows were prerecorded if the team was traveling. In the weekly talk show, Coach Knight answered questions from Don Fischer and IU fans, and covered in more depth issues that were of interest to him.

This book contains excerpts from both programs, 50 broadcasts in all. Some of what was said on one program was repeated on the next show, and I have edited the transcripts to avoid unnecessary repetition and remove inconsistencies in the use of present and past tense.

Bob Knight's inflections, sentence structuring and pacing add meaning to his words. Some people refer to it as "Knight speak" and it is an important part of what makes him an excellent communicator. Occasionally, "Knight speak" in writing carries a different meaning than it does in audio. In some instances, I made grammatical and structuring changes to improve the clarity of Coach Knight's comments. When necessary, assumptions were made to preserve the consistency of Coach Knight's comments or to insert words that were lost in the recording.

ACKNOWLEDGEMENTS

Among the many people responsible for this publication, I am especially grateful to Judy Rogers. Judy recorded and transcribed every *"Bob Knight Pre-game Show"* and *"Bob Knight Talk Show"* for eight years. Without her commitment to this project and her skill at deciphering the sometimes blurred tapes of the interviews, this unique history of Indiana basketball and Coach Bob Knight would not be possible.

Don Fischer conducted the interviews of Coach Knight and provided information for the game summaries. Don is the consummate broadcast professional and one of the most dedicated men I have had the honor to work with. His knowledge of basketball and understanding of Coach Knight kept the interviews interesting and focused. Don knew how to press a question and when to give Knight some leeway.

I would like to thank Board member and longtime friend Judith Hamilton for her assistance in printing and publishing this book. Her ideas, energy, support and encouragement have been vital in bringing this book to life.

Joseph Angotti assisted with the early drafting of the manuscript in 1993. What is notable about his introduction is that it was written ten years ago, and it has endured without requiring change. Joe has been an inspiring brother in many ways, and I gained a better appreciation for his journalistic brilliance while working with him on this book.

Many associates at Artistic Media Partners have assisted in the research, preparation and editing of this book. I want to thank Stephanie Schmitz, Carol Hume and Jeremy Gray who were especially helpful in gathering information. I also want to thank the Artistic Media Partners Board of Directors for allowing this book to be published.

The assistance of RR Donnelley and Sons Company has been invaluable. The professional and courteous support of the Donnelley organization goes far beyond printing. My thanks to the staff in Chicago, Allentown, Elgin and Crawfordsville who helped with the design, layout, artwork and printing for this book.

The Media Relations office of the Indiana University Athletic Department has been particularly helpful in gathering box scores, player information and basketball records. I have worked with Jeff Fanter and his associates for many years; however I have not appreciated the complexity and the historical importance of their job until working on this book.

Basketball at Indiana University has a long and proud history. This book is about one season, yet the Indiana tradition has grown from the dedication of players, coaches, administrators and staff over many seasons. My thanks to all of them for making Indiana athletics all that it is and all that it has meant to the Angotti family for the past 60 years.

I would be remiss if I did not acknowledge the central role Bob Knight plays in this book. His primary contributions as coach and narrator are evident; however there were other areas that were equally important to the success of the radio broadcasts. Bob runs his basketball operation the same way a chief executive runs a corporation. It is organized, efficient and businesslike. The proficiency of his approach to basketball carries over to his business interests, and he is a very good businessman. That made it easier for me to work into his operation when I assumed the contract for these broadcasts in 1992. Bob's cooperation was crucial, and we worked through the wrinkles of his previous contract and negotiated a new agreement without much time to get ready for the season. He cooperated with the new broadcast technology we used and did a nice job of bringing his sense of humor into the interviews. Bob, thank you for a very good basketball season. Thank you also for the informative and entertaining radio broadcasts. They are interesting and enjoyable today just as they were ten years ago.

Finally, I want to thank the student athletes of the 1992–93 Indiana University basketball team. The players are listed on the following page. I did not understand the demands of a grueling 35-game schedule or the incessant challenges of competing for a Big Ten Championship until undertaking this project. Thank you for giving me and IU fans everywhere a season we can all remember. Your outstanding performance provided the story line of this book and the drama of the exciting 1992–93 season.

1992–1993 Indiana Basketball Team

No.	Player	Pos.	Ht.	Wt.	Yr/Elig	Hometown
22	Damon Bailey	G	6-3	200	Jr/Jr	Heltonville
40	Calbert Cheaney	F	6-7	209	Sr/Sr	Evansville
34	Brian Evans	F	6-8	211	So/Fr	Terre Haute
20	Greg Graham	G	6-4	183	Sr/Sr	Indianapolis
33	Pat Graham	G	6-5	209	Sr/Jr	Floyds Knobs
44	Alan Henderson	F	6-9	214	So/So	Indianapolis
25	Pat Knight	G	6-6	210	Jr/So	Bloomington
30	Todd Leary	G	6-3	180	Sr/Jr	Indianapolis
50	Todd Lindeman	C	7-0	235	So/So	Channing, MI
24	Matt Nover	C	6-8	230	Sr/Sr	Chesterton
21	Chris Reynolds	G	6-1	187	Sr/Sr	Peoria, IL
11	Malcolm Sims	G	6-4	207	Fr/Fr	Shaker Heights, OH

INTRODUCTION

More has been written about Robert Montgomery Knight than any active coach in college basketball. Some of it has been critical, some laudatory, and some of it has been untrue. This book does not attempt to describe Bob Knight or to offer an opinion of him. It allows Bob Knight to explain himself.

By taping hours of pre-game and weekly interviews during the 1992–93 basketball season, Bob Knight created an intimate, behind the scenes view of his life as head coach. We find a different Bob Knight in his private locker room before a basketball game than the Bob Knight we know trying to motivate a lagging effort on the basketball court or questioning an official's call. Knight is often introspective and self critical in this private setting, much different than the taskmaster he is thought to be during a game. Most of the time, Knight uses these interviews to do what he enjoys the most, analyze and teach the game of basketball. No one is better at that than Coach Knight. Even his detractors agree on that.

These shows were not rehearsed, and there were no scripts. Bob Knight is open and spontaneous as he answers questions from veteran announcer Don Fischer and Indiana basketball fans. In the process, he created a history of Indiana basketball and a unique time exposure of himself.

There are no small words to describe Bob Knight. When journalists write about him the adjectives are always towering: intense, brilliant, volatile, contemptible, fiery, arrogant. Bob Knight's accomplishments place him at the vanguard of college coaches. His basketball technique is highly regarded by other coaches, and his insistent, scorching appearances on the sidelines of basketball games are legendary. Even with the occasionally brutal criticism of Bob Knight from the media, or possibly because of it, when Bob Knight steps on a basketball court before a game he carries an aura of celebrity.

Several books have been written about Knight. John Feinstein's best seller "A Season on the Brink," covering Knight during the 1985–86 Indiana basketball season, presents Knight in a one-season capsule. Bob Knight along with Bob Hammel published "Knight: My Story" in 2002 which covers among other things the troublesome termination as Indiana basketball coach. But there is not much written about the years in between. These were transitional years in an exceptional career as head basketball coach and teacher at Indiana University.

This is the first in a series that will describe eight years of Bob Knight and Indiana basketball, game by game, week by week, in Bob Knight's own words. By taping over 350 "Bob Knight Pre-game Shows" and "Bob Knight Talk Shows" for broadcast on the Indiana basketball radio network, Bob Knight explains himself over this sometimes turbulent period. Coach Knight answered questions spontaneously and openly from veteran Indiana play-by-play announcer Don Fischer or from Indiana basketball fans. In the process, he gave the listener, and now the reader, insight into Knight the man as well as the coach. He gives a behind-the-scenes view of what it is like to run one of the leading college basketball programs in the country.

In these radio shows, Knight is talking directly to Don Fischer, Indiana basketball fans, and occasionally, to his players. His comments are not filtered through the media. Most of the time, Knight is teaching, instructing, and explaining the game of basketball. His approach is much different than it is in a press conference, and his message is communicated clearly and concisely.

Radio is the most intimate of all of the mass media. Unlike television, radio requires no lights, no cameras and no trips to a studio. Many of these interviews were recorded in Knight's private locker room. Bob Knight is not alone when he says he finds radio the most direct means of explaining thoughts, ideas and concepts to a mass audience.

Among other things, Bob Knight's sense of humor is revealed on these radio programs, occasionally at Don Fischer's expense. Yes, Bob Knight has a sense of humor. Television analyst Dick Vitale thinks "Knight is one of the funniest guys in the business, but not many people see that side of him." One listener asked Coach Knight why he looked so angry on a basketball court. Knight responded, "Well, we have a problem. The chair I sit in is broken, and if I sit in it the wrong way it pinches me."

When Art Angotti assumed the contract for the Bob Knight Talk Show in 1992, he was surprised to learn that previous shows were not archived. So he and his assistant, Judy Rogers, began to tape, transcribe and copyright each show beginning with the 1992-93 basketball season. The contract with Coach Knight continued for eight years, through the final season that Bob Knight coached at Indiana University. Now, after ten years of sitting in a file cabinet, these transcripts are brought to you to enjoy and ponder.

Knight is now building another successful basketball program at Texas Tech University. His replacement, Mike Davis, has established himself as Head Basketball Coach at Indiana. Myles Brand, former president of Indiana University, is now head of the NCAA, and Clarence Doninger, former Athletic Director at IU has resumed a successful law practice. The resentment and anger that filled the air when Knight left Indiana has settled somewhat, and it is time to bring this publication to light to pay tribute to the 1992–93 team and to once again hear Bob Knight's views on Indiana Basketball.

This is Bob Knight, in his own words.

Joseph A. Angotti
Professor and Chair
Broadcast Program
Medill School of Journalism
Northwestern University

SECTION I

PRESEASON NIT

"How much better mentally are we going to be?"

Murray State
Tulane
Florida State
Seton Hall

The 1992–93 campaign was a good year for me to begin to work with Bob Knight. He had a talented and experienced group of players returning from a 27-7 team that made it to the NCAA Final Four earlier that spring. Coach Knight would say at the end of the season that he liked this team, he liked the players and he liked what they tried to do together. This would be a good year for Bob Knight.

Bob strives for excellence in basketball. When his team plays the game as well as it possibly can, he is at his best as a teacher and coach. He is also playful and sometimes mischievous. Despite the grueling schedule, it was an exciting and enjoyable year for the team, the coaches and for me.

Coach Knight's teams won NCAA National Championships in 1976, 1981 and 1987, so it had been six years since Indiana won a national championship. IU fans began to look forward to national championships just as Coach Knight expected excellence from his teams. The potential for this squad was vast. It had an outstanding player in Calbert Cheaney surrounded by a lot of other very good players with considerable experience. It had four seniors returning who had won 56 games over the past two seasons, the second highest number of victories of any IU team in a two year period. Expectations were high for Indiana. The players realized that they had the potential to improve on last year's Final Four appearance, and they worked hard in the off season to be ready for the new campaign.

Bob Knight saw the NIT as an excellent opportunity to learn about his team's strengths and weaknesses. This was the second time Indiana played in the NIT in eight years, and Knight talks about the Preseason NIT and his opponent for tonight's game, Murray State. He also covers the new four week practice rule established this year by the NCAA.

Coach Knight finished with an analysis of what his team had to do in order to be better than the Final Four team it was last year.

I think that the NIT Committee came up with a really great idea for college basketball with this preseason tournament that usually involves a number of the better teams in the country going into any given year. A couple of the rules are very good ones. Only one team from any conference can participate in any given year, and a team can only play once every four years. We're coming back into the tournament after having played in it in December of 1988. So we have had a four year wait before we could get back into it.

The idea of having anywhere from one to four games to play prior to the opening of your regular schedule is good for all sixteen teams that are participating. The NIT is to be congratulated by all of us in college basketball for having started this tournament eight years ago. This is now a tournament that teams all over the country are anxious to play in.

I have always felt that four weeks was plenty of time to set up a season. In previous years, when we had those six weeks of practice from October 15th to the 1st of December, we would get to the end of the fourth week and the players began to tire out. I think they're tired of playing against one another. You have a tough time getting them to concentrate and reach the level of performance that you want in practice. Too much effort goes into just getting the players ready to practice on a six week practice schedule. So given those four weeks, you have ample time to prepare for the season. I think that four weeks is going to be plenty adequate.

This year we're not actually experimenting with four weeks, because we've just got the two weeks prior to playing this game tonight against Murray State. Everybody else in the NIT has only had two weeks also, so we're not in a disadvantage as far as this tournament is concerned.

To fully understand the Murray State squad we play tonight, you've got to look back over the last five years. They played in the NCAA Tournament four times, and they played a very close game with Arkansas last year. I think the year before that they had Michigan State beaten and then lost at the end of the game in overtime. They are a team that will be coming here with a lot of physical characteristics very similar to our team, the same size, same quickness, same kind of athletic ability. They will be saying, "We can play Indiana or anybody else."

Our team, on the other hand, has got to be able to take the challenge, has got to be able to come out and play with the kind of intensity that enables us to execute offensively those things that we need to execute as far as obtaining good shot selection. Defensively, we need to have a combination of aggressiveness and positioning that enables us to put the offense of Murray State in a difficult position to score.

We are coming off an exhibition game against Athletes in Action that raised a number of questions. First of all, we gave up too many points, regardless of what combination we used at what stage of the ballgame. We gave up over 100 points, and that's just too many. We scored points at a pretty fast clip, yet we've got to be able to refrain from giving them up at almost the same clip.

We got off to a very good start in the second half. With not a lot of time gone, maybe seven minutes, we put a new group of players on the floor using five of our most experienced players. We were able to take a halftime tie to where we had a 20 point lead. So, we have to be fairly pleased with what we were able to do there. We had good individual performances offensively by several different players. We had moments defensively, but we also saw some mistakes that we made defensively that didn't just cost us a basket, but three or four times cost us 3 points.

The improvement of this year's team over last year's team has to center almost exclusively around how much better mentally are we going to be? How much tougher are we going to be to play against? How much more consistent are we going to be from game to game? Will we, in fact, be able to eliminate bad games from our play? If we can do that, then we have a chance to be a better team.

GAME SUMMARY

INDIANA 103   MURRAY STATE 80

For the 18th time in Bob Knight's 22 years at Indiana, the Hoosiers won a season opener. Indiana started the game slowly but gradually built a 17-point lead at halftime when the score was 53 to 36. IU allowed Murray State to come back to within 1 point early in the second half, but then gradually built the lead to 20 points and maintained that lead throughout the remainder of the second half.

Indiana had five players in double figures, and hit 53 percent from the field in each half. Greg Graham had 22 points, while Calbert Cheaney and Alan Henderson earned 13 points each, and Damon Bailey and Pat Graham had 12 points apiece. IU outrebounded Murray State 38 to 28.

Bob Knight was not happy with his ball club in two areas. One was the 20 turnovers the team had, compared to 17 assists. The second was the number of second chance baskets given up off offensive rebounds. Murray State gained 13 of its 28 boards on the offensive end.

MURRAY STATE

No.	Player		Total FG FG	FGA	3-point FG	FGA	FT	FTA	Rebounds Off	Def	Tot	PF	TP	A	TO	Blk	S	Min
20	Hoard, Antwan	f	2	3	0	0	0	0	0	2	2	1	4	1	6	0	0	15
24	Cannon, Maurice	f	4	10	1	5	2	2	2	1	3	4	11	1	2	0	2	28
44	James, Michael	c	4	6	0	0	0	0	1	2	3	4	8	0	2	1	0	18
53	Brown, Marcus	g	4	6	0	1	3	4	1	0	1	5	11	0	2	1	1	26
33	Allen, Frank	g	6	13	3	4	4	4	1	3	4	5	19	4	3	0	0	30
00	Taylor, Kenneth		2	5	1	1	1	2	4	1	5	3	6	1	4	0	2	26
03	Teague, Antione		1	4	0	0	1	2	0	1	1	3	3	0	0	1	0	11
14	Wilson, Jerry		1	2	0	0	0	1	0	1	1	1	2	0	1	0	0	9
23	Bailey, Tony		3	6	0	0	3	4	2	0	2	3	9	0	4	0	1	18
25	Bussell, Lawrence		1	3	0	0	0	0	2	2	4	1	2	0	2	0	0	10
43	Sivills, Scott		0	0	0	0	1	2	0	0	0	0	1	0	0	0	0	5
04	Gumm, Cedric		2	3	0	0	0	0	0	0	0	0	4	0	0	0	0	4
	Team								0	2	2							
	TOTALS		30	61	5	11	15	21	13	15	28	31	80	7	26	3	6	200

Total FG%: 1st Half .433(13/30) 2nd Half .548(17/31) Game .492(30/61) Deadball
3-Pt. FG%: 1st Half .200(1/5) 2nd Half .667(4/6) Game .455(5/11) Rebounds ___1___
FT%: 1st Half .692(9/13) 2nd Half .750(6/8) Game .714(15/21)

INDIANA

No.	Player		Total FG FG	FGA	3-point FG	FGA	FT	FTA	Rebounds Off	Def	Tot	PF	TP	A	TO	Blk	S	Min
40	Cheaney, Calbert	f	5	12	1	3	2	2	1	4	6	1	13	2	3	0	0	26
44	Henderson, Alan	f	6	8	0	0	1	2	2	7	9	3	13	1	3	2	2	24
24	Nover, Matt	c	3	4	0	0	3	6	2	1	3	2	9	1	2	0	0	26
20	Graham, Greg	g	5	13	0	1	12	13	4	3	7	1	22	1	1	0	0	31
21	Reynolds, Chris	g	2	2	0	0	8	8	0	2	2	3	12	4	4	0	2	23
22	Bailey, Damon		5	6	0	0	2	2	2	0	2	3	12	2	2	0	0	15
33	Graham, Pat		1	4	0	2	2	2	0	0	0	0	4	1	2	0	0	8
30	Leary, Todd		2	3	0	1	3	3	1	0	1	2	7	3	0	0	0	13
24	Evans, Brian		3	6	1	2	2	2	2	2	4	1	9	0	1	0	0	18
11	Sims, Malcolm		0	1	0	0	2	2	0	0	0	1	2	0	1	0	0	9
25	Knight, Pat		0	1	0	0	0	0	0	0	0	0	0	2	1	0	0	7
	Team								4	4	5							
	TOTALS		32	60	2	9	37	42	15	23	39	17	103	17	20	2	4	200

Total FG%: 1st Half .533(16/30) 2nd Half .533(16/30) Game .533(32/60) Deadball
3-Pt. FG%: 1st Half .200(1/5) 2nd Half .250(1/4) Game .222(2/9) Rebounds ___3___
FT%: 1st Half .909(20/22) 2nd Half .850(17/20) Game .886(37/42)

Officials   Mike Panco, JC Liembach, Gene Millentree
Technical Fouls
Attendance   13,619

Score by Periods	1	2	OT	OT	Final
Murray State	36	44			80
Indiana	53	50			103

Two nights later, Indiana faced its second round opponent, Tulane in Bloomington. Tulane, which was ranked seventeenth at the time, was similar to Murray State in many ways, but a better basketball team in terms of talent. It would be Indiana's first test against a pressing and trapping defense. Knight begins by analyzing the Murray State game, and then turns to Tulane.

The Murray State game was a ballgame against an experienced team that I thought played very aggressively. There were some things that we weren't totally pleased with and some areas where we felt we made some mistakes. Even with that, we looked up at the scoreboard and with ten minutes to go in the game, we were ahead by 25, so we couldn't have been playing all that badly. I felt that we played well and that we did a lot of good things in the ballgame.

This was a quick team, but there will be some bigger, quicker teams that we'll play also. I really was impressed by how hard they played and how they stuck to what they wanted to do throughout the entire course of the ballgame.

I'm not really sure sometimes whether stats keepers know just exactly what an assist is. I don't have any problem with them knowing what a turnover is, but we scored 30 some baskets and had just 17 assists against 20 turnovers. And there weren't all that many individual baskets, although we got some offensive rebound baskets. But maybe that's a fairly accurate count? If it is, then I have to be a little disappointed because we have to have a much better ratio for assists and turnovers than that.

What I was more disappointed with, however, were some of the defensive errors that we made. Some of the errors I thought that we made were just simple play where we over-committed ourselves, we lost our balance, or we took ourselves out of the play. We were just careless, and the elimination of careless mistakes is going to be a very important thing to us with this ball club.

We did a good job of getting to the free throw line. This has always been important, just as trying to get to the basket is important. You're trying to get an offense set up that gives you an opportunity to score from high percentage areas. You're trying to get to the free throw line, because that may be the highest percentage shot of all.

Tulane is practically a carbon copy of Murray State, but they are a lot bigger and probably just a better basketball team from the standpoint of the total amount of talent they have. They are a very experienced, aggressive team. Also, there will be a very interesting facet to this game tonight. Our best player against full-court pressure, maybe for as long as I've been here, was Jamal Meeks. In a game where we were really being pressured, where there was a lot of trapping going on, either on full-court or half-court, Meeks handled it extremely well. You could almost count on Jamal having 10 or 12 assists, and maybe no turnovers. This was a part of the game where he truly excelled. Now without Meeks, we'll have to rely on spreading his responsibility through the rest of our team, because Tulane does a lot of trapping, does a lot of half and three-quarter court pressing. We'll just have to see at this point in the season if we can handle it. It may very well be that we can't. With the loss of Meeks and our not being very far along into the season, we may find that their defense and their pressure will be somewhat advanced compared to where we are offensively. That's the biggest question for us tonight.

GAME SUMMARY

INDIANA 102   TULANE 92

The Hoosiers blasted past the Green Wave of then 17th ranked Tulane in a game where the score made it seem closer than it really was. The Hoosiers conducted a clinic on how to break the full-court press, roaring to a 26-point first half lead. They built a 36-point second half margin before the reserves let it slip away with 8 minutes to go. Then Tulane scored 11 points in a row to cut the lead to 94-78. With 4:09 remaining, Knight re-inserted his starters for the remainder of the ballgame, and they held on for the victory. He was very disappointed that the bench could not hold on to a lead.

Indiana shot 62 percent from the field. For the second straight game, the Hoosiers got to the free throw line decisively more than their opponent. They hit on 24 of 37 attempts from the stripe, while Tulane was held to 21 attempts, connecting on only 14. Indiana was out rebounded in this game 36 to 33, but had 14 turnovers compared to 17 for the Green Wave.

The Hoosiers had three players in double figures: Alan Henderson had 28 points and 9 rebounds, Calbert Cheaney had 21 points and 7 boards, and Greg Graham added 12 points.

TULANE

No.	Player		Total FG FG	FGA	3-point FG	FGA	FT	FTA	Rebounds Off	Def	Tot	PF	TP	A	TO	Blk	S	Min
44	Popp, Matt	f	1	1			0	0	0	0	0	2	2	1	0	0	0	7
55	Reed, Anthony	f	7	17	3	3	1	2	1	2	3	2	18	0	2	1	0	37
34	Perry, Makemba	c	1	4	0	0	3	4	0	5	5	5	5	2	1	0	0	18
04	Williams, Pointer	g	5	10	1	3	2	4	0	1	1	3	13	6	4	0	2	26
23	Lewis, Kim	g	1	1	1	1	0	0	0	1	1	0	3	0	1	0	0	5
05	Hunter, G.J.		4	9	2	3	2	2	0	0	0	4	12	2	2	0	4	28
30	Greene, Matt		6	13	0	0	3	6	4	4	8	3	15	2	1	0	1	32
32	Hartman, Carlin		6	8	0	0	3	3	5	1	6	5	15	1	2	0	0	19
03	Simmons, Le Veldro		4	8	1	3	0	0	0	3	3	3	9	3	4	0	0	20
54	Rasche, Pete		0	2	0	0	0	0	0	3	3	1	0	0	0	0	0	8
	Team								3	3	6							
	TOTALS		35	73	8	13	14	21	13	23	36	28	92	17	17	1	7	200

Total FG%: 1st Half .313(10/32)   2nd Half .625(25/40)   Game .479(35/73)   Deadball
3-Pt. FG%: 1st Half 1.00(1/1)   2nd Half .615(7/12)   Game .615(8/13)   Rebounds ___4___
FT%: 1st Half .583(7/12)   2nd Half .778(7/9)   Game .667(14/21)

INDIANA

No.	Player		Total FG FG	FGA	3-point FG	FGA	FT	FTA	Rebounds Off	Def	Tot	PF	TP	A	TO	Blk	S	Min
40	Cheaney, Calbert	f	9	14	1	2	2	2	2	5	7	2	21	4	3	1	0	26
44	Henderson, Alan	f	10	12	0	0	8	11	4	5	9	1	28	2	1	1	2	27
24	Nover, Matt	c	3	4	0	0	1	4	3	2	5	3	7	0	4	0	0	18
20	Graham, Greg	g	6	10	0	1	2	4	1	3	4	0	14	2	0	0	2	32
21	Reynolds, Chris	g	2	4	0	0	1	4	0	5	5	1	5	5	1	0	0	28
22	Bailey, Damon		3	6	2	3	0	0	0	0	0	4	8	4	1	0	0	19
30	Leary, Todd		2	3	1	2	2	2	0	0	0	1	7	0	2	0	1	10
33	Graham, Pat		2	5	0	1	2	2	0	0	0	1	6	0	0	0	1	14
34	Evans, Brian		0	1	0	1	2	2	0	0	0	2	2	0	1	0	0	13
11	Sims, Malcolm		0	1	0	0	3	4	0	0	0	2	3	0	1	0	1	8
25	Knight, Pat		0	0	0	0	1	2	0	1	1	0	1	0	0	0	0	5
	Team								0	2	2							
	TOTALS		37	60	4	10	24	37	10	23	33	17	102	17	14	2	7	200

Total FG%: 1st Half .645(20/31)   2nd Half .586(17/29)   Game .616(37/60)   Deadball
3-Pt. FG% 1st Half .250(1/4)   2nd Half .500(3/6)   Game .400(4/10)   Rebounds ___3___
FT% 1st Half .765(13/17)   2nd Half .550(11/20)   Game .649(24/37)

Officials   Ed Schumer, Paul Castor, Bill Westbrook
Technical Fouls
Attendance   14,008

Score by Periods	1	2	OT	OT	Final
Tulane	28	64			92
Indiana	54	48			102

Indiana vs. Florida State
November 25, 1992
Preseason NIT—New York City
Pre-game Show

The victories over Murray State and Tulane sent Indiana to Madison Square Garden in New York during the Thanksgiving weekend for the Preseason NIT Semi-Final round. I was there along with a large number of IU fans who made the trip to New York for the game.

The Hoosier's first opponent in New York was Florida State, ranked seventh in the nation at the time. Knight begins by discussing the first two games of the tournament, then turns to the four teams in New York for the NIT Championship. He finishes talking about the performance of Alan Henderson and Calbert Cheaney.

So far we've played two teams that, I think, are fairly good teams. They are going to be good teams in their leagues. Tulane has a chance to develop into perhaps a nationally competitive team. Murray State has the capability of giving everybody some problems. I would think that these two teams are considerably better overall than the year that we beat Illinois State and Stanford in the NIT.

We thought in Murray State we were playing against a very aggressive team, a team that worked hard to play against us. Tulane was the same. I'm very pleased with some progress we made in our defense from the Murray State to the Tulane game. We were able in the Tulane game to play against a team that had successfully pressured a lot of teams last year. We were able to play against that kind of defense with some degree of productivity.

I was pleased in the Murray State game because we gradually worked, and worked, and worked, and worked. With about ten minutes to go against a pretty decent team, we had a 25-point lead. In the Tulane game, we were able to attack right off the bat, and very quickly we had a big lead.

Now we had the disappointment, in the second half of taking our starters out of the game and then not being able to maintain some semblance of the lead that we had developed with those starters playing. Yet, I would hope that would be a lesson to all of our players as to just what can happen quickly if they're not paying attention to what's going on.

So, I'm pleased with what we've done over two games and am looking forward to these next two games here in New York. Playing the two teams here will give us a chance to look at ourselves against the kind of team that we are going to have to be able to beat over the course of the season, if we are, in fact, going to be a nationally competitive team this year. By that, I mean one that can legitimately contend for the Big Ten title and can be a threat at winning a lot of games in the NCAA Tournament.

You have four teams here playing in New York, all of which were in the regional tournaments last year. So you've got 25% of the final sixteen teams from last season here in the NIT finals. Only UCLA has suffered large losses from last year's lineup. So more important than anything is the fact that we've got this chance to play two games here, and that will give all of us, players and coaches alike, further opportunity to evaluate where we are.

Florida State is a team that we have beaten the last two times we have played them in the NCAA Tournament. I don't think that means anything one way or the other coming into this game. I mean it is important for our guys to understand that this is a very good basketball team and a very deep front line, a very talented team. Florida State is going to be a nationally competitive team and is the type of team we're going to have to be able to beat and beat consistently if we want this to be the kind of year for us that we can remember.

Henderson has played, obviously, very well. He scored well, but beyond that he has done a very good job on the boards. I think he has still got a lot of things to do defensively, and a lot of things to do offensively. I believe he's in the process of developing into what will be a truly outstanding basketball player.

Calbert has worked very hard in these first two games. He has been a more consistently hard working player at the offensive end of the floor than he was last year. This is going to be very important to him. Calbert has got to be relentless in his movement on offense.

GAME SUMMARY

OVERTIME

INDIANA 81 FLORIDA STATE 78

Indiana's victory over Florida State was a bittersweet triumph. The victory vaulted IU into the championship game of the Preseason NIT Tournament, but it suffered the loss of junior Pat Graham. Graham broke a bone in his left foot after sparking IU with 14 points in the second half that helped Indiana out of a 12-point hole. The injury was similar to the one that caused him to miss all of last season and use his redshirt year. The break was of the same bone, but in a different location than his previous injury. Pat will probably miss most, if not all, of the rest of the season.

Indiana took an early 15-point first-half lead, but the Seminoles roared back to within 2 by halftime. At the start of the second half, the Hoosiers surged on top by 12. Graham and Calbert Cheaney led IU's comeback. Cheaney's 34-point effort was a new career high, and his 7 free throws in overtime salted away the victory.

This was Indiana's poorest shooting effort of the young season. The Hoosiers hit 44 percent for the game, but Florida State was held to just 36 percent shooting in a very impressive defensive effort by both teams. In addition to Pat Graham's and Cheaney's point totals, Greg Graham and Alan Henderson each had 12 points. Henderson also pulled down 12 rebounds.

It was Indiana's third consecutive game in which it was able to get to the free throw line more times than its opponent. Indiana hit 20 of 30 from the stripe (67 percent) and Florida State hit 14 of 23. This was IU's second poor performance at the line, however it did not draw much attention in these interviews. Free throws would become a problem as the season advanced.

INDIANA

No.	Player	Total FG FG	FGA	3-point FG	FGA	FT	FTA	Rebounds Off	Def	Tot	PF	TP	A	TO	Blk	S	Min
40	Cheaney, Calbert	12	22	1	3	9	10	2	6	8	3	34	1	5	0	2	42
44	Henderson, Alan	5	11	0	0	2	5	5	7	12	4	12	0	1	3	1	40
24	Nover, Matt	1	3	0	0	1	2	2	5	7	2	3	0	1	2	2	25
20	Graham, Greg	4	14	1	3	3	4	2	5	7	1	12	3	5	0	1	37
21	Reynolds, Chris	1	3	0	0	0	0	0	2	2	2	2	5	0	0	0	22
22	Bailey, Damon	1	5	0	2	0	2	2	2	4	2	2	6	0	0	0	24
34	Evans, Brian	0	1	0	1	0	0	0	1	1	0	0	0	0	0	0	8
33	Graham, Pat	5	6	1	2	3	5	0	1	1	1	14	2	2	0	2	21
30	Leary, Todd	0	1	0	0	2	2	0	0	0	1	2	0	0	0	0	5
11	Sims, Malcolm	0	0	0	0	0	0	0	0	0	0	0	0	0	0	0	1
25	Knight, Pat	DNP—															
	Team							0	1	1				1			
	TOTALS	29	66	3	11	20	30	13	30	43	16	81	17	15	5	8	225

Total FG%   1st Half .486(17/35)   2nd Half .407(11/27)   OT .250(1/4)   Game .439(29/66)   Deadball
3-Pt. FG%   1st Half .400(2/5)   2nd Half .200(1/5)   OT .000(0/1)   Game .273(3/11)   Rebounds 6
FT%   1st Half .600(3/5)   2nd Half .583(7/13)   OT .833(10/12)   Game .667(20/30)

FLORIDA STATE

No.	Player	Total FG FG	FGA	3-point FG	FGA	FT	FTA	Rebounds Off	Def	Tot	PF	TP	A	TO	Blk	S	Min
34	Dobard, Rodney	4	10	0	0	2	2	1	4	5	3	10	0	2	2	3	39
32	Edwards, Doug	7	17	0	0	2	6	8	4	12	5	16	2	4	0	1	41
44	Reid, Andre	0	3	0	0	2	4	3	3	6	4	2	0	1	1	0	23
10	Cassell, Sam	7	20	1	7	3	3	3	2	5	5	18	2	4	0	2	40
03	Sura, Bob	5	24	2	11	5	8	4	6	10	3	17	4	2	0	1	41
33	Wells, Byron	4	5	1	1	0	0	5	5	10	3	9	3	1	0	0	28
11	Hands, Lorenzo	2	4	0	1	0	0	1	0	1	1	4	0	1	0	0	4
15	Shepherd, Scott	1	1	0	0	0	0	0	0	0	0	2	0	1	0	0	5
21	Carroll, Derrick	0	0	0	0	0	0	0	0	0	1	0	0	0	0	0	4
	Team							3	4	7				1			
	TOTALS	30	84	4	20	14	23	28	28	56	25	78	11	17	3	7	225

Total FG%   1st Half .385(15/39)   2nd Half .344(11/32)   OT .308(4/13)   Game .357(30/84)   Deadball
3-Pt. FG%   1st Half .300(3/10)   2nd Half .000(0/7)   OT .333(1/3)   Game .200(4/20)   Rebounds 5
FT%   1st Half .400(4/10)   2nd Half .769(10/13)   OT .000(0/0)   Game .609(14/23)

Officials   Mark DiStaola, Joe Mingle, Sean Corbin
Technical Fouls
Attendance

Score by Periods	1	2	OT	OT	Final
Florida State	37	32	9		78
Indiana	39	30	12		81

Making the Preseason NIT Championship Game had Indiana fans hoping for great things from this campaign. But Knight's pre-game comments initially were focused on the loss of Pat Graham. Then, Coach Knight talked about the inconsistency of the team's play. He analyzed Seton Hall, which was ranked sixth in the nation at the time, and he finished by discussing how they would represent an entirely different type of challenge for the Hoosiers.

The first thing that I want to talk about from our standpoint is the loss of Pat Graham. And it's not our loss as a team that concerns me. It's Pat's loss as an individual. Here's a kid who really enjoys playing basketball, loves to play basketball. He's 21 years old. Basketball has been a great part of his life to this point. He went through three different surgical procedures on his foot when it was broken last year. Then to break it again, as he has, is very disappointing. We've had some really disappointing injuries that have hurt us in terms of accomplishment over the years. Because this is the second major injury that he has suffered, I don't think we've ever had one that has been more disappointing for me as a coach. It has taken a kid who likes to play so well and who has been a very, very big part of our team out of basketball for possibly the remainder of the season. Here we are, just in the third game, and he came into the ballgame in a difficult situation and his play actually was what made it possible for us to win the ballgame. So that's my first thought about the Florida State game. I would hope beyond anything else that Pat will get a chance to come back before this season is over.

In looking at the Florida State game, we got off to a good start from an offensive standpoint, and got a good lead, a 15-point lead, in fact. In the other two games we had played against Florida State over the last two years, we started out even, at best. In fact, I think when we played them in Louisville, we might have been as many as 12 points behind early in that ballgame. As I recall, we were 6 behind when we went off the floor, although we were starting to play better when we went off at the half.

We jumped out to a really good lead in the ballgame, much like we did in each of these last two games in the second half. They cut our 15-point lead down to 2 by halftime, and I think at one point in the second half, they had a 12-point lead.

So they had outscored us during that period of time by 27 points, and during that time we lacked any degree of patience on offense. We did not do a very good job at all on the backboard. Our defense was very shoddy. We had a lot of lunging, a lot of off balance play on defense. We just got ourselves through a variety of poor efforts, in a real hole.

Once, when we got down by 12, I thought we came back and played really well. It was actually a game that should never have gone into overtime. We make a mistake at the end of the game by not calling a time out when we were trapped. A time out would have prevented us from going into overtime.

In this ballgame, I had to be very pleased with our start and our finish. We outscored Florida State at the start and finish by 30 points. They outscored us by 27 in the middle of this. So it was an odd game for two fairly good teams to play against one another. It was not a back and forth game. It was a game of decided advantages being taken away from the team that held the advantage.

Looking ahead to Seton Hall tonight, the last time we played them was in the Regionals in Denver in 1989. They were a very, very tough, hard-nosed team. The guards were very tough. They had real strong inside play, and went on to lose in the championship game to Michigan. So they were certainly the equivalent of any team in the country in 1989.

This year, it's a completely different team. P.J. Carlissimo, who I think is one of the really good basketball coaches in the country, has done a great job resurrecting basketball at Seton Hall, putting it back into a national spotlight. And Seton Hall is to be commended. P.J. started out with four or five tough years to begin with and just worked, and worked, and worked. Through his determination and perseverance and his ability to coach, P.J. has put Seton Hall in a very elite position in the country for the second time—that '89 team, and now this team four years later. I think this is always the mark of somebody who's really doing a good job. Not necessarily to have *a team* that does well, but to have *teams* that do well. And now he's here with a team that would be very, very tough for anybody to beat.

I think that the personnel are Seton Hall's biggest strength. DeHere is perhaps as good as any guard in the country. They play roles extremely well. They have a very good third guard come in. They have two centers, and when one center plays the other can play forward. When the former is out, the latter can play center, and he's extremely difficult to play against. They have three forwards, plus they have really good athletes backing up everybody. They've got the kind of personnel that can score on the break, that can shoot from the outside, and that can be extremely tough to play against inside and on the boards. It's just a *tough* group of players for anybody to play.

GAME SUMMARY

INDIANA 78   SETON HALL 74

Indiana won the eighth annual Preseason NIT Basketball Tournament and conquered its third consecutive ranked team in sixth-ranked Seton Hall. Senior All-American Calbert Cheaney was sensational in his two games at Madison Square Garden. He hit a career high 34 on Wednesday against Florida State, then rewrote his career best in the championship game with 36 points. His two-game output earned him the NIT's Most Valuable Player Award. Joining him on the All-Tournament Team was teammate Alan Henderson.

Indiana also had a solid performance from Greg Graham with 14 points while Henderson had 11 points and 7 rebounds. Indiana hit 44 percent from the field compared to 45 percent for Seton Hall. The Hoosiers, however, out rebounded Seton Hall 41 to 34. Once again, Indiana went to the free throw line more often than its opponent for the fourth straight game. This time Indiana connected on 20 of 32, while Seton Hall hit 14 of 22.

Bob Knight's Indiana team had an encouraging start on the 1992–93 season with wins over three highly ranked and regarded teams.

INDIANA

No.	Player		Total FG FG	FGA	3-point FG	FGA	FT	FTA	Rebounds Off	Def	Tot	PF	TP	A	TO	Blk	S	Min
40	Cheaney, Calbert	f	14	27	2	4	6	10	3	1	4	2	36	3	3	0	1	39
44	Henderson, Alan	f	4	8	0	1	3	6	2	5	7	4	11	1	4	1	1	30
24	Nover, Matt	c	2	6	0	0	2	2	2	3	5	2	6	2	0	0	1	22
20	Graham, Greg	g	4	8	1	1	5	8	1	3	4	3	14	4	1	0	0	33
21	Reynolds, Chris	g	0	2	0	0	3	4	1	2	3	1	3	5	1	0	2	29
22	Bailey, Damon		0	1	0	1	1	2	2	2	4	3	1	3	0	0	0	16
30	Leary, Todd		0	1	0	1	0	0	0	0	0	1	0	0	1	0	0	6
34	Evans, Brian		3	9	1	3	0	0	3	5	8	1	7	1	1	0	0	22
25	Knight, Pat		0	0	0	0	0	0	0	0	0	0	0	1	0	0	0	1
11	Sims, Malcolm		0	0	0	0	0	0	0	0	0	1	0	0	1	0	0	2
	Team								3	3	60							
	TOTALS		27	62	4	11	20	32	17	24	41	18	78	20	12	1	5	200

Total FG%	1st Half .455(15/33)	2nd Half .414(12/29)	Game .435(27/62)	Deadball	
3-Pt. FG%	1st Half .333(2/6)	2nd Half .400(2/5)	Game .364(4/11)	Rebounds	6
FT%	1st Half1.00(5/5)	2nd Half .556(15/27)	Game .625(20/32)		

SETON HALL

No.	Player		Total FG FG	FGA	3-point FG	FGA	FT	FTA	Rebounds Off	Def	Tot	PF	TP	A	TO	Blk	S	Min
55	Karnishovas, Artur	f	8	11	3	5	5	6	3	5	8	5	24	2	0	1	0	30
21	Walker, Jerry	f	1	4	0	0	2	2	1	1	2	4	4	2	4	0	0	35
50	Wright, Luther	c	2	9	0	0	2	5	4	7	11	2	6	0	1	1	0	26
10	Caver, Bryan	g	3	6	1	3	1	2	0	3	3	5	8	5	3	0	1	23
24	Dehere, Terry	g	6	14	3	6	2	2	0	1	1	5	17	4	4	0	1	36
15	Hurley, Danny		3	6	1	2	2	4	0	0	0	1	9	1	1	0	0	21
30	Leahy, John		2	5	2	4	0	0	0	2	2	2	6	0	2	0	0	21
04	Griffin, Adrian		0	0	0	0	0	1	0	1	1	2	0	1	0	0	0	5
32	Shipp, Tchaka		0	0	0	0	0	0	0	0	0	0	0	0	0	0	0	2
22	Duerksen, Craig		0	0	0	0	0	0	0	0	0	0	0	0	0	0	0	1
	Team								2	4	60							
	TOTALS		25	55	10	20	14	22	10	24	34	26	74	15	15	2	2	200

Total FG%	1st Half .444(12/27)	2nd Half .464(13/28)	Game .455(25/55)	Deadball	
3-Pt. FG%	1st Half .429(3/7)	2nd Half .538(7/13)	Game .500(10/20)	Rebounds	4
FT%	1st Half .750(6/8)	2nd Half .571(8/14)	Game .636(14/22)		

Officials   Jody Silvester, Tim Higgins, Tom Lopes

Technical Fouls

Attendance   14,338

Score by
Periods	1	2	OT	OT	Final
Indiana	37	41			78
Seton Hall	33	41			74

BOB KNIGHT TALK SHOW

November 30, 1992

Following the NIT, Indiana prepared to take on the Cuban National basketball team in an exhibition game. This was Bob Knight's first talk show of the season. It provided him with more time to talk about different aspects of the team's performance that he felt were important, such as leadership and what it takes to be a great basketball team. Coach Knight talks about the difference between a good team and a great team.

Because of the exhibition game this evening, this show was prerecorded, and there were no questions from fans.

We are allowed by the NCAA to play two exhibition games, one with a foreign team and one with a domestic team. Our game before the NIT with Athletes in Action based out of Cincinnati was obviously the domestic team and the Cuban National game is the foreign team. We've tried over the last couple of years to make sure we have those two games on our schedule to give us a chance to do whatever it is that we might want to do with our own players relative to preparing them for the season.

I think this game tonight comes at a really good time for us. It's a very opportune time, in fact, because we're able to get a look at a lot of players that we need to develop if we're going to have any bench strength. The substitutes did not do a particularly good job, in fact they did a very poor job, in the second half of the game against Tulane. We're going to start four of those players tonight, along with one of our normal starters and we may alternate a little bit through that one starting position, but giving the other four players as much opportunity to play as we possibly can in tonight's game.

I want to see exactly where they are and what they can do. We had everybody come in the ballgame the first half against Tulane and everyone played very well. Then we had everybody come in the first half against Seton Hall and play very well. So that's the kind of thing we want to develop with this 10-man roster that we now have.

We only had two practice weeks before the NIT, but sometimes, even a twelve-week practice session would be difficult with a less experienced team coming in. That's something you would always have to take into consideration. But, you know, you're not going to have more than three or four new players on any given team. I think you're going to be able to have the experience that's coming back become even more involved with the development of the younger players and their teaching. It still seems to me that by the time four weeks are over, you're going to be ready.

We had some dedicated work being done over the course of the summer by our players, relative to stamina and strength and skills. But I would expect that any year. I think that one of the things that was kind of interesting was that one of our doctors, Larry Rink, who does a lot of testing with our players relative to conditioning prior to the start of the season, felt that when these kids came back to school and were tested, as a group, they were in the best shape of any team we've ever had. So that's a good indication, I think, that these players were very seriously working during the off season, anxious for this season to get started, wanting to be in the best condition possible. So the shorter practice time didn't hurt us from a conditioning standpoint.

Last year's team went 27 and 7 and got to the NCAA finals. They had to be pretty dedicated to do that. This team has won 56 games in the last two years. That's the second most that an Indiana team has ever won over a two year period.

To be a great basketball team—and this team has been a good team, it has not been a great team—I think to elevate itself from being a good team to being a great team, it has to have a much, much stronger mentality than it had over the last couple of years. The difference between being really good and being great may only be three or four games, but you've got to have a team that just does not lose games that it can win. And our team has done that.

I don't think that we had as much improvement as I would like to have seen as far as our mental approach to basketball was concerned last year. I thought that it was a team that on occasion played as well as any team I've ever coached, and yet in playing that well on occasion, there were other times when it just was not as good as it should have been.

I have been on record many times, I think, in saying that our leadership wasn't good last year. It wasn't good from the beginning of the season until the tournament when we changed the leadership. When we told the juniors it was going to be up to them to provide leadership, I thought that our cohesiveness, our togetherness, and our cooperative efforts were much stronger than before. And I would hope that would continue to be a source of strength for us. I would like to think that we can get Cheaney, Nover, Reynolds and Greg Graham to give us the kind of leadership we need.

You have to have a guy in the locker room that's constantly saying the same things, trying to get the same things done as you as a coach are trying to get done. You've got to have a guy that isn't going to worry about anybody getting upset because he says something.

Todd Lindeman, who has been redshirted this season, was operated on when he was 11 or 12 years old. It was a serious elbow surgery. And it really didn't work out as well as he hoped. It particularly didn't work out because he became a basketball player. He was unable to get the kind of extension that he had to have. Jim Strickland and his group in Indianapolis did a great job with surgery. Now Todd is pretty much recuperated from that, simply because he has worked hard at it. Yet, I think it would be unfair to him to throw him back in playing right away, until he had a chance to do some things relative to the rehabilitation of that injury. I think he's really going to be ready to go after this year, but not now.

I felt that Murray State was an excellent first game for us. They had back a team that was very good, quick, aggressive, experienced, hungry to get going in competition, anxious for another shot at the NCAA Tournament. As the game unfolded and progressed, we were able to gradually work into a position with about 12 or 14 minutes to play in the game, we had a 25-point lead. What goes with a 25-point lead is really pretty much a real control of the ballgame. And I thought we had it there. So Murray State ended up being a very good start for us and I thought that we handled that start pretty well.

You can't be aggressive unless you're quick, and the defensive aggressiveness that Murray State brought with them was a really good test for our offense. We turned that around in playing two nights later against a very experienced team in Tulane that bases its full approach to the game on its press. So right away in those first two ballgames, we got a couple of good things to go against.

We played extremely well against Tulane, until we had that 35 or 37-point lead and then we let things slide away from us a little bit. That's why, as I mentioned a little while ago, we're going to go right back in this exhibition game tonight against Cuba using those players for the most part who were in the ballgame when things slipped away from us in the Tulane game. Now each of those kids has come back and made some really good plays or played very well in either the Florida State or the Seton Hall games or in a couple of cases in both games. But things really got away from us in that game with Tulane, and we want to see where we would be with that same kind of lineup playing tonight.

I was glad that we had a chance to go against the press. Tulane was a very good pressing team last year with really good results. We went into the game asking what are we going to be able to do against the press? We answered that question at least in part for ourselves in the Tulane game with Chris Reynolds handling the ball, or whoever. With good passing and good movement, we were able to get some very good things done against the press.

I think that Henderson and Graham have both improved as far as ball handling is concerned. We have seen an overall improvement in our ball handling which then enables us to handle the press better.

I felt that in New York, we were playing against a team that really works at it, a team that makes it difficult for you to do some things offensively. That goes back to the pressure in the Murray State game or in the press in the Tulane game. It's always interesting to me to see if we are going to be able to do some things against those teams that have a definite plan or approach in trying to prevent you from doing certain things.

Pat Kennedy, the coach of Florida State, asked a year or so ago about coming up and just came up to practice. Some people have a problem with this, but we do this often. What difference does it make whether we're going to play them or not? It isn't like this is a CIA operation. We don't have a lot of things that are ultra secret. I don't have anything marked "for eyes only" or "top secret" or "for nobody to look at but me." What we do is pretty much open to anybody that's in basketball.

I was pleased with the fact that we got off to a good start against Florida State. I think that in the start of that game we were up by maybe 15 points and then the thing just kind of went away from us from that point on. We got back ahead by 2 points at the half. We were a little careless on offense, we shot too quickly. One pass or two passes at the most to the shot was not my idea of really getting things done offensively, the way we did in getting to the 15-point lead.

On defense, we made some very careless plays insofar as getting into position was concerned. That had us going from an excellent start to a very, very poor performance in the middle of the ballgame, one that ended up with our being 12 down.

Once we got 12 down, we went ahead and played pretty well from that point to the end, right through overtime. And I really believe that this would not have been a game that our team could have won a year ago. So maybe we have made some strides with our mental approach to the game. Of that I am not really certain. I just know that we had a let up, didn't follow through with what we were doing early in the ballgame against Florida State. I'm pleased that we came through, but I don't like that approach. That's not the way I look at it. We played very poorly to get in that position in the first place. Being 12 points down was not a position that we should have ever been in, given the start that we had in the ballgame.

In the Championship game against Seton Hall, we felt they were going to be a very, very tough man-to-man defensive team. I felt that we were going to have to work for everything that we got. You know when we played them in the first round of the Regional in 1989, in Denver, they were a very, very tough-minded team.

P.J. Carlissimo is a guy that I've known since he was 10 or 12 years old. His mother and father are good friends of mine. I've really enjoyed watching him develop and move and grow as a coach. He's done a great job resurrecting basketball at Seton Hall and he does an excellent job with what they are doing defensively. They were a team that we were going to have to work awfully hard against at both ends of the court. It was going to be difficult to keep them from scoring. It was going to be very hard for us to get anything at our end.

There's tremendous half-court pressure from them. They move their feet very well. They use their hands extremely well, and make it difficult for you to cut and to move offensively. You don't get easy shots against them. You only get things against them by working hard. All of that together made things, I think, very good for us simply because it was another team we had to work very hard against.

In general, I felt in our first ballgame in New York against Florida State that while Calbert had scored very well, 34 points, he had not played real well. I think after looking at the tapes, Calbert would have agreed with this. I think that in the second game, however, Calbert was just really very conscientious about trying to play well in addition to scoring. His scoring is obviously very important to our team, but just as important is his playing well in every phase of the game. I thought he did that maybe as well as I've ever seen him play in the game with Seton Hall. I think that he moved very well. I thought he was very difficult to play against.

Chris Reynolds provided leadership for us at both ends of the court. He was enthusiastic; he was tough-minded. I was really pleased with what we got from Chris.

I thought that Brian played well in both games. We got a lift from him in the game against Florida State, and then we got a lot of really good play from him in the game against Seton Hall.

I don't think Alan Henderson rebounded as well in these two games or was as active as he had been in the Tulane game. Alan kind of sat around and watched a little bit more than he is going to be able to do if he's going to be effective.

I think that Greg's defense in our game against Florida State was very poor and improved immensely in our game against Seton Hall. He and Chris Reynolds did almost all of the guarding of DeHere, but Damon Bailey figured into it also. Greg did a very good job.

Damon Bailey has played basketball very well for the most part. He's made some mistakes defensively. He has not scored well. He has not shot well. One of the areas that he has to be conscious of and work through is moving to get open. Damon moves, but he doesn't always really work to get open, and there is a difference.

I think Pat Graham has handled his injury very well. There isn't anything that he is going to be able to do other than to just work to rehabilitate the foot when that time comes. He's been dealt a certain hand and he has to play it. He can't look over at the dealer, give him his cards back and say, "I want another hand."

THE DECEMBER SCHEDULE

"THIS HAS NOT BEEN A PARTICULARLY GOOD NON-CONFERENCE SEASON."

Kansas
Notre Dame
Austin Peay
Western Michigan
Cincinnati
St. John's
Butler
Colorado
Kentucky

Coming off the NIT Championship, Indiana faced a highly regarded Kansas team at the Hoosier Dome in Indianapolis. Ranked third in the country at the time, Kansas was Indiana's toughest opponent of the season. A crowd of 31,000 was on hand along with a national television audience. Indianapolis has hosted the NCAA Tournament several times and the Hoosier Dome was set up in a Final Four lay-out for the game. Even though it was still early in the season, I was surprised by how effectively the organizers created an NCAA atmosphere in the Dome that day. This setting would repeat itself later in the season when Indiana and Kansas would face off again in the Midwest Regional title game.

Coach Knight began by talking about this week's practice sessions, and he also covered the recent Cuban National game in which he kept four starters on the bench throughout the game.

Finally, he analyzed the Kansas team Indiana will play today. This is the first of several times during the season when his pre-game comments foretell the outcome of the game.

I remember one time when I was at Army, and we were playing Notre Dame in the NIT in 1968. We came into the game with a really good practice week. We were playing on Sunday afternoon in Madison Square Garden. We went in on Saturday to work out, and we were practicing so well that I cut our workout in half. The next day we played very poorly in the first half against Notre Dame, and got behind by I think 9 points at the start of the second half. We were never quite able to catch-up. We ended up losing at the end of the game. I use that analogy simply to preface what I say about our week's practice.

It's been a really good week of practice for us. I like very much what I've seen in practice, both offensively and defensively, and yet I always think back, as I usually do, to things that have gone wrong from that point. I've seen times when the night before a game I'm not sure we could have beaten anybody. By game time, a night later, we played about as well as we could play. So we were really pleased with what we saw this week, but how that translates as far as today's game is concerned, is anybody's guess.

In the game against the Cuban team, we were simply trying to give as much game experience to players as we possibly could. We're going to need all ten of our players at different times during the course of the year. They're all going to have to be able to come in and help. They did do that in the Tulane game in the first half. I think they did well in the Seton Hall game in the first half. We're going to need our whole roster, so we try to give them as much experience in playing as we possibly can. The Cuban game was perfect from that standpoint. We used Nover because we've got to get Matt and his athletic ability more involved in our play, and he's got to do some scoring for us. I think it was good in the Cuban game that he scored as well as he did, accumulating 37 points during the time that he was in there. I wanted to play Bailey a little bit just to have him do some shooting in competition, which he did, and Damon shot well and scored well in the time that he was in there. So, among those six players that we have used most often, we just used Damon and Matt in that game to hopefully get them back on track offensively and then gave our other kids as much playing time as we possibly could.

The Kansas team that we play today is a team very similar to our own. They are about the same size as we are, they have essentially the same kind of depth, maybe a little bit more depth than we have. They're athletic and they have people that can shoot the ball. The two teams, I think, match up in most respects very evenly. Plus the fact that they are a team with a lot of players that played on a very good Kansas team last year, just as our players played on a very good Indiana team. I look forward to the game at this point, to see what we are able to do with the various challenges that a team like Kansas presents at both ends of the floor. It's a very well set up team, a team that knows exactly how it wants to play and plays as it has been taught to play.

If we're able to do things well offensively and take away some things defensively, then that's a very good indicator for us that we are going in the right direction. If we can't, then it is not a good indication, because Kansas is in the upper echelon of teams across the country that we are going to have to play well against if we want to be any kind of contender in the Big Ten. So today is a good barometer for us.

I think that Kansas differs a little bit from Indiana. Both teams try to play very hard and I think both teams try to read what is happening out there on the offensive end. Kansas uses a few more things defensively than we do and they're probably a little bit more patterned on the offensive end than we are. But I think in general, in philosophical terms, both teams are fairly similar.

It really does not do much good to look at the previous game against Kansas. We were playing with Meeks and Anderson and Pat Graham in that game. Kansas didn't have Walters. They had Randall playing and they're different players to some extent. On the other hand, when we play somebody, we sometimes do look at the most recent game we've had with them. If it's been in the last couple of years, we look at that game from the standpoint of what did we not do or what did they do that really hurt us.

I don't think that the team can live very long on the idea promoted so often in the news media of trying to get even or trying to beat somebody that has beaten you. If that in fact is the case, what do we do with the team that we've beaten three times in a row? Do we just not pay any attention to that team? It seems to me that if you do one, you probably do the other. Maybe many teams do that, and that's why a lot of them get beaten in games when probably they shouldn't get beat.

For tonight's game, we will change the starting lineup around just a little bit with our guards, as I think we'll do often throughout the course of the year, and for specific reasons. We'll go with Reynolds and Bailey at the guards to start with, but this will not affect in any way the minutes that Graham plays. Then we'll go with Cheaney, Henderson and Nover in the front line.

A crowd of 31,000 was expected for the game in Indianapolis, and Knight had this to say.

I think that from the first time we played here in Indianapolis in single games, we've had really good receptions. The whole idea of playing in Indianapolis has been interesting with the advent of the Hoosier Dome. The crowds that we've had in the Dome have numbered among the highest in the country for a single basketball game during the regular season.

GAME SUMMARY

KANSAS 74   INDIANA 69

Indiana played its fourth consecutive opponent ranked in the top 20. This time, third-ranked Kansas came out the winner, and the Hoosiers suffered their first loss of the season. This loss was especially disappointing because many felt that the Hoosiers outplayed the Jayhawks for much of the game. Statistically, IU outshot and outrebounded Kansas, but at crunch time, when the plays had to be made, the Hoosiers simply didn't get the job done.

At the end of the first half with a little over a minute remaining, Indiana owned a 9-point lead, but frittered it away to just a 2-point margin at the break. From there it was a dog fight the rest of the way.

Indiana had some other problems which also led to its downfall. Free throw shooting was a real problem in a couple of ways. First, the Hoosiers didn't get to the line as often as Knight wanted them to or as much as they had in the previous four games. Second, the Hoosiers hit only 4 out of 13 free throw tries against Kansas. So they managed only a 30 percent performance on a shot that Knight earlier referred to as a high percentage shot.

Indiana shot 45 percent from the field. Kansas shot just 41 percent, but the Jayhawks connected on 15 out of 20 free throws. Indiana also turned the ball over three more times than did Kansas. Indiana outrebounded Kansas 43 to 39.

The biggest disappointment to Bob Knight was his team's lack of effort. He felt the free throws were not the deciding factor. It was the lack of effort that hurt them, and effort is something that the Hoosiers will need each and every time they take the floor.

KANSAS

No.	Player		Total FG FG	FGA	3-point FG	FGA	FT	FTA	Rebounds Off	Def	Tot	PF	TP	A	TO	Blk	S	Min
	Hancock, Darrin	f	1	5	0	1	1	2	2	1	3	1	3	1	1	0	0	22
	Scott, Richard	f	6	11	0	0	1	3	1	2	3	5	13	0	3	0	1	14
51	Pauly, Eric	c	1	8	0	0	0	0	3	3	6	3	2	2	1	1	0	27
23	Walters, Rex	g	6	15	2	11	2	3	1	3	4	4	16	3	2	0	0	27
30	Jordan, Adonis	g	4	6	2	4	6	6	0	2	2	0	16	3	0	0	1	34
12	Richey, Patrick		0	1	0	1	1	2	0	4	4	1	1	1	0	0	1	23
20	Woodberry, Steve		4	12	1	3	4	4	4	3	7	0	13	1	0	1	0	29
00	Ostertag, Greg		1	2	0	0	0	0	0	5	5	1	2	0	2	2	0	13
21	Pearson, Sean		2	3	1	2	0	0	1	0	1	2	5	0	1	0	0	7
10	Rayford, Calvin		1	1	1	1	0	0	0	0	0	0	3	1	0	0	0	4
	Team								1	3	4							
	TOTALS		26	64	7	23	15	20	13	26	39	17	74	12	10	4	3	200

Total FG%   1st Half .441(15/34)   2nd half .367(11/30)   Game .406(26/64)   Deadball
3-Pt. FG%   1st Half .308(4/13)   2nd half .300(3/10)   Game .304(7/23)   Rebounds   3
FT%   1st Half .667(4/6)   2nd half .786(11/14)   Game .750(15/20)

INDIANA

No.	Player		Total FG FG	FGA	3-point FG	FGA	FT	FTA	Rebounds Off	Def	Tot	PF	TP	A	TO	Blk	S	Min
40	Cheaney, Calbert	f	11	19	2	3	2	4	3	6	9	4	26	0	4	0	0	35
44	Henderson, Alan	f	3	6	0	0	0	0	1	8	9	4	6	0	0	2	1	23
24	Nover, Matt	c	8	16	0	0	2	7	8	2	10	2	18	1	2	1	1	35
32	Reynolds, Chris	g	0	2	0	1	0	0	2	3	5	2	0	4	2	0	0	24
22	Bailey, Damon	g	5	11	1	5	0	2	0	3	3	4	11	4	1	1	0	35
20	Graham, Greg		3	11	2	5	0	0	0	1	1	2	8	3	1	0	0	29
34	Evans, Brian		0	1	0	0	0	0	0	2	2	0	0	1	1	0	0	14
30	Leary, Todd		0	0	0	0	0	0	0	1	1	0	0	0	1	0	0	3
25	Knight, Pat		0	0	0	0	0	0	0	0	0	0	0	0	0	0	0	1
11	Sims, Malcomb		0	0	0	0	0	0	0	0	0	1	0	0	1	0	0	1
	Team								1	2	3							
	TOTALS		30	66	5	14	4	13	15	28	43	19	69	13	13	4	2	200

Total FG%   1st Half .486(17/35)   2nd half .419(13/31)   Game .454(30/66)   Deadball
3-Pt. FG%   1st Half .833(5/6)   2nd half .000(0/8)   Game .357(5/14)   Rebounds   3
FT%   1st Half .167(1/6)   2nd half .429(3/7)   Game .308(4/13)

Score by
Officials   Stan Reynolds, Paul Caster, Scott Thornley
Technical Fouls
Attendance   31,197

Periods	1	2	OT	OT	Final
Kansas	38	36			74
Indiana	40	29			69

BOB KNIGHT TALK SHOW

December 7, 1992

Coach Knight is often introspective and analytical after a loss, and his concern after the loss to Kansas was apparent in this second talk show of the season. You can sense some of the frustration that Bob feels about his team's performance. As he often does, he focuses on the things that have gone wrong, and on what he feels is necessary for his players to reach their full potential. He lets the listener and now the reader know his thoughts about who should start the next game and why.

Bob begins by differentiating between the loss and the disappointment he feels about the game.

First of all, it was very disappointing to me, but the loss has nothing to do with the disappointment. The disappointment for us is in the way we played and some of the things that we did or did not do in the ballgame. Ours is a team that just hasn't been able to mature mentally as a team over the last couple of years. It seems as though when we have been able to have some kind of accomplishment such as winning the Preseason NIT, then we turn around and have a very difficult time playing as well the next time out. I don't know what it is. I don't know if it's because we relax or because we have a tendency to think that we can just come out and play, or just exactly what it is. We have had that problem with this team now going into the third year.

There were obviously moments in the Kansas game where we played pretty well, but it isn't a game of moments; it's a game of playing well for 40 minutes. We just absolutely did not do that. We get down to the end of the game and there were a lot of things we haven't done. We haven't had the kind of effort in execution that we have to have. Our effort is there sometimes, but it just isn't there enough. We don't work at getting the ball where we have to have it in our offense enough.

Our practice during the week was much better than our play on Saturday was. We had probably as good a week of practice as we've had all season. Norm Ellenberger, who's in his third year here, thought it was the best week of practice that we've had since he's been here. I thought it was extremely good. That's a mystery to me, and the biggest puzzle I've had with this team.

We had opportunities at the defensive end to make three different plays that would have really put us in a great position at the last few minutes of the ballgame, and then didn't make them. There comes a time, well, it's like football. You've got to hold the team at third down and four yards to go at the end of the game, and you've got to get the ball back. And they run a play and you miss a couple of tackles. And you don't get the ball back. That's exactly what happened to us three different times at the defensive end. We had to make the play. The play was there to be made. Shots were missed, we missed a block out, we fouled a guy throwing up a drive on a bad shot. We got out scrambled for the ball again. Those things are going to all add together and they're going to make it difficult for us to beat good basketball teams. It was a very disappointing game from my standpoint in terms of our execution and our effort throughout the ballgame.

We talk about the mental part of the game. The mental thing! We've talked about that a lot over the years, and you know how much emphasis we've tried to put on the mental thing. Let me give you a little bit of an idea and use this last game as an example. I'll talk about some individual plays that occurred in this game that involved the concentration that's necessary to win against good teams.

We have a switch setup that is an easily recognizable switch and one that we have to execute to enable us to maintain our defensive pressure. The first time the switch occurs, we foul it up and Kansas gets a lay-up out of it. All right. That's an early mistake, and people have a tendency to pay more attention to late mistakes than early mistakes. But a mistake that costs us 2 points is a mistake that costs 2 points, no matter at what time it occurs. And when the final score is tabulated, a mistake in the first minute that has cost two points is just as damaging as one in the last minute that has cost two points. I am not sure that everyone understands this.

Like going back to when I talked about Cheaney's play in the Florida State game, a game in which he had scored 34 points. People absolutely could not believe that I didn't think that Cheaney had played a great game. I thought he scored really well and he had taken advantage of his opportunities to score, but he had not played basketball particularly well that night. The next game that we played against Seton Hall, Cheaney was much better. His concentration was much better. He did far more things in the Seton Hall game than he did in the Florida State game. So, his concentration on what he had to do was just much better. We had a tempo that we wanted to play defensively in the Kansas game and it slipped away from us. There were three or four times when our guards could have positioned Matt Nover in the post. We really didn't get any direction from our guards when it was important for us to get direction.

What really hurts this team is that we just don't have things going at full tilt or as hard as we can go all the time. And that's a little bit of our concentration slipping. That's a little bit of relaxing at the wrong time. There's just no point out here when you can relax. If a kid feels that he has to relax then he has to ask to be taken out, until he gets to a point where he is not going to have to relax on any play. The great game for people who have to relax is baseball, because you can sit down half an inning and then go back out and play in the field. But in basketball, you just can't do it. We have these moments and periods when they lose their concentration. I've said all along, the whole key to this team is not shooting or passing or skills. This team has got plenty of skill and plenty of talent to play. Mental toughness is the absolute key to this team, and we lost a game again this Saturday because of a lack of mental toughness.

We're 4 and 1 right now, right? Then we were 27 and 7, so that makes us 31 and 8. And then we were 29 and 5 before that, so that's a total of 13 games that we've lost and 60 that we've won, if my elementary math is correct. So we're 60 and 13. I'd be willing to bet now that between 6 and 8 of those games we have lost for an assortment of reasons all related to the same thing. Either we didn't think the opponent was going to be that good, and we concentrated on the fact that we had beaten the team badly the first time, instead of concentrating on beating them the second time, or we got into the game and it almost seemed like it was a game that wasn't worth our total effort. It's like saying "this is a team that isn't going to be a problem for us."

All of this comes back to the fact that the best teams, and certainly the best teams I've ever had, are teams that are able to go out and play each game as though it's the most important game of the season.

People say this team is struggling at the free throw line this season, going 4 for 13 against Kansas. Let's take the number first of all. Thirteen is not a very good number for us to shoot from the free throw line. That's an indication that we aren't doing enough things offensively and we're not into enough things defensively to draw fouls. My first thought is not that we missed 9 of 13, but that we only shot 13 free throws. Our team should definitely be able to shoot more than that.

Now, let's look at the free throws that we missed. The first thing about missed free throws is that it is easy to say, "well, if we had made free throws." Let's say that we would have shot ten out of thirteen. That's another six points, and at that point where we had a three point lead, we'd have had a nine point lead, and that would have had the game in a pretty good position to go down to the wire with it, OK?

But the free throw is like the shot. It's like fouling off a baseball instead of getting a piece of it. It's like, "gee, another foot and I'd have cleared that bunker." Or even a little thing like fishing. When I fish, there are days when I can put a fly at 50 feet on a quarter. And some days I couldn't put it in a dump truck sometimes. I get too quick or my concentration slides, whatever. By the time this season is over, we'll be able to look back and see that the free throw would have been very, very important to us, and we would have won a lot of games because of good free throw shooting.

The small number of free throws, as I said, was far more of concern to me. That's an indication that we weren't working hard enough on offense to get fouled. We were too easy to guard. We didn't present enough problems to the defense to only shoot that many free throws.

I don't think it was a poorly officiated game. I think there were some calls in the game that just shouldn't happen with three alert officials in a game. But overall, the officiating really didn't hurt us any more than it helped or hurt the other team.

But the mechanical slippage in a shot, in a swing, in whatever, I pay attention to. What things I do that throw things off a little. Like when I'm hunting and a bird flushes. Sometimes I don't get completely down on the gun, and I shoot over it. Usually I'm a pretty good shooter, but I'll make mistakes like that.

It's easy to blame things on shooting when you don't shoot real well, but basically in any game that's lost, it's lost for two reasons. It is very possible in a lot of games that Team A just has far superior talent than Team B and beats them because of that. Particularly if there is organization and structure involved with Team A's talent. Secondly, in games that are lost, there usually are basketball reasons why the game is lost: a failure to block out; a failure to contain the ball in one-on-one situations; help not being given at the proper time. All basketball things: poor shot selection; not working to get open without the ball. Those are the things that cost us the Kansas game, not 4 out of 13 from the free throw line.

One thing that concerned Knight about the Kansas game was the way the Jayhawks were able to drive against Indiana.

The most important thing to us is not what the driver does in terms of scoring but what the driver is able to do if we are forced to help stop the drive. Individuals have to be contained. You try and set up a defense to take away something on a one-on-one situation, all right? You take that away and in taking something away, you put less of a burden on the individual defensive player. Let's say you take away the drive back to the inside or the drive to the outside, or you can play him head up and try and keep him on an angle going from mid court to the corner.

Any one of those ways is fine, but in our case, occasionally, we'll try to force a guy to the outside. When we do force him to the outside, we want him going toward the corner because going toward the corner provides him with less opportunity to do something than going in any other direction on the floor. So if a guy drives over the top of us and we feel that a guy coming back for the middle he has an opportunity to really make some plays when he gets into the middle of the floor, if we don't prevent that. If we let him come back to the middle, he will hurt us. If we don't do a job containing the driver and somebody else has to come over and help, no matter what we're trying to do with that driver, then that's left somebody open momentarily. And when we've left somebody open momentarily, that's a potential score against us. So, a team that drives is able to create a play and able to make something happen not because necessarily the driver is a threat to score, but the fact that if you haven't contained him, then he can get somebody else to score.

Looking ahead to the rest of this campaign, Notre Dame is the next ballgame. Knight talks about how he will direct this team.

I've always felt that if we have not played well and if particular players have not played well, then we go away from those players and we start again. Now I still don't know what I will do in the Notre Dame game, as you and I are recording this, but my choice as a coach is one of two. I take the players that really played well in the Kansas game, that would be Nover and Cheaney, and build around them to see what we can do against Notre Dame. And if I do that, then I don't play Reynolds, Henderson, Bailey and Graham. At least don't start them in the ballgame. Now, I've built almost a completely different team with that. I have done that in the past and have usually had pretty good results in doing it. I'm not sure that's the thing to do with this team. I think that this team has the kind of talent that can be a very good basketball team. The mental toughness factor that we have talked about and talked about has got to be there, however, for this team to realize the talent that it has.

So now the question I've asked myself is this, "who played well in the Kansas game and who, through their play will play in the next game?" I don't think very many people understand that players dictate who plays. The player's performance in practice and the player's performance in a game determine how much he's going to play and in fact whether or not he's going to play. I don't determine that. That's all done for me on the practice floor and in game situations.

Vince Lombardi made many great comments and one about winning stands out in my mind. "Winning is not a sometime thing." You can't win some of the time, you can't win part of the time, you can't win most of the time. If you're going to win, you have to win all of the time. Winning is an all the time proposition, period. You're going to win for 40 minutes. You can beat mediocre teams, but you cannot beat good teams without beating them for 40 minutes. And that more than anything is what we have to do.

Now, that's the thing that has really pleased me about Cheaney. I think Cheaney's work effort is approaching his talent level, which will make Cheaney a great player. And I've said that for two years.

Now this second question that I ask myself probably comes out that we've got to come back with players that we have. They are our most talented players. Somehow we've got to get them playing as they can play. I think what you want is to have the best possible thing going at the beginning of the ballgame for you, and at the beginning of the second half. Now, you pick a lineup to start the ballgame based on the previous game and practices which led up to that game. I think you pick the lineup to go into the second half based on what's happened in the first half and who's played well and who hasn't played well. Then you just go from there with your starting lineup.

But of equal importance is developing play off the bench. And I think we have, perhaps this year, tried harder than ever to get people some critical minutes in ballgames. Every game that we've played, we've turned to the bench just to get them in there, rather than riding with our starting players. And we've had some good play and we've had some mistakes made. We had a couple mistakes in the Kansas game, but hopefully as we get on down the season, we'll have developed to the point where we can come into the game with players that for a minute or two minutes give somebody else a break and really do a good job for us.

But how we get some players really into the game mentally, I don't know. If I had an answer to that, we would have done it already. Whether it's to put them on the bench and let them sit and watch or to try to get them to do it by playing them, I really don't know what the answer to that one is.

We've got a game tonight that I think is going to be really interesting to us because Notre Dame is just coming off a couple of good wins against Loyola and Evansville. They have to be all pumped up about having the chance to play us at South Bend early in the year. It is a chance for them to get a lot of recognition and accomplish a lot in beating a team that's supposed to be a good team. So, there will be a real challenge, I think, for our players in this ballgame. How will we go about handling it, I just don't know. As I said, the disappointment from Saturday's game doesn't come with the score; it comes with how we arrived at the score.

Don Fischer spent some time prior to the show watching the tapes of the Kansas game with Knight and the way Indiana has performed. Don saw first hand how detailed Coach Knight's analysis is of each game, of each player and the various segments of a game. Fischer comments that he doesn't think people see the details of what goes on in a basketball game unless they can break it down like Coach Knight is able to do in looking at tapes. Knight responds with a classic statement.

Well, basketball is my business. That's all I've ever done, so I should be able to sit and see what's going on.

I wish I could have come out of the Kansas game just feeling that if we had made free throws we would have won the ballgame. But it was impossible to do that and even more so after watching the tape of the game. We can shoot 95 percent at the free throw line the rest of the season and play the same way we did against Kansas, and we're going to lose a lot of basketball games. Believe me; we will lose a lot of basketball games playing like we did Saturday.

Indiana vs. Notre Dame
December 8, 1992
South Bend
Pre-game Show

Indiana had only two practice days to prepare for Notre Dame; however Coach Knight continues to review the Kansas game and look at the things that were lacking, especially on defense. The lessons from a loss stay in Knight's mind for years, and he replays those losses over and over again. He repeats himself in this show as I am sure he did with his players during practice this week.

He takes a moment to talk about Calbert Cheaney and Matt Nover, who played well against Kansas. While Knight looks back, the season goes on, and playing the Irish in South Bend is always difficult. This year's Notre Dame team, which comes into the game with a 2-0 record, would present a real challenge for the Hoosiers. At one point in the game it seemed that the entire season was hanging in the balance as Indiana worked to overcome a 2-point deficit.

I think the thing that concerned me the most about the way we played in the Kansas game was just simple effort. There's effort from a mental standpoint and there's effort from a physical standpoint. Every situation that develops in a game defensively requires a particular reaction on the part of every defensive player. There were some times that we just gave a careless reaction. We did not give a well-timed, well-conceived reaction to the situation. The careless reaction usually meant that we over committed on recovery or we got hung up in some kind of an angle in the post. Then, the other thing that we did was just have a pure lack of effort. We had people driving past us throughout the entire course of the ballgame that enabled Kansas to set up opportunities to take the shot. They made four or five three-point shots as a result of our simply not working to contain the ball, or putting the ball in a position where we had to slide to help and that would free somebody for the shot and then knocking it down. That became probably as much a part of their offense as anything they did throughout the course of the game.

Fischer asks how Cheaney and Nover are emerging, and Knight has this to say.

Cheaney's not emerging. I mean he has been here as a pretty good player for a long time. Matt Nover has played very well at times in the past. I think the word "emerging" is ill advised here. I think they, as seniors, certainly in the Kansas game, went to the forefront as far as our own personnel were concerned. They totaled 44 points and 19 rebounds between them, but each made some mistakes that proved to be very costly to us. Yet, in tallying up everything, their good plays and their contributions far outweighed the mistakes.

Now that wasn't the case with our other players. We had negative contributions from everybody else with any degree of playing time. And that, in the final analysis, was what decided the game—not the play of Cheaney and Nover.

Looking ahead to Notre Dame, they are a very good offensive team. They've got the capability of putting five players in the game, all of whom can shoot the ball, so you really don't have anybody that you can drop away from. It requires you to play a lot of really good individual defense against them. They've never had fewer than three and most times four good post players in the ballgame at the same time. So the combination of the players' abilities to shoot outside and post inside requires really good defensive play from whoever is playing against them.

GAME SUMMARY

INDIANA 75   NOTRE DAME 70

Indiana broke out to a 17-point lead in the first 15 minutes of this game with some ferocious defensive play which took the Irish out of its offense. Indiana could not sustain that level of intensity and Notre Dame was within 10 points by halftime. The second half almost looked like a reversal, with the Irish playing more intensely and IU trying to hang on.

Calbert Cheaney again led Indiana's attack with 19 points, but took only ten shots against great defensive pressure. He handed out six assists that were just as damaging to Notre Dame. Matt Nover hit a key basket in this game, with Indiana up 73 to 70 and the shot clock winding down to zero. With about 18 seconds to go, Nover, under heavy pressure, drilled a 15-foot field goal that gave Indiana the insurance it needed to pull out the win.

Nover had 16 points and 8 rebounds in the game, while Greg Graham added 15 points. Indiana shot just over 52 percent for the game while holding Notre Dame to 40 percent from the field. But the Hoosiers struggled from the free throw line, connecting on just 19 for 30, for 61 percent.

INDIANA

No.	Player		Total FG FG	FGA	3-point FG	FGA	FT	FTA	Rebounds Off	Def	Tot	PF	TP	A	TO	Blk	S	Min
40	Cheaney, Calbert	f	6	10	2	4	5	8	1	2	3	3	19	6	4	0	2	36
44	Henderson, Alan	f	4	10	0	0	1	2	5	8	13	2	9	0	4	2	1	33
24	Nover, Matt	c	5	9	0	0	6	12	0	8	8	3	16	1	5	0	0	30
20	Graham, Greg	g	5	10	2	3	3	4	0	2	2	5	15	2	2	1	2	34
22	Bailey, Damon	g	2	3	0	0	0	0	0	2	2	2	4	3	1	1	0	27
32	Reynolds, Chris		1	1	0	0	0	0	0	0	0	2	2	3	2	0	0	22
34	Evans, Brian		1	3	1	2	4	4	1	2	3	2	7	0	0	0	0	10
30	Leary, Todd		1	2	1	2	0	0	0	0	0	0	3	0	0	0	0	4
25	Knight, Pat		0	0	0	0	0	0	0	0	0	0	0	0	0	0	0	3
11	Sims, Malcomb		0	0	0	0	0	0	0	0	0	0	0	0	0	0	0	1
	Team								3	0	3							
	TOTALS		25	48	6	11	19	30	10	24	34	19	75	15	18	4	5	200

Total FG% 1st Half .548(17/31) 2nd half .471(8/17) Game .521(25/48) Deadball
3-Pt. FG% 1st Half .600(3/5) 2nd half .500(3/6) Game .545(6/11) Rebounds 3
FT% 1st Half .667(6/9) 2nd half .571(13/21) Game .613(19/30)

NOTRE DAME

No.	Player		Total FG FG	FGA	3-point FG	FGA	FT	FTA	Rebounds Off	Def	Tot	PF	TP	A	TO	Blk	S	Min
3	Williams, Monty	f	5	12	2	2	3	4	5	7	12	5	15	1	4	1	1	21
21	Russell, Malik	f	3	8	0	0	0	0	0	3	3	4	6	4	5	1	1	35
53	Ross, Joe	c	0	1	0	0	2	4	1	3	4	2	2	0	0	1	0	14
5	Hoover, Ryan	g	2	6	2	5	0	0	0	1	1	1	6	1	3	0	0	16
30	Taylor, Billy	g	3	14	1	3	2	5	1	1	2	3	9	2	1	0	2	39
54	Ross, Jon		2	5	0	0	3	4	1	2	3	4	7	0	0	0	0	27
24	Justice, Lamarr		4	4	2	2	2	2	0	2	2	1	12	6	4	0	2	24
50	Cozen, Carl		3	6	3	5	2	2	2	2	4	4	11	0	0	0	0	18
15	Boyer, Brooks		1	1	0	0	0	0	0	0	0	0	2	0	1	0	1	5
23	Williams, Jason		0	0	0	0	0	0	0	0	0	0	0	0	0	0	0	1
	Team								4	1	5							
	TOTALS		23	57	10	17	14	21	14	22	36	24	70	14	18	3	7	200

Total FG% 1st Half .387(12/31) 2nd half .423(11/26) Game 0.404(23/57) Deadball
3-Pt. FG% 1st Half .600(6/10) 2nd half .571(4/7) Game .588(10/17) Rebounds 2
FT% 1st Half .750(3/4) 2nd half .647(11/17) Game .667(14/21)

Officials Tom Rucker, Sid Rodheffer, Tom Clark
Technical Fouls
Attendance 11,418

Score by Periods	1	2	OT	OT	Final
Indiana	43	32			75
Notre Dame	33	37			70

Austin Peay vs. Indiana
December 11, 1992
Indiana Classic—Bloomington
Pre-game Show

Indiana has won 36 straight games in the Indiana Classic during the 18 years it has been played at Bloomington and the Hoosiers will add to that run in the 1992 Classic with two impressive wins. Knight begins by talking about the 75-70 win over Notre Dame and the problem with Cheaney getting only 10 shots a game. He also talks about the loss of intensity in the second half. Then he gave his thoughts on the Austin Peay team.

I thought that we started out obviously really well in the ballgame. I told John McLeod, the Notre Dame coach, the afternoon of the game that I thought they were going to have a real fine team this year and I expected it to be, you know, a very tough ballgame for us. And yet, we got off to such a good start and were ahead by 17 points. We ought to be able to play with that lead and play pretty well from that point on, but we just didn't.

We ended up, I think, getting down by what, as much as 2? So we lost 19 points. You know I can say, "well I was really pleased that we came back, and we came back really strong, and we did this and we did that." The thing that concerns me more than anything else is not the fact that we came back strongly at the end of the Notre Dame game; it's the fact that during that period of time, we were outscored by 19 points.

Calbert really went into the game trying to get everybody else involved in the offense. He made three or four really good passes in the first half of the game. But we can't live with him taking ten shots in the ballgame. That's just not enough for our offense. We've got too much tied up in him to do that.

The inability to maintain intensity is a continuing concern to Knight.

If I knew the reasons behind the drop in intensity, I'd correct it. I don't know what happens when intensity slips away from us. I don't know why we have it to the point where we get 17 ahead and then we don't have it to the point we're two behind. I wish I knew. If I knew the answer to it, believe me I would correct it. I would change it. I'd rectify it. I'd bottle it, and I'd sell it to all the media people.

I saw Austin Peay in their game against Mississippi State, and I really liked what I saw. They were patient, they went to the things that they could do well. They jammed things up a lot defensively, and made Mississippi State score from the outside. I'm sure that is something that we're going to have to be able to do in this ballgame.

I'd like to look for 40 minutes of good, consistent play. Defense is team play, and overall, I think our defense has been decent. Some individuals have not played well and some have played well. Those that have not played well have made our defense decent instead of very good.

Fischer then asked Knight to talk about Western Michigan and Pacific, the teams that play in the second ballgame tonight. Knight quips in response:

Well, the first time that I'll get a chance to see either one of those two clubs play will be watching them with you in the second half. So at this point I can't really comment on something that I haven't seen or know very little about. Unlike people in the news media, Don, I only talk about those things that I know something about.

I do know that Western has an outstanding coach in Bob Donewald, a guy that had an awful lot to do with getting our basketball situation going here at Indiana. We had two of his players, Laskowski and Abernathy, and then Bob was with us for a long time in the '70s and '80s and we really enjoyed having him here as a part of our staff.

Fischer often asked Knight who would start in the game that day and Knight would often dodge the question. Naming the starting lineup became an ongoing battle for Fischer, as you will see from the following exchange.

FISCHER: Coach, how about the lineup tonight?

KNIGHT: We're going to go with the same lineup that we used yesterday in practice.

FISCHER: Do you care to review who that was?

KNIGHT: I forget.

FISCHER: All right. Well, best of luck in tonight's ballgame.

KNIGHT: Where are we playing?

FISCHER: We're playing here at the Assembly Hall tonight.

KNIGHT: This season is early, Don, and I seem to have lost . . . .

FISCHER: This has been the *"Bob Knight Pre-game Show"* with discussion and commentary on tonight's ballgame with Austin Peay. Now this is Don Fischer inviting you to stay tuned for tonight's game.

GAME SUMMARY

INDIANA 107   AUSTIN PEAY 71

Indiana ran its record to 6-1 with the opening-round victory in the 19th annual Indiana Classic Tournament topping Austin Peay. This was a game in which Bob Knight was able to use his entire roster and five players scored in double figures, led by Alan Henderson with 25 points. He also had a team high 18 rebounds. Joining Henderson in double figures: Calbert Cheaney, Damon Bailey and Chris Reynolds all had 16 points. Greg Graham added 12. For Chris Reynolds, the 16 points was a season high. Damon Bailey also added 6 assists which led the team in that category.

The most pleasing aspect of the game for Bob Knight was the fact that his Hoosiers maintained full concentration and intensity, along with effort, for the full 40 minutes of this ballgame. Indiana found its free throw shooting touch once again, connecting on 22 out of 29 for 76 percent. The Hoosiers shot 56 percent from the field and outrebounded Austin Peay 35 to 30.

AUSTIN PEAY

No.	Player		Total FG FG	FGA	3-point FG	FGA	FT	FTA	Rebounds Off	Def	Tot	PF	TP	A	TO	Blk	S	Min
25	Yudt, Rick	f	12	23	1	3	0	1	0	6	6	3	25	1	2	0	0	37
42	Jenkins, John	f	1	2	0	0	1	2	0	1	1	1	3	0	5	0	0	21
5	Dupree, Reggie	c	2	4	0	0	0	0	1	1	2	3	4	0	1	1	0	16
20	Franklin, Greg	g	4	6	0	0	0	1	0	1	1	3	8	2	6	0	1	24
22	Meriwether, Carlosg		0	2	0	1	2	2	1	2	3	4	2	4	6	0	1	27
44	Beck, Tyrone		2	3	0	0	2	2	4	4	8	2	6	1	3	1	1	23
3	Casbon, Cole		0	2	0	0	0	0	0	0	0	0	0	1	1	1	0	8
23	Savage, Jermaine		2	4	1	2	0	0	1	0	1	0	5	0	2	0	1	20
31	McCormick, Malcomb		3	5	0	0	2	2	0	3	3	0	8	1	2	0	1	13
24	Bell, Devlin		0	3	0	0	0	0	0	0	0	3	0	0	0	0	0	9
50	Heien, Jason		0	0	0	0	0	0	0	1	1	0	0	0	1	0	0	1
55	Key, Otis		0	1	0	0	0	0	0	0	0	1	0	0	0	0	0	1
	Team								3	1	4							
	TOTALS		26	55	2	6	7	10	10	20	30	20	61	10	29	3	5	200

Total FG% 1st Half .423(11/26)   2nd half .517(15/29)   Game .473(26/55)   Deadball
3-Pt. FG% 1st Half .400(2/5)   2nd half .000(0/1)   Game .333(2/6)   Rebounds __1__
FT% 1st Half .800(4/5)   2nd half .600(3/5)   Game .700(7/10)

INDIANA

No.	Player		Total FG FG	FGA	3-point FG	FGA	FT	FTA	Rebounds Off	Def	Tot	PF	TP	A	TO	Blk	S	Min
40	Cheaney, Calbert	f	6	11	3	4	1	1	0	1	1	1	16	3	0	0	2	20
44	Henderson, Alan	f	10	15	0	0	5	6	5	3	8	3	25	2	2	1	3	22
24	Nover, Matt	c	1	4	0	0	5	8	0	3	3	1	7	0	1	1	0	17
20	Graham, Greg	g	4	8	0	1	4	5	2	2	4	2	12	3	1	0	1	22
30	Leary, Todd	g	2	5	1	2	0	0	1	2	3	1	5	0	1	0	0	18
22	Bailey, Damon		7	13	1	1	1	1	1	4	5	4	16	6	0	0	1	26
21	Reynolds, Chris		7	7	0	0	2	4	0	0	0	1	16	1	1	0	3	22
25	Knight, Pat		3	6	0	0	0	0	1	3	4	1	6	1	0	0	0	21
34	Evans, Brian		0	0	0	0	0	0	1	1	2	2	0	1	2	0	1	17
11	Sims, Malcomb		0	2	0	0	4	4	0	1	1	2	4	0	2	0	2	15
	Team								3	1	4							
	TOTALS		40	71	5	9	22	29	14	21	35	18	107	17	10	2	13	200

Total FG% 1st Half .469(15/32)   2nd half .641(25/39)   Game .563(40/71)   Deadball
3-Pt. FG% 1st Half .571(4/7)   2nd half .500(1/2)   Game .556(5/9)   Rebounds __4__
FT% 1st Half .706(12/17)   2nd half .833(10/12)   Game .759(22/29)

Officials   Randy Drury, Sam Lickliter, George Demos
Technical Fouls
Attendance   16,482

Score by Periods	1	2	OT	OT	Final
Austin Peay	28	33			61
Indiana	46	61			107

The game against Western Michigan brought Knight against his former assistant Coach at IU, Bob Donewald. As fiercely competitive as Knight becomes during a game, his respect and regard for Donewald is apparent in his pre-game interview. Coach Knight begins by talking about the Austin Peay game, a 107-61 triumph, with the Hoosiers playing well during the entire game.

One of the things that we have got to be able to do is play steadily and consistently well throughout the course of the ballgame and not have just isolated periods where we play really well.

Take the Florida State game as an example. We jump out to a 15-point lead, and then we wind up going from that point of 15 ahead to 12 behind at the start of the second half. We've got to be able to keep things going steadily. We're a lot better off to be playing well and to be playing relatively even with somebody than we are to have great ups and downs in the course of a ballgame.

I think even more indicative was our game against Notre Dame where we had a 17-point lead, then saw it not only dwindle but actually become a 2-point deficit. What I'm getting at is that when you lose that kind of a lead it is very difficult to ever get the thing going back to where you had it in the beginning. So last night we had things go pretty well for us throughout the whole ballgame with everybody playing. That's the kind of basketball I like to see us play.

Before I talk about Western Michigan, I want to talk about Bob Donewald, a really outstanding coach. He did a great job at Illinois State, but he had a president and an athletic director over there who I think epitomize what's wrong with intercollegiate athletics when they let Bob go in that job. Then Bill Orwig who had hired me here was very instrumental in helping Bob get the Western Michigan job, which I think was a real improvement for him. Bob has done a great job there. He's really kind of resurrected things at Western Michigan. Of all the coaches that I've worked with, none does a better job or understands the game better than Bob does.

So we are really happy to have his team here. They did a great job and they played a pretty good Pacific team last night.

Looking to the Western Michigan team, their size or lack of it wasn't a real key factor in their last ballgame. What was really important for them in the game was their ability to maintain their composure early in the game when they got behind and they just kept chipping away and chipping away. Once they got into a position where they had to lead, they didn't make any mistakes from that point on and went ahead to put Pacific away.

Against Austin Peay, Henderson did a very good job during that stretch when he scored 14 straight points, getting a lot of points off the offensive board. I think that he was able to get up and down the floor well and certainly capitalize on the opportunities that he had. At the same time, Alan missed a couple of block outs that led to a couple of buckets for the other guys. And that concerned me as much as I was pleased about what he had been able to do at the offensive end.

Fischer then asked Coach Knight: You have to be pretty pleased with a guy we don't talk very much about, your son Patrick? He seems to see what's going on the floor very well.

Well, he's been around it long enough. He ought to know what's going on.

GAME SUMMARY

INDIANA 97   WESTERN MICHIGAN 58

Every Indiana basketball team since the inception of the Indiana Classic Tournament, 18 years ago, has won this event, and the 19th Indiana Classic was no exception. The Hoosiers prevailed easily in this title ballgame over former assistant coach Bob Donewald and his Western Michigan Broncos.

In this tournament, neither opponent could match IU in manpower, although the Broncos kept it interesting for a half. The best news from the two-day event was that the Hoosiers maintained their intensity level for a full 40 minutes in each of the two wins, despite numerous lineup changes and the shuffling in and out of different combinations.

Chris Reynolds joined Co-Most Valuable Players Alan Henderson and Calbert Cheaney on the All-Tournament Team. Cheaney became IU's fourth player in history to score 2,000 career points. Cheaney and Henderson each had 38 for the two games, while Henderson had 8 and 13 rebounds, to lead IU in that department.

The only real negative was 20 turnovers in the title game, but when you win by 39, it's hard to dwell on that kind of a problem. Indiana had balanced scoring with Cheaney's 22, 19 out of Matt Nover, 13 points from Alan Henderson, and 10 from Damon Bailey. The top assist man, Greg Graham, had 6 in this contest, and Indiana hit a blistering 65 percent from the field while holding Western Michigan to just 38 percent for the ballgame. Indiana outrebounded the Broncos 44 to 20 as well.

Indiana now stands 7-1 on the season.

WESTERN MICHIGAN

No.	Player		Total FG FG	FGA	3-point FG	FGA	FT	FTA	Rebounds Off	Def	Tot	PF	TP	A	TO	Blk	S	Min
12	McGee, Leon	f	5	11	0	2	0	0	1	1	2	2	10	1	2	0	0	21
32	Whightman, Sean	f	5	13	3	7	3	4	0	0	0	2	16	1	3	0	2	37
50	Van Abbema, Matt	c	2	6	0	0	0	1	3	0	3	3	4	0	1	0	0	23
4	Sanders, Ebon	g	3	6	1	3	2	4	0	0	0	2	9	2	4	0	1	29
23	Brooks, Darrick	g	5	14	1	6	0	0	1	1	2	1	11	2	0	0	4	32
24	Jackson, Shawn		0	0	0	0	0	0	0	0	0	3	0	1	3	0	1	5
35	Handlogten, Ben		1	2	0	0	0	0	1	3	4	5	2	0	1	0	1	6
11	Sanders, Janocus		0	0	0	0	0	0	0	1	1	0	0	0	0	0	1	10
21	Johnson, William		2	5	0	0	0	0	1	0	1	0	4	0	0	0	1	11
34	Whightman, Sean		0	4	0	2	0	0	1	1	2	0	0	1	0	0	0	2
33	Mosely, Mike		1	2	0	0	0	0	1	2	3	0	2	0	1	0	0	13
30	Schaffer, Doug		0	0	0	0	0	0	0	0	0	0	0	0	0	0	0	2
10	Bennett, Vinton		0	0	0	0	0	1	0	0	0	1	0	0	0	0	0	4
22	Pearson, Michael		0	0	0	0	0	0	0	1	1	1	0	0	0	0	0	5
	Team								0	1	1				1			
	TOTALS		24	63	5	20	5	10	9	11	20	20	58	8	16	0	11	200

Total FG%	1st Half .441(15/34)	2nd half .310(9/29)	Game .381(24/63)	Deadball
3-Pt. FG%	1st Half .250(3/12)	2nd half .250(2/8)	Game .250(5/20)	Rebounds 2
FT%	1st Half 1.00(4/4)	2nd half .167(1/6)	Game .500(5/10)	

INDIANA

No.	Player		Total FG FG	FGA	3-point FG	FGA	FT	FTA	Rebounds Off	Def	Tot	PF	TP	A	TO	Blk	S	Min
40	Cheaney, Calbert	f	9	14	2	4	2	2	4	3	7	4	22	3	3	0	2	28
44	Henderson, Alan	f	4	6	1	1	4	7	3	11	14	3	13	0	4	1	1	23
24	Nover, Matt	c	8	8	0	0	3	4	1	5	6	0	19	2	1	1	0	23
20	Graham, Greg	g	3	6	0	0	3	4	1	1	2	4	9	6	2	0	2	35
30	Leary, Todd	g	3	5	1	1	0	0	1	0	1	1	7	3	4	0	1	21
22	Bailey, Damon		3	5	0	0	4	4	0	2	2	1	10	3	2	0	1	19
21	Reynolds, Chris		2	3	0	0	4	4	0	1	1	1	8	1	3	0	1	23
34	Evans, Brian		2	3	0	1	3	4	1	6	7	0	7	1	1	0	1	15
25	Knight, Pat		0	2	0	0	0	0	0	1	1	0	0	0	0	0	0	9
11	Sims, Malcomb		0	0	0	0	2	2	0	2	2	1	2	1	0	0	0	4
	Team								0	1	1							
	TOTALS		34	52	4	7	25	31	11	33	44	15	97	20	20	2	8	200

Total FG%	1st Half .615(16/26)	2nd half .692(18/26)	Game .654(34/52)	Deadball
3-Pt. FG%	1st Half .750(3/4)	2nd half .333(1/3)	Game .571(4/7)	Rebounds 2
FT%	1st Half .765(13/17)	2nd half .857(12/14)	Game .806(25/31)	

Officials   Sam Lickliter, Randy Drury, Rick Wulkow
Technical Fouls 1 - Indiana 15:51 2nd Bench
Attendance 16,528

Score by Periods	1	2	OT	OT	Final
W. Michigan	37	21			58
Indiana	48	49			97

BOB KNIGHT TALK SHOW
December 14, 1992

Due to the team's travel schedule, previous talk shows were pre-recorded and Knight did not take questions from listeners. This was the first "call-in" show of the season, and it originated from his locker room. The audience began to hear more of Knight's sense of humor.

We were concerned about the air quality of the program and some of tapes were garbled or inaudible. When I visited with Coach Knight for one of the shows, I found that he often talked "off mic" as he moved around his locker room during a broadcast. I asked our engineer Gary Kline to find a solution to this problem. For this show, a wireless microphone was used to try to improve the quality of the broadcast. We suspected that Knight would have some fun with the freedom the new microphone gave him, and we weren't disappointed.

FISCHER: Coach, the team was victorious in three ballgames this past week. Talk a minute about those three games and the way you felt your ball team performed.

KNIGHT: Probably the best that we played was in the beginning of our game with Notre Dame. Can you hear me, Don?

FISCHER: I hear you.

KNIGHT: This is a strange microphone we have here.

FISCHER: It is a little bit different, Coach, but it picks you up just about any place you go in your room.

KNIGHT: Well, that will be beneficial, Don, for a lot of reasons. That will help immeasurably.

FISCHER: All right.

KNIGHT: We had good defensive awareness and alertness. The audio here kind of bothers me, Don.

FISCHER: How about the first ballgame against Austin Peay?

KNIGHT: In that particular game, Don, what we wanted more than anything else was to get 40 minutes of good playing time out of our players. I thought we were able to pretty much accomplish that. We didn't have any slippage at all in what we were trying to do. So that game was good both offensively and defensively. We pretty much dominated the game and were able to establish the kind of control of the game that we thought we should have.

Then with Western Michigan, it was a different type of a ballgame because

Western Michigan was going to be a more aggressive ball team, a more difficult team to play offense against than Austin Peay was, and they proved to be that. Any time a team works as hard as it can and works to do things at the defensive end with rules and principles in aggressiveness, it's going to be a difficult team.

One of the interesting things, I think, from perhaps a fan's standpoint might be something Norm Ellenberger said early in the game. People may not know this, but Naismith, the inventor of the game of basketball, detested the dribble. I think somewhere, perhaps in the year 1927, they actually worked to get the dribble out of basketball. It happened for a year, and it was put back into basketball. Well, from that assessment of the dribble in the late 1920's, we're here in 1992 where the dribble is probably the most difficult offensive weapon there is to play against.

A guy that really uses the dribble, that works with the dribble, is a very, very difficult guy to play against. A guy that really can use the dribble makes it tough for you to completely contain that offense. If he uses the dribble to penetrate, it keeps you off balance, you can't get the ball away from him. Eventually the defense is going to break down somewhere and there is going to be an opportunity for the offense to get a good shot or to score a basket.

Western Michigan became a very tough team for us to play against at both ends of the floor because of the way Bob had them set up defensively. The good movement and screening that they had in their offense were a real challenge. It was a different test for us in the three games, all hopefully contributing to our development to be ready to play by the time our conference starts.

Don, can you hear me?

FISCHER: Yes, I can hear you.

KNIGHT: This new microphone gives me a lot of freedom.
Then listeners could clearly hear a toilet flush and Knight chuckling in the background.

FISCHER: I was afraid of that. All right. Let's take some phone calls here this evening. Our first call of the night is from Fishers, Indiana. Last week you talked about your disappointment with the intensity of many of your players in the Kansas ballgame. Did that improve this weekend?

KNIGHT: We're working to improve it. Let me put it that way. I don't think that we are anywhere close to where we have to be or what we have to have as a team in terms of our intensity. We just have to put that into play if we're going to be a really competitive team.

FISCHER: From Jasonville, Indiana. What do you think of the Big Ten schedule, and is there a way to make it any better? My assumption here is that he is talking about the Penn State addition.

KNIGHT: The best way to set up the schedule is to play everybody twice, and I don't believe that's going to happen. I'm probably the only coach that voted in favor of that. So what I'm sure we'll continue to have the 18 game schedule, playing two teams once and then doing that on a rotating basis.

FISCHER: Our next caller is from Glendale. Do you think Calbert Cheaney loses some intensity when he sits on the bench during the ballgame?

KNIGHT: What would you want us to do? Play Calbert Cheaney 40 total minutes? Cheaney's got to be taken out and given a breather here and there. I think that his intensity and his retention of intensity has been the best this year that it has ever been.

FISCHER: This is from Clarksville, Indiana. Do you think Quinn Buckner would take a head coaching job or the one that you would leave when you retire?

KNIGHT: Well, actually it's going to be announced tomorrow. In fact Quinn will be the new head coach at Indiana and his first game will be the Cincinnati game on Saturday.

FISCHER: This is from Indianapolis. Damon Bailey doesn't seem to be shooting well this year. Do you think he'll get over this situation or is it that he's just not a good shooter?

KNIGHT: Well, I'm not sure that he isn't shooting well right now. Bailey has hit 26 shots of 50 attempts. He's shooting 52%. As a team, we're shooting 52%, so Bailey is shooting right where we are as a team. 52% is pretty good.

FISCHER: Our next caller is from Westminster, Maryland. Saturday night you seemed at times to have problems in calling a time out. Do you want your kids to get themselves out of trouble in situations like this?

KNIGHT: I really don't have any problem in calling a time out. I actually do know how to do it. You just kind of stand and make a "T" sign with your hand. I don't think that a time out is necessary at every moment something goes wrong. I think it is important to have time outs near the end of the game for a variety of reasons.

FISCHER: This is a question from Columbus, Indiana. Has this senior class lived up to your expectations?

KNIGHT: I think this senior class has played on teams in the last two years that have won the second most number of games that any Indiana team has ever won in a two-year period. I would think that would be something that would fulfill the expectations of any Indiana fan.

FISCHER: All right. This question is from Bloomington, Coach. Can you give an evaluation of Todd Lindeman's progress? What weight you'd like to see him playing at next year?

KNIGHT: I'd like to see Todd play at somewhere between 240 and 245. He's just under 230 now, and I think his progress has been outstanding. I have really been pleased with the way he has worked and the progress that he has made. I think that we are going to be looking next year at Todd as a very, very good basketball player.

FISCHER: This next question is from Bloomington. Has Alan Henderson's intensity level dropped this year or is he playing up to his capability?

KNIGHT: I think that Alan's intensity has improved. I don't think that anybody could come in here as a freshman and have exactly what we want in terms of intensity, but last year Alan may have come about as close as anyone we ever had. I think it has been, for the most part, pretty good this year.

FISCHER: From Oolitic, Indiana. What's the biggest fish you've ever caught and where was it caught?

KNIGHT: Well, I caught Jaws once. I was fishing off Montauk Point once with red worms for blue gill, and I caught Jaws.

FISCHER: No damage done, though?

KNIGHT: To the worms or Jaws? The biggest fish I've ever caught was probably . . . I don't know. I've never really fished much for big fish. I've caught blue gill that weighed over a pound and a half, which is really big for blue gill. I've caught Atlantic salmon that weighed over 20 pounds, snook that weighed over 20 pounds. Salmon in Lake Michigan that probably weighed 26 to 28 pounds. Those are probably the biggest fish. It isn't the biggest fish in fishing that's important. It's the challenge of catching a specific fish under certain conditions that makes fishing so interesting.

FISCHER: This is from Indianapolis. Have you changed your philosophy over the years on substituting for fatigue?

KNIGHT: No. When guys are tired, I usually take them out.

FISCHER: This is from Spencer. Who was the tallest player you've ever coached?

KNIGHT: I had a kid that played for me when I was at West Point that was 9-2, and we really weren't able to use him because they commissioned him as an officer without ever having gone through the Academy. They disguised him as a palm tree and they used him as a forward artillery observer at the desert war-fare training site on the Mohave Desert. I just don't know how Lamont would have done had we been able to keep him.

FISCHER: He never had to go through the Academy to get commissioned, huh?

KNIGHT: No. I mean they took him out right away. Actually, he reached the rank of two-star general, was in charge of the Army's string of convenience stores in the California desert. He was in charge of all of them because, disguised as a palm tree, he would spend time outside of each one, observing the work habits of the employees as well as anything that took place from the standpoint of robbery or petty theft or whatever. That string of stores became the most profitable chain in the United States Army.

FISCHER: A New Albany listener would like you to assess Brian Evans' play so far this year.

KNIGHT: I think that Brian is like what we would expect of any first year player. He played very well on occasion and has made some really good contributions to the games that we've had thus far. He's got a lot to learn about consistency of play and consistency of effort. As soon as he does, I think he'll improve immeasurably.

FISCHER: This is from Atlanta, Georgia, Coach. How do you prepare your players mentally for a ballgame?

KNIGHT: Sometimes not very well, Don.

FISCHER: Do you deal with their mentality at all, prior to a contest?

KNIGHT: No, we don't think that the mental part of basketball has anything to do with playing. We simply deal with the physical aspects of the game. Where have you been for 20 years?

FISCHER: I'm just giving you a question from a guy in Atlanta.

KNIGHT: Well, then you asked me if we deal with the mental aspect of the game. I mean, why ask that question? Why don't you just answer it? You've heard me answer that a thousand times.

FISCHER: Listener, you must understand that the mental is the physical.

KNIGHT: At least.

FISCHER: At least that. And that's primarily how much importance Coach puts on the mental part of the game. So virtually every contest, they are much more interested in their mental frame of mind than their physical being.

FISCHER: From Columbus, Indiana. His son in Portland, Oregon, would like you to know that he would love to have you come to Portland, Oregon, any time to go sturgeon fishing.

FISCHER: This is from Bloomington, what . . .

KNIGHT: Wait a minute, Don. I really appreciate the offer to go to Portland to go sturgeon fishing. That was nice of him to extend that.

FISCHER: All right. This is from Bloomington, Coach. How is Jamal Meeks doing now?

KNIGHT: Playing in the Global League in Cedar Rapids, Iowa. They like Jamal out there very much.

FISCHER: This is from St. Joseph, Michigan. Is there any possibility that you would go to another university if a large amount of money would be offered to you?

KNIGHT: Right now I'm contemplating a move to the University of the Antarctica. As Buckner takes my place on Saturday, I may be coaching Antarctica on Saturday. The problem is that they've had two penguins quit. That's kind of an interesting situation. Down there, Don, you don't have black players or white players. You have black and white players.

FISCHER: Can you assess Dan Dakich's coaching and how well he will he do in the future?

KNIGHT: Danny has done an exceptional job for us. I think he has an excellent future in basketball.

FISCHER: This question from Schererville, Indiana. You coached many years without the three-point shot. Has it been difficult to adjust to having it?

KNIGHT: Don, my memory fades in and out, but it seems to me that the first year of the three-point shot we won the NCAA Championship.

FISCHER: From Bedford, Indiana. From seeing other college games this year, who has impressed you?

KNIGHT: The only games that I've seen are the games that we have played. And I think several of these teams will do well in the NCAA tournament.

FISCHER: This is from Indianapolis. Todd Leary was in a starting role in the last two games of the tournament. How did you assess his play and will he continue in that role?

KNIGHT: I think Todd has done some really good things for us this year, and I expect that to continue throughout the course of the season.

FISCHER: This is from Fort Wayne. Please talk about Calbert Cheaney becoming the fourth player in Indiana history to go into 2,000 career points in the scoring column.

KNIGHT: Well, what I'm more interested in as far as Calbert is concerned is his all around play. We have had some great players here that didn't come close to scoring 2,000 points, but that's a great accomplishment for a kid. That's a singular accomplishment insofar as scoring is concerned. And for a kid to score that much, he has had a lot of help from people, a lot of screening and getting him the basketball in a lot of situations where he can shoot it. What I want for Calbert is for him to be as good an all around player as he can possibly be.

The non-conference season continued with Cincinnati visiting Assembly Hall to play Indiana which is now ranked fourth. Cincinnati was also a Final Four contender last year and represented another formidable challenge to Indiana.

One unexpected loss was Malcolm Sims, whose decided to transfer to another school for the second semester. I remember seeing Malcolm after the team meal in New York City, prior to the Preseason NIT championship game. He was telling one of his teammates that he was having a hard time with the ritual of the pre-game meal, among other things. Sims played in eight games and averaged 1.3 points and five minutes per game.

With Pat Graham out with a broken bone in his foot and Sims gone, Knight's team was down to nine players. This would require changes in several aspects of the team's practices and its game strategy.

Because of final exams, the Hoosiers were limited in their practice time during the week. Knight begins by talking about the preparation process this week, working around semester exams.

We started the week by not practicing on either Sunday or Monday, and then came in and started our practice for the game on Tuesday. We had a little bit of an unstable schedule, a scattered kind of a schedule, because of the exams. We did all of our practicing, last year, in the mornings during exam week. This year we did not do that. We did practice in the afternoon, but the times varied between 3:00 and 5:00 as starting time. And yet I think we had all the time that we needed and got in all the work that we had to get in.

The results thus far from the exams and the grades that the players have had this year have been pretty good. So I think we have accomplished both things this week that we set out to do.

One of the things that we tried to work toward achieving in those two games this past weekend was to maintain a steady and a level increase in our play throughout the course of the ballgames. And I think for the most part we did that.

This ballgame today will be another example of where we can't have dead spots. We've got to be able to play well. If they get a bucket, we've got to be able to get a bucket. If we don't score, we've got to keep them from scoring. I mean, we've got to be able to play in such a way that we don't have long dry spells offensively or spells at the defensive end where we are easy to score against.

The Cincinnati basketball team has three or four players among their first seven back from last year. They are a very athletic and quick team, a team that has an offensive weapon. They utilize three-quarter court and half court pressing and trapping techniques, trying to get you into a position where you don't handle the ball well. In their first three ballgames, I think their opponents have averaged 30 turnovers a game, and that's an awfully lot of opportunities given to the offense by the defense.

We'll have to first of all handle their half court and three-quarter court trap situation. If we can do that, then we create offense opportunities for ourselves, and that's what I think will be a real determining factor in today's ballgame.

They're very similar to Tulane's defensive alignment in terms of what they want to get from their defense and how they go about playing defense. I think that Cincinnati may be a little bit quicker than Tulane was.

Recognition is a key to beating the press. You know you're going to get trapped, and before the trap can be established, you try to get rid of the basketball. If you can bypass the first trap, then automatically you have four on three somewhere through the rest of the court. In some situations, you're going to be able to create a two on one. And that's what we're trying to eventually establish when we are playing against a trapping or aggressive team, getting to the point where you've got two guys against one of theirs, and then make the play.

For the most part, we have rebounded fairly well. We have played against a couple of teams that are very good rebounding teams. What we want to do is to be able to come out of the board play even. We don't want a situation arising where we just get hammered on the board, like we did in the Florida State game. It was remarkable, in fact, that we were able to win the ballgame as badly as we were beaten on the boards.

We came back against Seton Hall and played them pretty well on the boards. We need to be able to get a little more off our offensive board. We had some moments where we've done well on the offensive board, but we've got to get a little more scoring out of the offensive board than we have thus far.

We'll keep bringing Reynolds off the bench, and then just see what happens. As long as we are able to accomplish what we want with Chris or whomever coming off the bench, then that's the way we'll go about it. And we will stay with that at least tonight.

GAME SUMMARY

INDIANA 79   CINCINNATI 64

In the first half, Indiana played like a highly ranked team as they ripped apart number 19 Cincinnati. The halftime score was 38-18. Then they coasted to a 79-

64 triumph. Bob Knight was very upset with his ball club for letting up in the second half.

The Hoosiers played frantic defense that took the Bearcats out of their game plan, then cut up UC's pressure defense to get that 20-point halftime lead. The second half play was almost like Indiana was going through the motions. Bob Knight was frustrated with his team's lack of effort and inability to maintain intensity, concentration and focus for the full 40 minutes, especially against good basketball teams.

All five starters hit for double figures, with Calbert Cheaney's 17 the top output. Cheaney and Alan Henderson each pulled down 10 rebounds. Knight felt that his front line play was the worst it has been all year, which means when final exams are completed for the semester, there will be plenty of time spent rectifying the current problems prior to Wednesday night's match up with St. John's.

Indiana hit 52 percent from the field while Cincinnati managed only 34 percent. Indiana hit just 63 percent from the free throw line, 26 of 41. The Bearcats were no better, hitting 11 of 18 for just 61 percent. Indiana edged out Cincinnati in rebounding 42 to 37. In the turnover department, Indiana had one less than the Bearcats, 15 to 16. But again, it was Indiana's inability to take control of the game when it had the opportunity that will receive a lot of attention in practice over the next few days.

Cincinnati vs. Indiana

CINCINNATI

No.	Player		Total FG		3-point		FT	FTA	Rebounds			PF	TP	A	TO	Blk	S	Min
			FG	FGA	FG	FGA	FT	FTA	Off	Def	Tot	PF	TP	A	TO	Blk	S	Min
21	Gregor, Keith	f	0	2	0	1	2	2	1	2	3	5	2	3	3	0	0	32
43	Bostic, Curtis	f	2	5	0	0	0	1	1	3	4	5	4	0	2	0	0	21
4	martin, Erik	c	1	7	0	0	3	3	4	2	6	5	5	0	1	0	2	22
31	Van Exel, Nick	g	8	26	4	14	2	4	0	1	1	0	22	3	3	0	2	38
52	Jackson, Allen	g	5	11	1	3	2	2	1	3	4	5	13	2	2	0	1	31
10	Gibson, Tarrance		2	4	1	3	0	0	2	2	4	2	5	1	4	0	1	19
23	Durden, LaZelle		1	4	1	3	0	0	0	0	0	3	3	0	1	0	0	13
32	Harris, Mike		4	8	0	0	2	5	6	4	10	4	10	0	0	0	0	22
54	Ford, Darrick		0	0	0	0	0	0	0	0	0	0	0	0	0	0	0	2
	Team								3	2	5							
	TOTALS		23	67	7	24	11	17	18	19	37	29	64	9	16	0	6	200

Total FG%	1st Half .207(6/29)	2nd half .447(17/38)	Game .343(23/67)	Deadball
3-Pt. FG%	1st Half .333(3/9)	2nd half .267(4/15)	Game .292(7/24)	Rebounds ___1___
FT%	1st Half .600(3/5)	2nd half .615(8/13)	Game .611(11/18)	

INDIANA

No.	Player		Total FG		3-point		FT	FTA	Rebounds			PF	TP	A	TO	Blk	S	Min
			FG	FGA	FG	FGA	FT	FTA	Off	Def	Tot	PF	TP	A	TO	Blk	S	Min
40	Cheaney, Calbert	f	6	16	0	3	5	6	2	8	10	1	17	4	1	0	1	37
44	Henderson, Alan	f	3	7	0	0	5	6	4	6	10	3	11	0	1	1	0	31
24	Nover, Matt	c	5	7	0	0	4	8	1	4	5	4	14	0	3	0	0	23
20	Graham, Greg	g	5	6	2	2	3	5	0	4	4	4	15	3	4	0	0	23
22	Bailey, Damon	g	4	7	1	2	3	5	2	3	5	4	12	3	2	0	0	30
32	Reynolds, Chris		1	1	0	0	5	8	0	1	1	2	7	2	0	0	1	24
34	Evans, Brian		0	1	0	0	0	0	0	3	3	1	0	1	1	0	1	13
30	Leary, Todd		1	3	0	1	1	2	0	0	0	0	3	0	1	0	0	9
25	Knight, Pat		0	0	0	0	0	0	0	0	0	0	0	2	2	0	1	10
	Team								1	3	4							
	TOTALS		25	48	3	8	26	40	10	32	42	19	79	15	15	1	4	200

Total FG%	1st Half .556(15/27)	2nd half .476(10/21)	Game .521(25/48)	Deadball
3-Pt. FG%	1st Half .200(1/5)	2nd half .667(2/3)	Game .375(3/8)	Rebounds ___9___
FT%	1st Half .583(7/12)	2nd half .655(19/29)	Game .634(26/41)	

Officials	Ed Hightower, Mac Chauvin, Ed Schumer
Technical Fouls	
Attendance	17,124

Score by Periods	1	2	OT	OT	Final
Cincinnati	18	46			64
Indiana	38	41			79

Bob Knight Talk Show
December 21, 1992

FISCHER: Indiana ran its record to 8 and 1 for the season with a victory over the Cincinnati Bearcats on Saturday. I know you felt that your team performed quite well in the first half, but you did not have the same feeling on the second half of action.

KNIGHT: Well, we got ahead, progressed well, and after halftime came back and regressed well.

FISCHER: Certainly the intensity level did not come back the second half like it was in the first.

KNIGHT: We talked a lot during halftime about coming out with the score at zero just to see what we could do with the second half. We just didn't have the same kind of approach the second half that we had for the first half. What causes that? I don't know. I don't know whether it's something that we don't do, don't discuss, don't get across, don't emphasize properly. We try different things, and that is a real problem for this team and has been a big problem for this team as we have gone along. This team has been able to make some pretty good plays in tough situations, has been able to play a lot of good basketball. They also have created problems for themselves by not doing the same things from the standpoint of execution throughout the course of a ballgame, the things which enabled them to get into a position where they were in fact in control of the game.

FISCHER: You made some comments about your front-line play, that it was not anything close to what it should be in the ballgame.

KNIGHT: I didn't think that we helped out very well defensively. I thought our defensive awareness from our front-court people was very, very poor. We had a lot of drives to the basket where we just weren't alert to what was happening. And then we also had an awful lot of missed block-outs through the course of the game that enabled Cincinnati to get a couple of extra shots off the offensive board.

FISCHER: Let's turn to call-in questions now. Our first caller is from Indianapolis. Does the NCAA require HIV virus testing of players?

KNIGHT: No, it does not.

FISCHER: This is from Syracuse, Indiana. If the captain is chosen by his fellow ball players, does this help in developing leadership?

KNIGHT: In all the years that I have coached, our captain has never been chosen by his fellow players. The captain is my captain. He's the guy I want as my representative. He's the guy that I want on the floor to handle what it is that I think is important out there in terms of playing and in the establishment of the atmosphere around playing. That captain has always been my choice. This year our seniors are the captains. All four of them handle the responsibilities that a captain would have.

FISCHER: From Seymour, Indiana. What are you most pleased with so far this year and what things do you need to work on most before the Big Ten season?

KNIGHT: I think that our team has played basketball very well. We have had some periods in most games where things have slipped away from us. Our intensity has not had the continuity throughout the course of the entire ballgame that we want it to have. That, more than anything else, is a major area for us so far as improvement is concerned. If we could get that, then I think our team will be difficult to contend with. If we don't, then our team is going to have a problem when we get into the Big Ten.

FISCHER: This question is from Columbus. Who is responsible for Assembly Hall decor and why is there just an "I" in the middle of the floor rather than an "IU?"

KNIGHT: The person responsible for the decor of the floor is me, and the "I" in the middle of the floor I think is very easy to understand when one realizes that the "I" is placed in the center of the outline of the state of Indiana.

FISCHER: This is from East Gary, Indiana. Is IU considering the new style trunks that are longer in length?

KNIGHT: We're considering those trunks for our Field Hockey team.

FISCHER: This question is from Henderson, Kentucky. What are your impressions of Rick Patino and the job he has done at Kentucky thus far?

KNIGHT: Oh, I think he has done an excellent job. I think that the Kentucky team has obviously gotten off to a good start, has played well, and will have an outstanding season.

FISCHER: A South Bend listener asks, what approximately is the average GPA of the team this year?

KNIGHT: I'd imagine that the average would be about, oh somewhere around a 2.8 for this last semester's work.

FISCHER: This is from Indianapolis. What part of the process of recruiting do you play and what part do you delegate?

KNIGHT: Well, we're all involved. There are three of us who can really go outside and recruit: Dan Dakich, Ron Felling, and me. We all go out and look at players. We look at those players that have through one way or another shown some degree of ability to play at this level. We try to assess, we try to determine which kids are the most suitable for the way we want to play, and then we determine what players are most interested in coming to Indiana. Then we make our decisions relative to recruiting after that.

FISCHER: From Noblesville comes this question. I notice three offenses that you run: triangle, motion and high set. Am I correct? When and why do you use them?

KNIGHT: Well those are three basic alignments that we go out in, but our offense then moves into what we would usually call our regular offense. It depends upon what of kind pressure we're playing against, what we are trying to accomplish, who we have at any particular time. There are several things that determine which set we try to utilize at any given moment.

FISCHER: From South Bend, what can you tell me about the stress you place on players' abilities in the classroom?

KNIGHT: All we try to do is to make it a very simple proposition. You either go to class and do well or you don't play. The most important thing to us is that these kids earn a degree.

FISCHER: From Indianapolis, what is the situation as far as the number of players a team can currently carry and why does Indiana have but nine?

KNIGHT: You know with Sims having quit put us down to ten with Todd Lindeman being redshirted. I really think that twelve is a very good number, but the problem with just having twelve is that's what we started with, and Pat Graham is hurt and Sims has quit. So now we're down to ten and now you're getting kind of a situation where you don't have nearly as much flexibility in practice as you would if you had at least twelve kids.

FISCHER: Would you look at walk-ons again, intramural players, anything like that?

KNIGHT: No thanks.

FISCHER: A Centerville, Indiana, listener wants to know if you are still satisfied picking Alan Henderson in your recruiting as compared to Glen Robinson?

KNIGHT: Very satisfied. If I could just get Alan to block out on the boards a little more. We have been working with him the past two days a little bit, trying to get him to go after the ball a little harder on the boards.

FISCHER: This is from Heltonville, Indiana. If you were coaching a timid player, how would you bring out aggression in a player that is timid?

KNIGHT: Sometimes you don't. Sometimes it is very difficult to change a personality. That is, I think, one of the very difficult things you have to do as a coach. What you have to do as a coach is deal with the different personalities and recognize what those personalities entail and what they have to be like for the kid to get the most out of his ability.

FISCHER: This is a question from Woodburn. Does mental toughness suffer fatigue the same way that physical toughness does?

KNIGHT: Not really. I think that kids that are really tough minded can maintain that mindset without fatigue.

FISCHER: From Indianapolis. Was there a team or two that impressed you, during your college days, with the way they played and in the way they were set up? And if so, why and who coached them?

KNIGHT: One of the best setup teams during the time that I was playing in college in 1959 and 1960 was the University of California. It was a team that was loaded with talent that won the NCAA in 1959 and went to the final game in 1960. Teams in the Big Ten, would include Michigan State under Fordy Anderson. This was a very, very good offensive team. A team that did some things offensively that were difficult to play against. There wasn't a lot of defense played in the Big Ten at the time. Probably outside of Ohio State, the team that perhaps played the best defense was Northwestern. Northwestern did it under Bill Rohr. Bill's teams were good defensive teams. Indiana and Illinois were teams that scored a lot, were teams that were very tough to play against, particularly, I think, Indiana.

This was an argument for including the best teams in NCAA play. Indiana in 1960, I thought, was the best basketball team in the country, other than Ohio State. And because of the Big Ten's stand against going to the NIT and only the Conference Champion going to the NCAA, Indiana with a great basketball team, had no where to go when the season was over.

FISCHER: Let's go to Bell Fountain. Is there any specific reason for the poor free throw shooting that this team is experiencing at times this year?

KNIGHT: If there was a specific reason for it, we'd do all we could to correct that, but I don't think there is. We are working on a variety of different things to improve that.

FISCHER: This question is from Athens, Georgia. Do you still get a chance to play basketball at all for recreation?

KNIGHT: I have absolutely, positively, no interest whatsoever in playing basketball.

FISCHER: All right. This is from New Albany, Indiana.

KNIGHT: I mean, like none.

FISCHER: All right. This is from New Albany, Indiana.

KNIGHT: I mean, like at no time. The next time you get a good look at me, try to imagine me playing basketball.

FISCHER: All right. This is from New Albany, Indiana.

KNIGHT: I couldn't play basketball today if you gave me 30 fouls.

FISCHER: Most Big Ten teams have player's names on the back of their jerseys. Is there a reason IU never has done this?

KNIGHT: My impression is that we have answered this for the 142nd time. We are all playing for Indiana, not Charlie Jones.

FISCHER: Has IU ever retired the number of a player?

KNIGHT: Not while I've been here.

FISCHER: And this is from Crawfordsville, Indiana. Since the zone defense is illegal in pro basketball, do you feel it should be outlawed at the college level as well?

KNIGHT: No, I think that the zones, presses, the various combinations of defenses that can be played all make college basketball and high school basketball very interesting. Trying to prepare for upcoming games and knowing the tremendous scope there is to defensive play is one of the most enjoyable challenges in coaching.

FISCHER: This question is from Evansville. Aside from this current basketball squad, what other of your clubs have struggled with their 40 minute intensity, and did you ever feel that you solved the problem with any of those groups?

KNIGHT: At times, everybody struggles with intensity. I think that there are going to be some games within even the best of seasons where there are some lapses in team intensity. That isn't something that is just totally peculiar to this team.

FISCHER: From Indianapolis. How many truly different types of offense are there in the game of basketball?

KNIGHT: Well, there are a lot of different alignments and there are a lot of different setups, but there are only some basic things which can be done: screen away from the ball, cross screen in the lane, down screen on the perimeter, pass up to the basket, flash into the lane from opposite pass and screen away. There are variances in screening, such as double screen or in one or two cases, a triple screen that can be used, but there are various ways of getting into these different things.

One thing we try to teach our players is there are only a couple of things that can ever be done to you as a defensive player, given any position you might be in on the floor, and it's important that you recognize this. Then you can be well prepared for what may happen.

FISCHER: This question is from Manchester. Please comment on Steve Alford's coaching at Manchester and the job he's done thus far.

KNIGHT: Steve has obviously done a great job in turning things around there. I did notice the other day where he held somebody to 103 or 105 points while scoring 119 and I would have to needle him a little bit about that. That sounds more like when he was a player than now that he's a coach. As a coach, he's got to pay a little bit more attention to defense than he ever did as a player. But, he's taken that situation and he's winning a lot of ballgames. He's had a little injury problem but I think it has been a really good experience for him, and I imagine the people up there have enjoyed what Steve has done.

FISCHER: From a car phone here in Indianapolis, Coach. Comment on St. John's, a team that you will be facing this coming Wednesday.

KNIGHT: They've got a very strong inside game. Scott is a 6-1, 250 pound center. Milton is 6-6 and 235 or 240, and they play back and forth in the post, and with those two people we've got to do a good job with our inside defense. It's going to have to be better than in the last ballgame in terms of our inside help and our blocking out on the board.

FISCHER: Coach, can you talk a little bit about Brian Mahoney? He's the new coach this year at St. John's.

KNIGHT: The last time we played against Brian he was a really good player at Manhattan. He almost beat us single handedly in Madison Square Garden. In fact, Manhattan won the ballgame, and Brian was basically responsible for that happening. I think that he will carry on in fine fashion the tradition, as excellent as it has always been, that is St. John's basketball.

FISCHER: This is from Indianapolis. Would you assess Damon Bailey's progress this year over the past two?

KNIGHT: Damon, like every player we have, is in a situation where constant progress is important. I think that he has grown as a college basketball player. I'm very pleased with what I have seen from him this last couple of weeks.

FISCHER: This is from Indianapolis. How do you set your practices up with just 10 players?

KNIGHT: We play a lot of 4 on 4, 2 on 2, 3 on 3. And the fact that there isn't much break I think has been a little bit of a plus for us, because I think to some degree it improves our stamina.

FISCHER: From Plymouth, Indiana. What is your success with designated shooters? Do you really use that strategy or do you simply have a situation where the guys that can shoot it, shoot it?

KNIGHT: We try to get the ball in position for our best shooter to be able to shoot the ball. We are trying to develop our offensive play with different roles for different people.

FISCHER: This is from Muncie. The listener heard you talk about your admiration for a man named Clair Bee. Will you talk a little bit about him and give me his background?

KNIGHT: Clair Bee was born in West Virginia and was I think one of the truly great giants in college coaching, the best winning coach in the history of college basketball, and was a pioneer in many, many aspects of the game. He coached at Rider University in Lawrenceville, New Jersey, and then went on to Long Island University where his team won the second NIT in 1939 and then won again in 1941. He was the author of a great series of athletic books for kids. It's an absolute shame they are not in print today, because they are the best set of books I have ever had the pleasure of reading. He was just an extraordinary man.

FISCHER: This question, Coach, believe it or not, is from my boss, Art Angotti. He would like to know if there's anything special you want this Christmas?

KNIGHT: A big raise for doing my call-in radio show.

FISCHER: Well, Art, you asked. You got the answer.

FISCHER: This question is from Indianapolis. What is your feeling about this particular pre-conference schedule as compared to years past and might this be the toughest one you've ever had.

KNIGHT: Oh, I think that we've had a lot of tough pre-conference contests. We have many times in the same week played Kentucky, Kansas and Notre Dame when all three were very good and very highly ranked teams. Some of the tournaments that we have played in, the Holiday Festival and the Tournament in Hawaii, have been tough.

Over the time that we have been here at Indiana, I think that other teams in this conference would be a real distant second to what Indiana has played in terms of difficulty.

FISCHER: That's all the time we have for tonight's program. Merry Christmas to you, Coach, and to the staff and the players as well.

KNIGHT: Don, do I get to say anything?

FISCHER: I was going to leave it open to you now.

KNIGHT: We have some fun, I hope, with the questions and I know I don't always answer the questions the way that everybody would like, but I try to have some fun with them. Some questions actually, I should bring about a little more serious response than others, and I do try to handle them that way.

But we do appreciate the interest you all take whether we have time for your questions or not. We're happy you participate in our show and we wish each and every one of you the Merriest of Christmases and the Happiest of New Years.

St. John's vs. Indiana
December 23, 1992
Bloomington
Pre-game Show

St. John's' timing for a visit to Assembly Hall could not have been worse. Indiana's poor second half effort against Cincinnati was the subject of much discussion during the practices leading up to the St. John's game. The Hoosiers were primed for a good performance and it would be at the Redmen's expense. Coach Knight talks about the St. John's team and also about their first year coach Brian Mahoney. It is interesting how much Knight knows about the other coaches in college basketball. He finishes with a few comments about Chris Reynolds and Patrick Knight, two players who had important roles during the season for IU, although they have not been regular starters.

St. John's is in the process of putting some new players together, but they have back Scott, who started against us last year, and Middleton who played very well against us last year. Cain also played quite a bit. They are a team that is very strong inside. Scott is 6-11, 260; Middleton's about 240, 6-6 or maybe 6-7. They post really well. A lot they do offensively revolves around the two of them playing in the post, and Minlend, who's a freshman, about the same size as Middleton, comes in, maybe not quite as bulky as Middleton and relieves either one of them in offensive post spots.

Cain is a guard, very much like the guard that Bob Donewald had with Western Michigan. He's going to control the ball on the dribble. You're not going to take it away from him. He's not going to give it up until he's ready to do so.

Also, the 5 second clock has been interpreted differently and changed a little bit as opposed to what it was a couple of years ago. It really works to the advantage of the good dribbler, which Cain is. He can go either way, and as I said, he is very clever with the basketball. We'll have to contain him. When he picks it up, we'll have to make it tough for him to do something with the ball.

Brian was an excellent player at Manhattan and then played in the pros a year or two for Lou Carnesecca when he was coaching the Nets in the old ABA, and has been an assistant with Lou for 10 or 11 years. And I would imagine that while doing some things differently, the basic approach to play will be very much the same as it has been.

I have been very pleased at what Chris Reynolds has been doing and the way he has played coming off the bench. He has done an excellent job, and I think he will continue to do so in whichever capacity we have him in.

I also like the way Patrick has played. He's played smart, I think, through his passing, he helped account for eight or nine points in the time he was in the game against Cincinnati. If he can continue to do that and maybe contribute a bucket here and there, he's going to be a real asset. I have been pleased with what he has done and how he's concentrated at both ends.

GAME SUMMARY

INDIANA 105   ST. JOHN'S 80

The Indiana basketball team gave Bob Knight an early Christmas present with 40 intense minutes of basketball that produced an easy victory over the Redmen of St. John's University. The Hoosiers hit 60 percent of their shots, including six three-point field goals, and dominated the boards 42 to 29. Five players hit double figures, led by Calbert Cheaney with 23 and Alan Henderson's double double of 20 points and 14 rebounds.

The biggest lead was 33, and it could have been much higher if Knight had kept his line up steady. The way he substituted his troops gave everyone good playing time and probably avoided embarrassing the Redmen.

In addition to Cheaney's and Henderson's point totals, Indiana also had 20 points from Greg Graham, 12 from Damon Bailey and 10 from Matt Nover. Indiana also had 29 assists in this game compared to just 10 for St. John's, and turned the ball over 14 times while St. John's gave it up 16 times.

Indiana now stands 9-1 on the season. The Hoosiers will have a couple of days off for Christmas before returning on Friday morning to begin preparation for The Hoosier Classic in Indianapolis.

St. John's

No.	Player	Total FG FG	FGA	3-point FG	FGA	FT	FTA	Rebounds Off	Def	Tot	PF	TP	A	TO	Blk	S	Min
31	Middleton, Lamont f	3	8	0	0	5	5	2	1	3	3	11	0	2	0	0	21
44	Lyson, Fred f	1	2	0	1	0	0	0	1	1	2	2	0	0	0	0	12
42	Scott, Shawnelle c	6	11	0	0	0	0	1	4	5	4	12	3	1	0	0	29
11	Cain, David g	1	8	0	1	0	2	0	3	3	2	2	2	5	0	3	31
23	Brown, Derek g	10	12	4	5	1	2	0	2	2	0	25	2	3	0	2	28
34	Minlend, Charles	3	6	0	0	3	3	0	0	0	3	9	1	0	0	1	19
24	Barret, Rowan	0	2	0	0	0	0	0	2	2	1	0	1	2	0	0	8
15	Foster, Mitchell	0	3	0	0	4	4	1	3	4	4	4	0	0	0	0	11
5	Brown, Maurice	1	3	0	1	0	0	0	0	0	0	2	1	0	0	0	9
13	Green, Lee	2	5	0	0	0	0	0	2	2	1	4	0	1	0	2	12
3	Luyk, Sergio	3	6	1	3	0	2	0	1	1	1	7	0	2	0	0	13
30	Beckett, Carl	1	1	0	0	0	0	1	1	2	0	2	0	0	0	0	7
	Team							1	3	4							
	TOTALS	31	67	5	11	13	18	6	23	29	21	80	10	16	0	8	200

Total FG%   1st Half .382(13/34)   2nd half .545(18/33)   Game .463(31/67)   Deadball
3-Pt. FG%   1st Half .333(1/3)   2nd half .500(4/8)   Game .455(5/11)   Rebounds 2
FT%   1st Half 1.00(2/2)   2nd half .688(11/16)   Game .722(13/18)

Indiana

No.	Player	Total FG FG	FGA	3-point FG	FGA	FT	FTA	Rebounds Off	Def	Tot	PF	TP	A	TO	Blk	S	Min
40	Cheaney, Calbert f	10	15	1	2	2	3	3	3	6	1	23	1	1	0	0	27
44	Henderson, Alan f	7	15	0	0	6	8	4	10	14	3	20	3	1	2	2	32
24	Nover, Matt c	5	10	0	0	0	3	1	4	5	4	10	2	2	0	1	21
20	Graham, Greg g	7	10	4	5	2	3	1	2	3	2	20	3	1	0	2	26
22	Bailey, Damon g	5	7	0	1	2	2	0	3	3	1	12	6	2	0	0	21
32	Reynolds, Chris	1	1	0	0	2	2	0	2	2	4	4	6	2	0	0	21
34	Evans, Brian	2	3	1	2	2	2	0	1	1	0	7	1	0	0	0	17
30	Leary, Todd	3	5	0	0	1	2	0	2	2	1	7	1	3	0	0	16
25	Knight, Pat	1	2	0	0	0	0	0	2	2	3	2	6	2	0	0	19
	Team							0	4	4							
	TOTALS	41	68	6	10	17	25	9	33	42	19	105	29	14	2	5	200

Total FG%   1st Half .629(22/35)   2nd half .576(19/33)   Game .603(41/68)   Deadball
3-Pt. FG%   1st Half .500(4/8)   2nd half 1.00(2/2)   Game .600(6/10)   Rebounds 3
FT%   1st Half .818(9/11)   2nd half .571(8/14)   Game .680(17/25)

Officials   Jody Silvester, Randy Drury, Steve Welmer
Technical Fouls
Attendance   17,051

Score by Periods	1	2	OT	OT	Final
St. John's	29	51			80
Indiana	57	48			105

The Hoosier Classic was developed in part to give Indiana fans in Indianapolis a chance to see Indiana play. Assembly Hall in Bloomington is sold out for most regular season games, so bringing two games to Market Square Arena gives more Indianapolis fans a chance to enjoy Indiana basketball.

The team had limited time to prepare for the Butler game due to the Christmas holiday, however Knight did not think that was a problem. He talks about the St. John's game and also about the game today against Butler, which is playing without Archibold, their leading scorer for the past four years.

I don't think that there's any problem with two days preparation time. We were able to practice twice yesterday, two actually good workouts. We could have gone as long as we wanted. Then we've had today to review what we went through and discussed and worked on yesterday.

There are a lot of times during the season when we have one day or two days to prepare for a Big Ten game, so this was really good in that regard. We took the 24th and the 25th off from practice and then practiced at 10:00 on Saturday morning and then again in the afternoon. And I think we had as much opportunity to prepare as we would have had prior to many other games.

Looking at the St. John's game; in the first half we probably played as well as we are capable of playing, perhaps at all phases of the game. We took on a St. John's team that I think is probably an above average basketball team. It certainly isn't a great team and isn't going to be a national contender, but it's a team that has some interesting facets to it.

We were able to play that game just about as we wanted. Our defense created some problems for them that resulted in some offensive opportunities for us, and we were able to get the game under about as good a control in the first half as I think you could possibly do with St. John's.

We had some good play in the second half. There are two things that happen in a ballgame when you have a 28 or 29 point lead at the halftime like we did. The other team basically knows that the game's over. They play with a relaxed attitude. They play with, "Hey, we're going to get beat; let's just try and work and do what we can do and see what we can make out of the second half."

The team that's ahead has a difficult time, after a 15 minute break, maintaining the same kind of intensity in getting back to where it was when the ballgame started. I just have never seen that fail. I've seen games where—maybe Western Michigan might have been an example for us—we lost a lead in the first half, an 11 point lead that was cut to one. We were back to 11 by the halftime. Certainly that game was in no way over on the scoreboard at halftime. Then in the second half, we came out and just steadily increased our lead in the ballgame. Rarely is a team able to have what amounts to an insurmountable lead at the half and be able to come out in the second half and duplicate that performance. This doesn't happen.

We used a lot of different combinations and maybe sometimes that detracted a little from the intensity. I don't know. I was very, very pleased with the first half where all nine of our players played extremely well, and made some very good plays in the second half as well.

In looking at the Butler team we face today, Archibold was obviously a great player for them during his four-year career at Butler, a really outstanding basketball player. They've got everybody back from a team that was pretty difficult for a lot of people to play against last year. They're off to kind of a disappointing start for them I'm sure, but I was very impressed with the fact that they could come back from their game with North Carolina to play as well as they did against Ball State. That's a very good indication of ability and even a better indication of the kind of character the players have. I think for them to come back with a really good game against an in-state rival like that speaks very well for the players.

They have a good guard in Bowen, another kid who is a very good dribbler, goes either way with the ball, and he's a kid that you're not going to steal the ball from. We're not going to try to take the ball from him. We're just going to try to play as well from a positioning standpoint as we possibly can.

Brens is 6-10 and, you know, that's all you need. They've got three interchangeable forwards that are athletic, have good quickness, and are about the same size, around 6-5. I think the game against Ball State will be an indicator of good things to come for them during the season.

The fans may be interested in our approach last night. You know, we left the players here last night with tapes of the last game we played because we want them to see some things that we did well and some things that we didn't do well, as well as some tapes and information on the upcoming game, which in this case would be Butler. We came back after dinner and after the players had looked at the tapes that we had left. We talked a little bit about what we did or didn't do in the St. John's' game and then what we are looking toward happening in this game. What we have to do, what we have to be aware of. Then we continue that through today, which is a game day.

GAME SUMMARY

INDIANA 90   BUTLER 48

The Hoosier Classic began its two day run at Market Square Arena, and the scenario was a familiar one for Bob Knight's Indiana squad as they dominated first-round foe Butler.

Butler shot just 30 percent for the game, while the Hoosiers made 55 percent of their field goals. Five players hit double figures: Calbert Cheaney, Matt Nover and Damon Bailey, all with 17 points and Alan Henderson and Greg Graham added 14. Henderson set a classic rebounding record in pulling down 19 boards.

This was another game in which Bob Knight was able to utilize his entire roster with no one playing more than 26 minutes in this contest and no one less than 16 minutes.

Indiana owned the boards in this contest, 45 to 32, had 23 assists to 12 for Butler, and turned it over 17 times to the Bulldogs' 21 turnovers. Indiana maintained a solid 40 minutes of effort in this ballgame, a factor that Knight feels must be maintained throughout the season.

BUTLER

No.	Player	Total FG FG	Total FG FGA	3-point FG	3-point FGA	FT	FTA	Rebounds Off	Rebounds Def	Rebounds Tot	PF	TP	A	TO	Blk	S	Min
12	Bowen, Tim	0	2	0	0	0	0	0	1	1	3	0	1	2	0	0	21
14	Taylor, John	1	5	0	1	0	0	2	2	4	5	2	2	1	0	1	19
22	Guice, Jermaine	2	11	1	4	0	0	2	1	3	1	5	3	3	0	1	23
34	Beauford, Brian	8	18	2	3	6	7	4	6	10	2	24	1	3	0	1	24
44	Brens, J.P.	0	0	0	0	0	0	0	4	4	4	0	2	4	0	0	31
30	Allen, Danny	1	6	0	1	0	0	1	2	3	2	2	0	1	0	0	10
32	Miskel, Chris	1	6	0	1	0	0	0	2	2	0	2	0	1	0	0	14
33	Reliford, Katara	3	7	0	0	0	0	1	1	2	0	6	1	2	1	2	26
20	McKenzie, Jason	3	6	1	4	0	0	0	1	1	2	7	2	2	0	0	21
10	Bowens, Quincy	0	2	0	1	0	0	0	0	0	1	0	0	2	0	0	10
45	Phillips, Burdette	0	0	0	0	0	0	0	0	0	0	0	0	0	0	0	1
	Team							1	1	2				2			
	TOTALS	19	63	4	15	6	7	11	21	32	20	48	12	23	1	5	200

Total FG%	1st Half _____	2nd half _____	Game 0.302	Deadball	
3-Pt. FG%	1st Half _____	2nd half _____	Game 0.267	Rebounds	1
FT%	1st Half _____	2nd half _____	Game 0.857		

INDIANA

No.	Player	Total FG FG	Total FG FGA	3-point FG	3-point FGA	FT	FTA	Rebounds Off	Rebounds Def	Rebounds Tot	PF	TP	A	TO	Blk	S	Min
20	Graham, Greg	4	7	0	1	6	7	1	2	3	0	14	2	3	0	1	26
22	Bailey, Damon	5	10	2	3	5	5	2	1	3	2	17	3	4	0	2	24
24	Nover, Matt	7	10	0	0	3	6	0	1	1	1	17	1	2	1	0	26
40	Cheaney, Calbert	8	14	1	2	0	0	1	4	5	2	17	2	1	0	0	24
44	Henderson, Alan	5	8	0	0	4	5	5	14	19	3	14	5	1	4	2	26
30	Leary, Todd	2	5	1	4	0	0	0	1	1	0	5	0	2	0	1	18
34	Evans, Brian	1	4	0	1	0	0	0	2	2	0	2	2	0	0	1	16
21	Reynolds, Chris	1	3	0	0	1	1	1	2	3	1	2	6	2	0	3	21
25	Knight, Pat	1	1	0	0	0	0	0	2	2	1	2	2	2	0	0	19
	Team							2	4	6							
	TOTALS	34	62	4	11	18	24	12	33	45	10	90	23	17	5	10	200

Total FG%	1st Half _____	2nd half _____	Game 0.548	Deadball	
3-Pt. FG%	1st Half _____	2nd half _____	Game 0.364	Rebounds	2
FT%	1st Half _____	2nd half _____	Game 0.75		

Officials   Ted Hillary, Tom Rucker, Dan Chrisman

Technical Fouls

Attendance   13,473

Score by Periods	1	2	OT	OT	Final
Butler	13	35			48
Indiana	37	53			90

The Hoosier record was 10-1 for the season as they entered the Hoosier Classic Championship for the 11th straight time. Indiana's dominance in the Butler game left the crowd at Market Square Arena in a high state of anticipation for the game against Colorado.

Knight begins by talking about the 90-48 victory over Butler. As is often the case, he analyzed the game as much from the standpoint of what the team can improve as he did what the team did well. In the Butler game, it was the lack of patience that he felt was the biggest detriment to this team.

Knight then turns to the game against Colorado. Knight's analysis of the Buffaloes is interesting. It shows how he applies his knowledge of the game of basketball to break down an opposing team.

We were able to reverse ourselves a little bit in last night's ballgame. I felt that in the beginning of the game, at least offensively, we got off to a slow start. We had two or three turnovers. I wasn't sure that either team was going to score very many points the way the game got going. I think we scored three points in the first four or five minutes of the half.

From that point, on we averaged about 12 points per five minutes, which is pretty good, you know. That's going to put you in the nineties if you can do that, which is what we ended up doing, hitting ninety. So, after a slow start we gradually moved into a position where we were in control of the game by the half.

Now, we have talked several times this year and in previous years with this team about coming off a good first half and that not always being a great position for us to be in as subsequent play has often shown in the start of the second half. Last night with three minutes gone in the second half, we had improved our half-time margin by 11 points, which was excellent for us. We continued to play pretty well right on down through the second half.

I thought Butler played hard and very aggressively defensively. I thought they had a good plan defensively, and we had to work to get good shots. Part of their defensive plan was to make us impatient, and we were. Until we developed a patience and developed the mind set that "Hey, we're not going to get easy shots against these guys. We've got to work to get what we get, and then go about doing it." Unless we showed some patience, we weren't going to get the kind of shots that we ended up getting.

So it was a good game from the standpoint of our acquiring patience as the game developed and also our getting off to a relatively poor start and going from there to playing pretty well.

Our lack of patience in the early stages of the ballgame created some problems for us. And as I said, that was brought about not so much by our player mistakes but by Butler playing very well defensively.

The Colorado Buffaloes are coached by Joe Harrington, who brought a Long Beach State team to the Indiana Classic a few years ago. This team is a very good basketball team. And I'm going to compare them to Seton Hall. Boyce is a very good player. You know he averages 20 points a game. Last year he scored 27 at Chapel Hill against North Carolina and he was just a freshman. He was the Freshman of the Year in the Big 8. So he is an outstanding player, like Cheaney is an outstanding player for us. He gives Colorado that one outstanding player very similar to what Terry DeHere is to Seton Hall.

Colorado has really strong, big inside players in Hodges and in Allen, 6-9 and 6-10, both are 230 or 235. Then they add a third inside player, Robinson.

So the front line, I think, is just about equal to what we played when we played Seton Hall. The second guard spot is filled by a kid named Hefty, a freshman who was an outstanding high school player in Colorado last year, along with two holdover kids named Pulliam and Terrill that have had considerable experience in the past couple of years there. Colorado is a team very similar in what it can do and how it plays to Seton Hall.

The first thing they try to do is get the ball down quickly, and either Allen or Hodges goes into the post. Whoever doesn't, stays on top. And they're trying to get the ball inside immediately. If they can't do that, they run a little game on the outside, the purpose of which is also to get the ball in the post. So they really take two shots quickly at getting the ball inside to one of their big post men, and then they go from there with a little three out game and two in, moving and trying to get the ball into the post, along with the drives and some outside shooting. They have two or three sets that they use, some structured stuff.

Our order of priorities would be to get down the floor and take away their posting in the break. And then to continue throughout the entire possession making it as tough as we can for them to utilize post play, which includes keeping the ball from getting back into their hands off the backboard once it's shot. So defending the post would be our biggest priority once we have established halfcourt play.

We have been pleased with the Indiana Classic, and everybody involved including the sponsors. Steve Downing, who is the tournament director, has done a really outstanding job making the teams comfortable, seeing to it that the teams have as good as stay as possible while playing their two basketball games. For the

Indianapolis fans, it's always been something that we have tried to do, just to give people a chance to see us play twice who might not otherwise be able to do so.

GAME SUMMARY

INDIANA 85   COLORADO 65

The Hoosier basketball team racked up its 11th straight Hoosier Classic Championship with a solid performance against the tall and talented Colorado Buffaloes. The triumph lifted Indiana to an 11-1 record on the year and kept a perfect streak alive at Market Square Arena where the Hoosiers have now won 13 straight games without a loss. The win also left Bob Knight one game shy of the 600 mark in career victories.

The victory produced five players in double figures, with Calbert Cheaney's 20 leading the way. Also hitting double figures in this contest were Alan Henderson for 19, 17 for Damon Bailey, 14 for Matt Nover, and Greg Graham turned in a 13-point effort. This was not a good shooting night for Indiana, however, hitting just 44 percent for the game, with Cheaney struggling more than anyone on a 9 of 23 performance.

The keys to this game were defense and rebounding. Although Colorado was much bigger and stronger, Indiana outrebounded the Buffaloes 50 to 43, with Alan Henderson pulling down 12 rebounds and a two-game tournament record of 31. Henderson and Cheaney both made the All-Tournament team along with Damon Bailey who received the Most Valuable Player honors with his best play of the year. His final stats showed 11 of 22 shooting from the field with 6 of 9 from three-point range, 6 of 7 free throws, 7 rebounds and 8 assists. Bailey had season highs of 17 points in each game. His defensive play had an intensity that carried over to his offensive production and also to his teammates.

Henderson, for the fifth consecutive game, hit double figures in both scoring and rebounding, pulling down 12 boards to lead the Hoosiers.

INDIANA

No.	Player	Total FG FG	FGA	3-point FG	FGA	FT	FTA	Rebounds Off	Def	Tot	PF	TP	A	TO	Blk	S	Min
20	Graham, Greg	3	6	0	1	7	8	1	6	7	2	13	6	5	0	3	31
22	Bailey, Damon	6	12	4	6	1	2	0	4	4	0	17	5	1	2	1	27
24	Nover, Matt	6	11	0	0	2	2	3	5	8	1	14	0	1	2	1	30
40	Cheaney, Calbert	9	23	0	5	2	2	4	1	5	2	20	2	2	0	1	31
44	Henderson, Alan	9	19	0	0	1	3	9	3	12	3	19	3	2	3	2	28
30	Leary, Todd	0	2	0	2	0	0	1	0	1	0	0	1	0	0	0	9
34	Evans, Brian	0	1	0	1	0	0	2	6	8	1	0	2	0	1	0	20
21	Reynolds, Chris	1	1	0	0	0	1	1	1	2	1	2	4	1	0	1	18
25	Knight, Pat	0	2	0	0	0	1	0	1	1	0	0	0	2	0	0	6
	Team							0	2	2							
	TOTALS	34	77	4	15	13	19	21	29	50	10	85	23	14	8	9	200

Total FG%	1st Half _____	2nd half _____	Game .442	Deadball
3-Pt. FG%	1st Half _____	2nd half _____	Game .267	Rebounds 2
FT%	1st Half _____	2nd half _____	Game .684	

COLORADO

No.	Player	Total FG FG	FGA	3-point FG	FGA	FT	FTA	Rebounds Off	Def	Tot	PF	TP	A	TO	Blk	S	Min
12	Hefty, Pete	1	4	0	2	0	0	0	4	4	2	2	2	4	0	2	22
24	Boyce, Donnie	7	19	1	3	1	2	5	2	7	2	16	4	4	0	3	40
25	Robinson, Randy	6	16	0	4	3	4	1	2	3	4	15	4	3	0	1	30
33	Hodges, Poncho	5	14	0	0	2	2	4	3	7	4	12	1	0	1	0	32
45	Allen, Ted	6	10	0	1	1	1	4	7	11	4	13	0	6	4	0	37
10	Pulliam, Anthony	1	4	1	3	0	0	0	0	0	0	3	4	0	0	0	17
21	Golgart, Sande	0	0	0	0	0	0	0	1	1	0	0	0	1	0	1	7
23	Williams, Kirk	0	0	0	0	0	0	0	1	1	1	0	0	0	0	0	2
32	Stephens, Joe	0	3	0	1	0	0	1	0	1	0	0	0	0	0	0	4
55	Schulte, Jon	2	3	0	0	0	1	2	1	3	0	4	0	1	1	0	9
	Team							2	3	5							
	TOTALS	28	73	2	14	7	10	19	24	43	17	65	15	19	6	7	200

Total FG%	1st Half _____	2nd half _____	Game .384	Deadball
3-Pt. FG%	1st Half _____	2nd half _____	Game .143	Rebounds 2
FT%	1st Half _____	2nd half _____	Game .700	

Officials Tom Rucker, Eric Harmon, Ted Hillary
Technical Fouls
Attendance 13,289

Score by Periods	1	2	OT	OT	Final
Colorado	30	35			65
Indiana	49	36			85

Indiana vs. Kentucky
January 3, 1993
Louisville
Pre-game Show

The Indiana-Kentucky rivalry is one of the most exciting in college basketball, and Kentucky is always hard to beat at home. With this year's Kentucky team ranked third and Indiana ranked second, interest in the game went far beyond the borders of these states.

The fact that the next win would carry Knight to 600 career victories made this an even more dramatic game for Indiana fans; though Knight did not attribute any special significance to that milestone. In 2003, Knight went over the 800 win mark.

Knight's analysis of the Kentucky team's strengths proved to be all too accurate. The pre-game interview again demonstrates some of Knight's keen insight into the game. Knight begins by looking back to his team's performance in the Hoosier Classic.

Getting things started well in the second half in both of the games in Indianapolis was important to us. That has been somewhat of a problem for us. In the Butler and Colorado games I thought that we worked to a position where we were in control in each case. So I thought there was some definite improvement in that regard.

I also thought that our overall play in both ballgames was pretty good. We were difficult to score against. At the defensive end last year, when we played Butler, we had a very substantial lead at the half. I think we had given up just 18 points in the first half and then Butler scored 55 against us in the second half. This year, again we were pretty stingy in the first half and Butler scored 35 in the second half against us. So that was a good plus for us.

Looking ahead to Kentucky, first of all, any time you get a chance to play against a team that you know is good, there are occasions when that team turns out to be better than you thought they were. Usually when that happens, you find yourself in some degree of difficulty insofar as the outcome of the game is concerned.

When the tournament was over in Indianapolis, everybody connected with our team knew that the next game was going to be against a very good team. There isn't any need to discuss Kentucky from the standpoint of how good they are. They have just developed into one of the better teams in the country at this point in the season.

They have a little different style of play than most teams have. They rely a lot on the three-point shot and they want as fast a tempo as possible in the ballgame. Our team has probably played some of its best basketball at a fast tempo, so that should be interesting from the standpoint of what kind of tempo this game develops into as it unfolds.

Mashburn is arguably the hardest player in the country to play against right now. He's very good inside, extremely good, and then he's a very good outside shooter as well. He did not play well in their last game against St. John's, so I'm sure that's an incentive to him coming into this game.

Rhodes is one of the better freshmen anywhere around. Then too, they have very good depth. They've used it well, they have developed their depth. They play a lot of people. They try to get you involved in an up and down game where they're going to have more numbers than you are, and you're going to get into the last five or six minutes and you're going to be a little bit tired, and you're not going to be able to maintain the pace. We've got to be very careful of that in today's ballgame.

I think that foul trouble could play an important part in the game today. They're better equipped to deal with it right now, I think, than we are. The foul is going to be important to us from two standpoints: first that we get to the free throw line, and second, that we keep them from getting there. Now this is always something that you want to do, but the circumstances of the game may prevent that from happening. In some cases actually, this is the reverse of what you want to do. If that would be the case with us today, it would be very hard for us to beat this team. We need to make them play defense.

One of the interesting things of playing against the press is that there are different degrees of shots. I have over the years felt that the one shot that you want to take against the press is the lay up. Whether you shoot a lot of other shots against the press depends on who shoots them and what kind of shots they are. There's a shot that's generally available against a pressing team once you've beaten the first trap in the press, and that's a driving 8 or 10 foot shot. It's a close shot, a relatively short shot, but it can be a very difficult shot. The problem with it is that if you miss it, then they've got the ball and they're going the other way. As you are coming toward the bucket, they're going the other way. It's a lot harder to get turned going the opposite way to play defense than it is to get turned going the opposite way to play offense.

When you're playing against the pressing team, you make a decision between two things. You're either going to shoot the ball or you're not going to shoot the ball against the press. That determines the tempo of the game. I think it's imperative that you attack the basket against the press, trying to get whatever the press will give you there.

If you come down and shoot the basketball against the press and don't pass at every opportunity, then what you do is put the game into a running game where there just will not be a lot of fouls, either on your part or on their part. Now, not fouling on our part is a good thing. Not fouling on their part is not a good thing for us. Taking the shot against the press, whatever shot is available, puts you in a situation where, from your standpoint offensively, you are not requiring the other team to play much defense. They're not going to be on defense a lot. So there's a real fine line that has to be drawn between attacking the basket and playing half-court offense, and we have to do both of those things.

I don't think that we can come down and be satisfied, nor do I think we can win shooting jump shots against the press. I just don't think that gives us enough things that we are going to be able to do in the ballgame. And I think that's the kind of game that Kentucky would win. And as I said earlier, we have to be very careful about not getting trapped into that kind of game.

GAME SUMMARY

Kentucky 81   Indiana 78

In what couldn't have been a more exciting atmosphere for a regular season basketball game, the third-ranked Kentucky Wildcats pulled out a pulsating 81 to 78 triumph over Indiana in Louisville. The record crowd of 20,060 in Freedom Hall was almost equally divided between IU red and Wildcat blue, and the national television audience created another game with a Final Four atmosphere. The fervor displayed by the fans was that of a great rivalry which always makes this matchup something special.

For Bob Knight's Hoosiers, it was another story of missed opportunities, especially from the free throw line, with IU connecting on just 50 percent of their 36 attempts. In three previous seasons, this team has never shot below 72 percent. This year, in both of their losses they've been far below their norm. Indiana, for the second game this season, was unable to perform with a full 40 minutes of effort from everybody on the floor.

Indiana did execute the game plan almost to perfection, forcing the ball inside, getting Kentucky into foul trouble and getting twice the number of free throws while keeping the Wildcats off the line. The problem was that Kentucky shot an incredible number of three-point shots, 41 to be exact, with 16 of those dropping, while Indiana couldn't find the range from the free throw line.

Scoring honors were a flat draw among four players, two from each team: Jamaal Mashburn and Travis Ford for Kentucky, and Calbert Cheaney and Matt Nover for IU each had 29 points. For Ford and Nover, the outputs were career highs. Indiana won the battle of statistics but lost the game. The Hoosiers hit 56 percent from the field to Kentucky's 39 percent. Indiana also was able to control the rebounds 40 to 35 over the Wildcats, and Indiana turned the ball over 14 times compared to Kentucky's eight.

INDIANA

No.	Player	Total FG FG	FGA	3-point FG	FGA	FT	FTA	Rebounds Off	Def	Tot	PF	TP	A	TO	Blk	S	Min
40	Cheaney, Calbert	12	19	5	6	0	0	4	4	8	3	29	5	4	0	0	38
44	Henderson, Alan	3	9	0	1	4	10	0	13	13	4	10	3	2	1	0	37
24	Nover, Matt	8	9	0	0	13	20	3	5	8	4	29	2	2	2	0	37
20	Graham, Greg	2	4	0	1	0	0	0	2	2	2	4	0	2	0	0	25
22	Bailey, Damon	1	6	1	4	0	1	1	3	4	1	3	3	1	0	1	31
32	Reynolds, Chris	1	1	0	0	1	5	0	2	2	3	3	1	1	0	2	23
34	Evans, Brian	0	0	0	0	0	0	1	0	1	0	0	0	2	0	0	5
30	Leary, Todd	0	0	0	0	0	0	0	1	1	0	0	0	0	0	0	2
25	Knight, Pat	0	0	0	0	0	0	0	0	0	0	0	0	0	0	0	2
	Team							1	0	1							
	TOTALS	27	48	6	12	18	36	10	30	40	17	78	14	14	3	3	200

Total FG% 1st Half .481(13/27) 2nd half .667(14/21) Game .563(27/48) Deadball
3-Pt. FG% 1st Half .500(3/6) 2nd half .500(3/6) Game .500(6/12) Rebounds 10
FT% 1st Half .438(7/16) 2nd half .550(11/20) Game .500(18/36)

KENTUCKY

No.	Player	Total FG FG	FGA	3-point FG	FGA	FT	FTA	Rebounds Off	Def	Tot	PF	TP	A	TO	Blk	S	Min
4	Dent, Rodney	0	3	0	0	1	2	1	3	4	3	1	0	1	0	0	12
5	Ford, Travis	10	15	7	12	2	3	0	1	1	2	29	2	2	0	2	37
12	Rhodes, Rodrick	1	4	0	3	1	2	0	0	0	4	3	1	0	0	0	17
24	Mashburn, Jamal	11	24	6	12	1	1	4	4	8	3	29	4	2	0	1	40
31	Brown, Dale	0	4	0	4	0	2	0	0	0	2	0	0	1	0	1	16
23	Braddy, Junior	2	6	2	5	0	0	3	2	5	3	6	2	1	0	0	24
10	Riddick, Andre	0	1	0	0	1	2	1	3	4	4	1	1	0	0	0	19
32	Prickett, Jared	1	7	0	2	1	1	5	2	7	2	3	0	0	0	1	16
14	Brassow, Jeff	1	4	1	3	0	0	1	2	3	2	3	0	0	0	0	10
44	Martinez, Gimel	2	3	0	0	2	4	1	0	1	5	6	0	1	0	0	9
	Team							1	1	2							
	TOTALS	28	71	16	41	9	17	17	18	35	30	81	10	8	0	5	200

Total FG% 1st Half .395(15/38) 2nd half .394(13/33) Game .394(28/71) Deadball
3-Pt. FG% 1st Half .417(10/24) 2nd half .353(6/17) Game .390(16/41) Rebounds 5
FT% 1st Half .333(2/6) 2nd half .636(7/11) Game .529(9/17)

Officials John Clougherty, Jim Burr, Jody Silvester
Technical Fouls
Attendance 20,060

Score by Periods	1	2	OT	OT	Final
Indiana	36	42			78
Kentucky	42	39			81

BOB KNIGHT TALK SHOW

January 4, 1993

FISCHER: Indiana ended its non-conference schedule yesterday falling to the Kentucky Wildcats 81-78. The defeat left the Hoosiers with an 11-2 record, and despite the loss of yesterday's outcome, a very successful non-league mark that included the championship of the Preseason NIT and titles in both the Indiana and Hoosier Classics. Coach, what are your thoughts on your team's performance in yesterday's ballgame?

KNIGHT: I don't think that losing to Kansas and Kentucky, the two best teams we played in the non-conference schedule makes it a good non-conference season. I agree with you that the NIT Championship was a good thing for us to win and something that we really worked to get and are pleased to have. But then when we lose to the two best teams that we play, from that point on, this has not been a particularly good non-conference season.

FISCHER: Coach, when you analyze the ballgame after you look at the films, what are your impressions of the performance?

KNIGHT: Our effort just wasn't real good and nothing disappoints me or frustrates me more than lack of effort. Talk all you want about missing the free throws. We may be a lousy free throw shooting team. There are some players that have never been able to be good free throw shooters. Then you'd have to win on other things.

Just plain effort is one of them, and our effort in this game was just not very good. We had very poor effort on the perimeter defensively, and then in individual situations, we had effort that just wasn't very good. And if you don't get good effort and you're playing a good basketball team, you can shoot well from the free throw line, you can shoot well from the floor and still get beaten. There isn't anything in this game that supplants just sheer, all-out effort.

FISCHER: Coach, you also were displeased with the effort in the Kansas ballgame. Was it no better in this contest than it was in the Kansas contest?

KNIGHT: It might have been worse in this game.

FISCHER: Let's turn now to our listeners. The first caller is from Coatesville, Indiana. Will depth be a problem with your ball club as the season wears on?

KNIGHT: Well, we've played a couple of games back to back so far, and we've played pretty good teams where in no case did I think our depth has hurt us in any way. I think that we've been able for the most part to play pretty good minutes off the bench, to give somebody a minute or two break, without being hurt at all. So at least to this point it hasn't, and I don't anticipate that being a real big problem.

FISCHER: A Salem, Indiana, listener would like to know if you adjust the length of practice as the season goes on?

KNIGHT: Our practices, because of the number of players that we have, are somewhat shorter in length than they normally would be. Once we get through with Christmas and start into the Big Ten play, we always reduce the amount of time we are practicing then as well. We probably start the season on November 1st with a practice that would begin at a 3:15 and end at 5:30. As the season goes on, we get to a point where, today, as an example, we worked for about an hour and thirty minutes, which would probably be a little bit longer than we work if it were not for the fact that school's not yet back in session.

FISCHER: From Bedford. Is there one person who helped you more than anyone else, and what did they do for you?

KNIGHT: Well, I played for a great coach in college in Fred Taylor at Ohio State, and I was able to get an excellent foundation for basketball from him. I then went to coach in high school in Ohio for another really outstanding coach named Harold Andreas and then developed a really good friendship with Pete Newell who I think is one of the two or three great coaches we've had in American basketball history. Then there have been a lot of other people along the way. I often say that I probably learned more about what it takes to win and what it takes to play from the players that played for me at West Point than anything else that I have had in my career in coaching.

FISCHER: From Indianapolis. Do you feel that this Hoosier ball club is ready for the Big Ten?

KNIGHT: Well, that remains to be seen, simply because the disappointment that I had in terms of our defensive effort in the ballgame yesterday. Had we been able to play that game with really good effort, then I would feel OK about our team going into the conference. But when the effort that we had was what it was, then that same effort in Wednesday night's game against Iowa will bring about the same results.

FISCHER: Again from Indianapolis. How do you motivate players to play so well?

KNIGHT: He must not have seen us play yesterday, because I didn't motivate anybody to do anything well yesterday.

FISCHER: This is also from Indianapolis. Did you change your defensive strategy in not picking up the Kentucky ball club at half court on Saturday?

KNIGHT: No, we really didn't. I was really concerned about Mashburn inside. He's a tremendous inside player. I thought that we could have some problems inside, as far as fouls were concerned, if Mashburn got going inside. We also came off the other big guy that they had and tried to jam up the inside and actually did a pretty good job of it.

But then, the pressure that we put on the perimeter on their guards was just non-existent. The game, forgetting the free throw part of the game, the game was decided by our inability to control their guard, Ford, up on top.

FISCHER: From Noblesville. How are the Big Ten schedules made up this year, and are they fair regarding the system that you don't play two teams but one time?

KNIGHT: When you only play two teams once, it isn't ever going to be completely equitable because let's say that in a given year there are two really good teams out there and we only had to play one of them twice, the other one we played just once and played here at Indiana. That becomes a real advantage to us. That's why I've always been against anything in the Big Ten schedule except a total round robin schedule that sees you playing everybody twice. Then people always get wrapped up with the idea of playing two games in a row on the road or playing three games away, but that all, I think, evens itself out over a period of time.

FISCHER: From Vincennes, why do you close a lot of your practices to the public?

KNIGHT: Well, for the same reason that the public doesn't go into the operating room when doctors are performing appendectomies or 'opterectomies' or whatever. We have a classroom situation where we are teaching and we're trying to get some things across. A situation like that I think requires a particular atmosphere and we just go about it that way. Generally for the past five years or so, we have had most of our Wednesday practices open to the public.

FISCHER: This call is from Evansville. By going to the foul line 38 times in yesterday's ballgame, did you feel that is what you wanted to do?

KNIGHT: One of the things that we wanted to do in that ballgame was to get to the free throw line. We felt that we could get the ball into position where we could get it to the free throw line, and that does a lot of things for us. That puts us in a position where we have a really good opportunity to score and it puts the other guy in a position where he's got foul problems and maybe can't play the people they want to play as much as they do. So with that part of what we wanted to do, we were very successful with getting to the line. We had an opportunity to get 41 points from the free throw line.

FISCHER: From Indianapolis, what is your opinion of this year's team's biggest weakness to date?

KNIGHT: Concentrated effort has been the biggest weakness that this team has had during the last two and one-half years. During the entire time that this team has been here it has been a pretty good basketball team.

FISCHER: This is from Kokomo. Do you feel Tom Davis of Iowa prepares his teams extremely well based on what you have faced over the past several years?

KNIGHT: I think that Iowa has always been very well prepared when we play them.

FISCHER: From Bedford. If the Big Ten would go to 12 teams, which new team would you like to see added?

KNIGHT: Uh . . . Vassar!!

FISCHER: This is from Indianapolis. Have you ever had a kid with a bigger heart than Chris Reynolds?

KNIGHT: Well, you see my problem with effort is that I've had a lot of kids with a heart like that. A lot of them have played here and a lot of them played at West Point. You know, we are all given some things in sports. We don't all walk into a store or onto an assembly line and choose what we want to be like. We can't choose a color or a size or a weight, or a height, or a sex, or anything else. You know, we're all born and we go from there. We're born with characteristics that we could change, that we didn't have. That's the hand that we are dealt and we play it as well as we can.

The one thing we all have is effort. Effort! Nobody has a corner on it. There's no patent on it. Everybody's got effort. And when you are as used to effort as I am from all the players that I've seen time and again just give total effort, when that effort isn't there, probably nothing creates more of a problem for me in coaching to deal with than that.

FISCHER: Coach our next questioner is from Indianapolis. During yesterday's ballgame when Kentucky went on a run of seven three-pointers, did you ever consider taking a time out to stop their run?

KNIGHT: Well, taking a time out wasn't necessarily the way to have much effect on stopping the run. Again, we go back to the same thing. We made a couple of changes and did some things without needing a time out. We used a time out, if you'll recall, to get the ball inbound against the press. When we stood around and didn't get the ball in, we had to use a time out to retain possession.

We actually just had two time outs left, and we used both of them at the end of the ballgame, and would really liked to have had just one more time out if we could.

That's not a thing to me. It was the kind of shot that was being taken, and how the shot was manufactured. Those were things that easily could have been straightened out just by simply saying, "We've got to do this or we've got to do that" and then do it. So, we get back again into the area of effort.

FISCHER: From Indianapolis, what did you think of the officiating in yesterday's ballgame?

KNIGHT: Oh, I can go through the tape and there are a lot of mistakes that were made. Again, I said if you looked at it from an Indiana point of view, as we did, you will find some mistakes that were made. And I'm sure if you looked at it from the other team's point of view, you'll find some mistakes that were made. Basically, I thought the officiating was such that it was fair and it was equitable for both teams.

FISCHER: This is from Oolitic, Indiana. What would cause you to finally retire from coaching basketball?

KNIGHT: A couple more efforts like yesterday.

FISCHER: From Indianapolis. It seems that Indiana beat Kentucky while the clock was running and lost to them when the clock was stopped for free throws. Were you not pleased with that part of the performance yesterday?

KNIGHT: Well, I go back to what I said earlier. Let's assume that we are a poor free throw shooting team. All right, then we've got to be able to win in other ways. Shot selection, defensive play, effort, rebounding all kinds of things. So just because we don't shoot free throws well doesn't mean that we can't play well against a lot of teams. And when we didn't, then I think it's a fallacy for us to say that we had a poor free throw shooting night or we would have won the ballgame. When you're deficient in a particular area, there have to be some things, other ways that will enable you to win.

FISCHER: Coach, our final questioner tonight is from Indianapolis, and he would simply like you to comment on the Iowa team you face on Wednesday.

KNIGHT: Iowa has played very well thus far. They really haven't been tested, I don't think, by any of the teams they have played. They have won by big margins all the way through, and they've been a pressing team. They're a very big, strong team. They've out rebounded their opponents close to two to one thus far and will present a problem that any big, strong team will present.

BIG TEN—FIRST ENCOUNTERS

"WE'VE GOT TO WIN THIS GAME DEFENSIVELY."

Iowa
Penn State
Michigan
Illinois
Purdue
Ohio State
Minnesota
Northwestern

```
┌─────────────────────────────────────────────┐
│                                             │
│             Iowa vs. Indiana                │
│             January 6, 1993                 │
│               Bloomington                   │
│              Pre-game Show                  │
│                                             │
└─────────────────────────────────────────────┘
```

Indiana began the conference schedule at home against Iowa, another compet-
itive and highly ranked opponent. The Hawkeyes were ranked eighth and the
Hoosiers were ranked fifth coming into the game.

The losses to Kansas and Kentucky neutralized some of the excitement of winning
the Preseason NIT. Often in the past few years, this group of players has struggled
with big games, and they did this season with Kentucky and Kansas prevailing in
games that Indiana could have won. Some fans were beginning to wonder if this
class could win a big game. Knight begins by discussing the campaign prior to the
Big Ten season, and he ends this pre-game show talking about the Iowa team he
faces tonight.

There are some really nice things that we were able to accomplish in terms of
play prior to the beginning of the Big Ten season. Most notably was the winning
of the Preseason NIT. I think with the exception of the NCAA Tournament itself,
the Preseason NIT is probably the most difficult of all tournaments to win. You've
got to win four games. There are some three game tournaments but the Preseason
NIT is going to provide a team with the greatest challenge. So, we were successful
in that regard.

Yet within the scope of the two most difficult games that we played, there
were really bad periods of play for us in each game, against Florida State and
against Seton Hall. Those were probably the things that I thought most about in
terms of evaluating our play in the Preseason NIT.

Then after the NIT was over, we had a chance to come back against Kansas and
Kentucky. In those two games, it's easy to say, "if we make free throws, we win
both games." We shot 49 free throws in the two games and made 22. Then we
probably add another 6 or 7 possible points to that in terms of one-and-ones that
we missed. We missed 5 one-and-ones in the Kentucky game and 2 or 3 in the
Kansas game, so let's say out of about 55 possible points from the free throw line,
we only get 22. Now that's 40%, and I've always felt that to be successful, really
successful, a team that isn't overpowering as a rebounding team, which we aren't,
has got to be able to convert 70% of the opportunities that it has from the free
throw line. Not 70% of the shots, but 70% of the total opportunities counting one
and ones that you have.

Well, we can easily say, "hey, you know if we can get our free throw shooting straightened around, we shoot better from the line, we're going to be all right." Well, that isn't the case, because we may not be a good free throw shooting team. We may wind up being a very poor free throw shooting team. I don't know. We do all that we can. The players work very hard at improving the free throw percentage, but maybe we just can't do it. Not everybody can hit a golf ball 260 yards, not everybody is a good putter, not everybody can hit a curve ball. There are things in all sports that people just can't do, and free throw shooting may be a real weakness for our team.

There are other things we can do to compensate. We can be really hard to score against; we can be difficult for somebody to get a basket against, hard to get good shots against. We can be really alert defensively to help situations, but we certainly weren't in either the Kansas or the Kentucky game. Being alert, difficult to score against, capable of making big defensive plays when we had to.

Unless we can get that turned around and unless we can develop an attitude toward how important defensive play is to the success of our team, then what happened in those two games is going to recur. It's going to happen again during the course of the Big Ten season.

So, I don't look back on November and December with any great thought about some of the outstanding play that we had, and we surely did have outstanding basketball play by our team, but I think back to the inadequacies that we exhibited from the standpoint of effort, which is the foundation of defensive play. Knowing that if we can't get that straightened out, if we can't get players to understand simply what effort is and what it means, then we're not going to be much of a factor in the Big Ten.

Iowa is a team that tries to score out of its defense and in doing so, it opens up some opportunities for you to score as well. I would imagine that for every point that Kentucky gained in its press in Sunday's game, we probably gained five. The press, I think, clearly worked to our benefit in that ballgame. If we could do that in tonight's ballgame, that would be a really big help to us.

On the offensive end, they're a team that, first of all, ends its offense, whatever it is, with exceptionally good offensive rebounding. If you don't battle Iowa at least fairly close to even on the boards, you're going to have a tremendous deficit to overcome right there. Earl is a very good inside player, a lot of good fakes and moves, excellent passer, particularly so for a big kid. They're able to do a lot of things off of Earl. You've got to cheat here and there to cover him, or he's going to score a lot of points. Then when you do, you open up some other things for them.

Barnes is a very good scorer, a good shooter. Street is tough on the boards. I mentioned earlier that they try and get offense from their defense, with their various presses. It's important that we handle the ball well and don't give them something for nothing in the press.

They are a well put together team, a team with really good experience that's played in this system for a long time. This is Earl's fifth year there, Street's third year, Barnes' third year, Winters and Webb have been there, I think, three and four years. Lookingbill's been there five years. It's a team that's got the kind of experience that a good team has to have.

Don Fischer then asked Coach Knight if fatigue has at all affected his ball club in dealing with the full-court pressure.

I don't think so. Let's just take the Kentucky game. We were 6 down with 7 minutes to play, and then ended up going ahead. So at that point, if fatigue is a real factor, we're six down, we go ten down. And we were able to just stay in there all through the second half and actually had three or four different opportunities when we got it to the six point halftime deficit down to three or four. Then we were finally able to go ahead and stayed ahead for three or four minutes until we made a couple of plays that put them back on top.

GAME SUMMARY

INDIANA 75   IOWA 67

Indiana's basketball team opened the Big Ten Conference campaign with a victory over eighth-ranked Iowa. In the process, there were a couple of milestones which were hit. The game was the 300th game played in Assembly Hall, giving Indiana a 265-35 record in the facility's 22 years. That's an 88% winning percentage.

It was Bob Knight's 600th career triumph, making Knight one of five active coaches and one of just fifteen in history to reach that mark. He reached 600 victories at a younger age than any coach in the 600-win club.

For the team, it was a solid, if not dominating performance, and proved a point Knight has talked about after each of IU's two losses this year. Even when the shots aren't falling at their normal rate, effort can pull you through. There was no lack of effort in this ballgame.

Despite just 45 percent shooting from the field, the Hoosier defense held Iowa to only 40 percent. The Hoosiers were outrebounded 45 to 30, as Knight feared they would be. However the Hoosier intensity forced Iowa into 18 turnovers, compared to 11 for Indiana.

Two players, Damon Bailey and Greg Graham, who were not big factors in Sunday's loss to Kentucky, came off the bench to lead IU with 21 and 17 points respectively. The two combined for 8 of 13 threes on a night when the Hoosiers fired up 23 in all, a new one-game IU record.

Also in double figures in this game were Calbert Cheaney with 14 points, and Todd Leary with 12 points. Leary also dished out 4 assists, a game high for Indiana, and he was 7 for 7 from the free throw line. Matt Nover, who didn't score a lot of points in this contest, pulled down 6 offensive rebounds and a total of 10 for the ballgame to lead Indiana in that department.

Indiana improved slightly at the line to 11 of 16 or 69 percent, which is closer to the 70 percent level Knight mentioned earlier in the season.

IOWA

No.	Player		FG	FGA	FG	FGA	FT	FTA	Off	Def	Tot	PF	TP	A	TO	Blk	S	Min
			Total FG		3-point				Rebounds									
23	Winters, James	f	5	10	0	1	6	8	5	3	8	5	16	0	4	0	3	22
40	Street, Chris	f	2	4	0	0	2	2	1	6	7	5	6	0	3	0	0	23
55	Earl, Acie	c	3	15	0	0	5	8	2	8	10	3	11	0	2	2	1	35
3	Murray, Kenyon	g	2	5	2	3	0	0	1	3	4	2	6	0	0	1	0	23
20	Barnes, Val	g	8	12	2	4	0	0	1	3	4	0	18	0	2	0	0	37
34	Lookingbill, Wade		2	5	0	1	2	3	2	2	4	2	6	0	2	0	0	23
10	smith, Kevin		2	5	0	0	0	1	0	0	0	1	4	5	3	0	0	23
42	Webb, Jay		0	1	0	0	0	0	0	0	0	1	0	0	2	0	0	13
13	Glasper, Mon'ter		0	0	0	0	0	0	0	0	0	0	0	0	0	0	0	1
	Team								5	3	8							
	TOTALS		24	57	4	9	15	22	17	28	45	19	67	5	18	3	4	200

Total FG%	1st Half .455(10/22)	2nd half .400(14/35)	Game .421(24/57)	Deadball
3-Pt. FG%	1st Half .000(0/1)	2nd half .500(4/8)	Game .444(4/9)	Rebounds 2
FT%	1st Half .667(6/9)	2nd half .692(9/13)	Game .682(15/22)	

INDIANA

No.	Player		FG	FGA	FG	FGA	FT	FTA	Off	Def	Tot	PF	TP	A	TO	Blk	S	Min
			Total FG		3-point				Rebounds									
40	Cheaney, Calbert	f	6	13	1	4	1	3	1	3	4	4	14	2	1	0	0	29
44	Henderson, Alan	f	2	11	0	0	1	1	1	4	5	2	5	0	0	2	0	29
24	Nover, Matt	c	2	4	0	0	0	3	6	4	10	5	4	1	2	1	0	38
21	Reynolds, Chris	g	0	1	0	0	0	0	0	0	0	0	0	0	0	0	0	10
30	Leary, Todd	g	2	6	1	4	7	7	0	3	3	1	12	4	1	0	1	21
34	Evans, Brian		1	5	0	2	0	0	0	2	2	1	2	2	1	0	0	18
22	Bailey, Damon		8	12	5	7	0	0	0	2	2	2	21	3	6	0	0	29
20	Graham, Greg		6	9	3	6	2	2	1	2	3	3	17	2	0	0	1	24
25	Knight, Pat		0	0	0	0	0	0	0	0	0	0	0	0	0	0	1	2
	Team								0	1	1							
	TOTALS		27	61	10	23	11	16	9	21	30	18	75	14	11	3	3	200

Total FG%	1st Half .438(14/32)	2nd half .448(13/29)	Game .443(27/61)	Deadball
3-Pt. FG%	1st Half .357(5/14)	2nd half .556(5/9)	Game .435(10/23)	Rebounds 2
FT%	1st Half .000(0/1)	2nd half .733(11/15)	Game .688(11/16)	

Officials _____

Technical Fouls _____

Attendance 17,020 _____

Score by Periods	1	2	OT	OT	Final
Iowa	26	41			67
Indiana	33	42			75

This was Penn State's first trip to Assembly Hall, which is considerably bigger than the arenas it had played in before it joined the Big Ten. What is the most striking about walking into Assembly Hall for the first time is the prominence of the red and white championship banners that are at both ends of the court. I was there when the Nittany Lions walked on the floor, and the players were consumed by the five NCAA Championship banners at one end of the Hall, and the other national banners at the other end.

I don't know if fans realize this, but when a player shoots a free throw at Assembly Hall, he or she looks right at the banners. They show through the glass backboard. They provide a constant reminder on the court for IU players and their opponents of the long tradition of winning we have at Indiana.

Then, as the game developed, the size and involvement of the 17,000 fans had its effect on the Penn State team. The Nittany Lions play was certainly below par in this game, but they would make a statement later in the season when IU visited University Park, PA.

Knight began by talking about the Iowa game, and then wrapped this show up with an analysis of Penn State.

We talked after last Sunday's game about the lack of effort we thought we had in our game with Kentucky last Sunday, particularly the lack of defensive effort that we had on the perimeter. I felt that we had an improvement in that area of play against Iowa. Iowa is probably one of the three best teams that we've played thus far into the season, without having played any of the other Big Ten games, very comparable to Kansas. We had a couple of opportunities in the Iowa game where we could have gotten a little better control of it than we had.

The final result of the game is really kind of indicative of what the three-point shot can do. I don't think the game was quite as close at the end as the score would indicate. We were able to maintain a pretty good margin of between 9 and 12 points in the latter stages of the ballgame, and I was pleased that we were down by 8 at two different times in the first half and then came back to have a 7 point lead at the half.

To give you an idea how my mind works, we've come from eight down to seven ahead at the half, and yet the thing that is on my mind most as I walk off the court at the end of the half is that we screwed up things at the end of the half and didn't get a good shot or a good attempt to score. We'd come up with a loose ball, good deflection and a loose ball recovery, to keep Iowa from getting a basket at the end of the half. Then it would have been great if we could have turned that over into a basket that would have enabled us to have gone from 8 down, I think at 19 to 11, to a lead of 35 to 26, that would have meant that we had scored 24 points in a period of time while Iowa was scoring just 7, I believe. We didn't do that, and yet we had outscored Iowa 22 to 7. We'd outscored them by 15 during that latter part of the first half.

Then we went from not real deep in the second half I think we'd gone ahead by 12 or 13 points. From then on, until just one brief moment toward the end, we maintained that margin. Mostly I thought our defense on the perimeter was good where it hadn't been against Kentucky. We shot the ball fairly well. We probably didn't take the ball inside nearly as much as we should have. But basically I thought it was a good comeback performance for us after what I thought was much less than an acceptable performance by us in the game prior to the Iowa game.

One of Todd Leary's greatest assets is his ability to shoot from three-point range, and I think he made just 1 out of 4 in the ballgame. He hit 7 free throws in a row. He made a tremendous three-point play driving on the basket in the latter stages of the game, not only scoring but getting fouled and making the free throw also. In the 3 minutes or so that he played in the Kentucky game, he was far and away more alert, quicker to react, much more on top of things. It was after reviewing the film and just that short amount of playing time that Todd had, and comparing it to the considerable minutes that we had other guys playing and comparing how alert and enthusiastic and aggressive he was in his play that without ever starting to work on the plan against Iowa, I had made up my mind that Todd would be in the starting lineup against Iowa.

I really like Bruce Parkhill, Penn State's coach. I think he is a very good coach, an excellent basketball coach, and a very good person. From a coaching standpoint, I think, he is a real nice addition to Big Ten basketball. They have had to cope with some injuries. Some kids that were starting for them early in the year were hurt. One of those kids, a ball-handling guard named Williams, may be back to play today. That would be a real help to them. They've got a couple of other kids that probably won't be back for a while yet.

In the Ohio State game, over the course of the game, they probably led Ohio State more than they were behind. In fact, Penn State led by as much as eight in the first half. Then they had a couple of chances, maybe three chances, to win or tie the game at the end, and just none of those things came about for them. So they played Ohio State to virtually an even game in their opening game in the Big Ten.

This, then, becomes just their second game and their first road game in the Big Ten, and I think that Bruce's team will be very solid at both ends of the floor. It's one that we're going to have to have good defensive aggressiveness and patience against, because they have good half-court offensive patience.

GAME SUMMARY

INDIANA 105 PENN STATE 57

Bob Knight's team ripped apart Penn State Saturday in Assembly Hall. The Hoosiers rampaged to a 53-20 halftime lead, and never looked back. The Hoosiers totally outmanned the Nittany Lions.

For the second straight game, Damon Bailey and Greg Graham came off the bench and led IU in scoring. Bailey had a season high 28 points, and Graham had 19. Each also had a hot hand in firing in three-point field goals, connecting on six out of nine attempts.

As a team, Indiana hit 62 percent from the field while holding Penn State to 36 percent from the field. From the free throw line, the Hoosiers connected on 14 of 19, for 74 percent. Penn State was just 6 of 9 in free throw shooting. Indiana turned the ball over just 7 times in this game to 18 turnovers for Penn State.

Individually, in addition to Bailey and Graham, Calbert Cheaney and Alan Henderson each had 14 points. Todd Leary had 11. Henderson led the Hoosiers with 9 rebounds.

The most pleasing aspect to Bob Knight was the sheer effort put forth for the full 40 minutes in each of the first two Big Ten games.

PENN STATE

No.	Player		Total FG FG	FGA	3-point FG	FGA	FT	FTA	Rebounds Off	Def	Tot	PF	TP	A	TO	Blk	S	Min
24	Hayes, Deron	f	5	14	1	2	0	0	2	3	5	1	11	0	0	0	0	20
30	Carr, Eric	f	3	5	0	0	0	1	2	1	3	1	6	0	0	0	0	20
13	Amechi, John	c	2	8	0	1	3	3	2	4	6	3	7	0	1	1	0	18
00	Jennings, Michael	g	3	7	1	2	0	0	1	2	3	1	7	0	2	1	0	28
22	Bartram, Greg	g	1	4	0	2	2	2	0	1	1	3	4	2	2	0	1	31
45	Joseph, Michael		2	3	0	0	0	1	4	2	6	0	4	2	0	0	0	18
33	Dietz, John		1	3	0	0	0	0	0	1	1	2	2	0	2	0	0	15
4	Carter, Elton		1	2	0	0	0	0	0	0	0	0	2	0	1	0	0	9
20	Wydman, Steve		1	4	1	3	0	0	0	1	1	1	3	2	6	0	0	16
15	Carlton, Rashaan		5	14	0	2	1	2	3	3	6	3	11	1	4	0	0	20
12	Williams, Donovan		0	3	0	0	0	0	0	1	1	1	0	0	1	0	0	5
	Team								2	1	3							
	TOTALS		24	67	3	12	6	9	16	20	36	16	57	7	19	2	1	200

Total FG% 1st Half .258(8/31) 2nd half .444(16/36) Game .358(24/67) Deadball
3-Pt. FG% 1st Half .222(2/9) 2nd half .333(1/3) Game .250(3/12) Rebounds ___0___
FT% 1st Half 1.00(2/2) 2nd half .571(4/7) Game .667(6/9)

INDIANA

No.	Player		Total FG FG	FGA	3-point FG	FGA	FT	FTA	Rebounds Off	Def	Tot	PF	TP	A	TO	Blk	S	Min
40	Cheaney, Calbert	f	7	13	0	5	0	0	2	5	7	2	14	4	1	0	0	30
44	Henderson, Alan	f	6	11	0	0	2	2	2	7	9	2	14	0	1	2	2	22
24	Nover, Matt	c	3	4	0	0	1	2	1	3	4	3	7	0	1	0	1	15
21	Reynolds, Chris	g	2	2	0	0	2	2	0	2	2	0	6	3	0	0	3	21
30	Leary, Todd	g	4	8	1	3	2	2	0	0	0	1	11	3	1	0	3	23
20	Graham, Greg		8	11	3	6	0	0	1	1	2	2	19	0	0	0	3	18
22	Bailey, Damon		9	11	3	3	7	9	2	3	5	0	28	6	0	0	1	23
34	Evans, Brian		1	3	0	1	0	0	1	6	7	1	2	5	1	0	1	25
25	Knight, Pat		2	5	0	0	0	2	0	2	2	2	4	3	2	0	0	23
	Team								0	1	1							
	TOTALS		42	68	7	18	14	19	9	30	39	13	105	24	7	2	14	200

Total FG% 1st Half .657(23/35) 2nd half .576(19/33) Game .618(42/68) Deadball
3-Pt. FG% 1st Half .444(4/9) 2nd half .333(3/9) Game .389(7/18) Rebounds ___2___
FT% 1st Half .600(3/5) 2nd half .786(11/14) Game .737(14/19)

Officials Tom O'Neill, Randy Drury, Mike Spanier
Technical Fouls
Attendance 17,265

Score by Periods	1	2	OT	OT	Final
Penn State	20	37			57
Indiana	53	52			105

BOB KNIGHT TALK SHOW

January 11, 1993

The team was traveling to Ann Arbor, and this show was prerecorded. Don Fischer was not able to take calls from listeners. In looking to the games ahead, Knight comes back to the fundamentals he has emphasized this season, the most important being effort and defense.

FISCHER: Coach, you have had two ballgames since the last talk show, starting Big Ten play with the Iowa contest on Wednesday night. Lets talk about that ballgame and the way your ball club performed.

KNIGHT: In the Iowa game it was important for us, especially after the Kentucky game where our effort in perimeter defense was not very good, to be able to come back and have some effort in our play. I thought that we got pretty good effort in what we were doing in the Iowa game. We were down two different times, yet in neither situation did I feel upset or irritated about the way we were playing, simply because there was effort involved. We were able to maintain that effort and gradually go from an eight point deficit to a seven point lead at the half. We had a better effort, and consequently we had a better result in the ballgame. I felt much better after our game with Iowa Wednesday night than I did going into the game.

FISCHER: In the game Sunday, Nover had 29 points, and in the game on Wednesday, he didn't come close to double figures. He had a great effort in the Iowa ballgame, despite not scoring a lot of points.

KNIGHT: The way that we set up things and the way that we handle our offense, the way it's run, there are going to be different opportunities for different players, as you go from one game to another. We explained to our team that we really didn't need a lot of help in the game against Kentucky. We had 29 points from Cheaney and 29 points from Nover. That's 58 points. We got 20 from everybody else. Seventy-eight points gives us enough to win the ballgame, if in fact, we're playing defense as well as we can play it. Kentucky was a game where we just gave up points too easily.

FISCHER: Let's talk now about the Penn State game, a ballgame that Indiana completely dominated throughout.

KNIGHT: I think the reason we played well against Penn State was that we had some carryover in our defensive play from Wednesday night's game. Our defense put us in a position where we were able to have control throughout the game.

Also, there were some very good things that happened to us offensively. By the same token what we were able to do in terms of scoring points in many cases was a result of what we did defensively. What we did defensively in the Penn State game, I think, was a direct result of what we were able to do in our first game of the week against Iowa. We had the kind of carryover that we would have liked to have had in the Iowa game.

We've just really not been able, and this will be very important from here on, we've not been able to operate from a point of view that we've got to win this game defensively. And then, if everything is going well offensively, then, we're that much more difficult to beat. If we could put the game in a position where through nothing but our defense we actually have a chance to play in the game, then the better our offense is, the more difficult we become to play against. And we just haven't been able to get the right kind of mental attitude toward defensive play that I think we have to have. Now, there were some obvious improvements here in these two ballgames, I think, that opened up the Big Ten season for us.

What's ahead of us? For us to be able to play well and to be competitive in everything that we do from here on, defense has to be the key for us. As we've discussed, our defense could have overridden anything that we did from the free throw line and we lost two ballgames. In those two games we've been 22 of 49 from the foul line. Of a possible 56 points that we could get, adding the bottom end of one and ones, we end up with 22. And you say, "gee, but nothing from the free throw line."

Well, all right, if we can't and we're not a good free throw shooting team, we can't and we're not.

What we have to do then is at the defensive end, and I've been going at this for a week now because of the results of our games with both Kansas and Kentucky. The defensive end. We've got to provide ourselves with an opportunity to win there, and that's just going to be extremely important to us all the way through this season.

FISCHER: The three-point shot was a much more prevalent thing for your ball club in both those contests.

KNIGHT: You've got to go back again to the game last Sunday against Kentucky. We really didn't need a lot of three-point shots because we shot 36 free throws. We were getting the ball where we wanted to get it. We wanted to go to the free throw line, we wanted to score from the foul line. We were able to get the ball inside, take it where we wanted, get the kind of shot that we wanted without a lot of threes

Then you go to the Iowa game, and Iowa plays a lot of zone. With our size, you're not going to do a whole lot inside offensively against Earl and Street.

Nover, you're talking about a kid that's a small 6-8 going against those two guys inside. I'm not sure how much we're going to get out of that.

So now we use some movement inside, we try to force the zone to cover certain areas, and now we have an opportunity to get some outside shooting involved in what we're doing. I thought we took pretty good advantage of it. I forget just how many we made, but I think we made 11, maybe, and probably took 22 or 23 shots in the game. And then, when we came back against Penn State, we continued to shoot a pretty decent percentage.

FISCHER: In the Penn State game it was 7 of 18.

KNIGHT: That's not quite as good as I would have thought. So what we've done is shoot a total of 18 of 41 in the two ballgames, which is probably the most threes we have taken in any two successive games, I would imagine.

There's a little zone play by both teams. We'll shoot the ball when we have the opportunity to do so against the zone, and we'll try to utilize the three-point shot. But when we are able to get the ball inside and take the ball where we want it and get to the line and get the kind of shots that are good for us with our inside movement, then the three-point shot just becomes a supplement in that regard.

Sometimes when a team goes to a three against us, perhaps it's an indication that we've done a pretty good job with our inside defense. Then we've got to have some perimeter quickness and I just keep coming back to the same thought: our perimeter quickness has just got to be better defensively. It's got to apply more pressure; it's got to be able to get more things done from the defensive standpoint than it did in the game that we lost to Kentucky.

FISCHER: Coach, how do you feel about Penn State joining the conference this year for the first time?

KNIGHT: No one has been able to explain to me why we needed an additional team to begin with. You know, why an additional team? Secondly, why a team from considerably far away from this general geographic area? If you are going to add a team, it seems to me you've got a couple of teams like Missouri and Nebraska and Iowa State that are much more similar to Big Ten schools in terms of facilities and everything else. So, as you can tell, I was not involved in the selection of the addition to the Big Ten and probably will not be consulted on any further additions.

I would guess I probably knew as much or more about Penn State than anybody in the Big Ten because we used to compete against them on an annual basis when I was at West Point. It's a great school, has a great athletic tradition, and a part of that tradition actually is in basketball. The teams out in this part of the country have not played a lot against Penn State over the years. Penn State played predominantly an Eastern schedule, but I think in 1954, Penn

State went to the NCAA Finals. They've been on and off a very good team in the East. And I think in these last maybe three or four years, Penn State has won 20 games each year. They knocked UCLA out of the first round of the NCAA Tournament a couple of years ago, and they've gone to the finals in the NIT.

I think Bruce Parkhill as a coach is an excellent addition to the conference. I think he is a very good coach and a very fine young man. I think he has a really good future in coaching basketball, should he have any real desire to do so. He has done an excellent job where he is.

The Eastern schools for years and years had a difficult time in recruiting against the Atlantic Coast Conference because it was a conference that drew more recognition. The ACC did considerably better on a national basis, played more of a national schedule than any of the Eastern teams did. But with the advent of the Big East, it has become very difficult now for people to go in and recruit in the East as they once did.

Now, you take St. John's, Villanova and Georgetown, and you add to that a team like Syracuse that had been pretty good. Syracuse simply became better with the advent of the Big East, to the point that it became a very strong team nationally. A team like Seton Hall, again simply because of the strength of the Big East overall, Seton Hall has risen to the point now where I think it's a very legitimate national basketball power.

Penn State has got to be able, through its association with the Big Ten, through what the Big Ten provides in terms of competition and national recognition, Penn State has got to be able to get itself into a position where it is exactly the same as a Seton Hall or as a St. John's in terms of the kind of player it can attract and in fact recruit. It will need that kind of player. They are going to have to get the majority of them from somewhere relatively close to home for you to be a power in a league, like the Big Ten.

FISCHER: I'd like to talk for just a moment about the work ethic of a young man that epitomizes that with your basketball team, Matt Nover, and where he's been through his five years here.

KNIGHT: Matt is absolutely the kind of kid that not only I want to recruit and have play for me, but everybody wants to recruit. We started out kind of on the wrong foot with Matt as a recruit. I actually didn't think that we were going to have a scholarship for Matt as recruiting was going when he was a senior in high school. We told him that. We let him know that, and then it developed that we did in fact have a scholarship, and we came back to Matt.

At that point, I'm sure there are a lot of kids that would have adopted the idea of "Well, you just as much as turned me down once. I have no interest in being recruited by you anymore." But Matt had a real strong interest in coming to Indiana and was just very pleased that things had worked out in such a way that we could in fact offer him a scholarship to come here. Then, because of the roster that we had at that point, we felt that it would be both to Matt's benefit and to ours to redshirt him for a year. He had absolutely no problem with that. He just worked to develop his skills through that redshirt year and again, not every kid is willing to be redshirted. We aren't ever going to redshirt somebody against his wishes. But the redshirt possibility is so important to a kid who perhaps isn't going to play a great deal as a freshman or a sophomore, but is going to play as a junior and senior. Because what the redshirt opportunity does is give that kid a third year to play. If we know he is going to play as a junior and a senior, then we hold him for a year, and he's going to play as a junior, senior plus one. That's what worked out with Matt.

Matt, beginning with his first year of competition, has been a very big factor in all that we've done. He's been a starter in a lot of games. He's been a sixth man perhaps when he hasn't started. And I think he has really worked and worked to improve himself as a basketball player. The one thing that I'd like to see us get from this point on that we really haven't gotten from Matt, and this isn't Matt's fault, it's probably mine, because we're not emphasizing this to him to a great degree, is to get Matt involved with his jump shot in our offense. He is an excellent 15 to 18 foot shooter, and we just have not really involved him inside a lot, trying to take advantage of his quickness inside. We have got to get him through the remainder of this season with his jump shot in our offense.

No one we've had here has put more time and effort into developing his skills to become an effective player at this level of competition than Matt has.

FISCHER: We've had several letters sent to us this week, and let's start our questions from Acton, Indiana. After watching the Iowa game, will you define what constitutes a traveling violation, since the NBA rules to my knowledge haven't been handed down to the colleges?

KNIGHT: Well, not only do you need to have defined what constitutes a traveling violation, the officials in the Iowa game needed to have defined for them what constitutes a traveling violation. Traveling is a very difficult thing to explain. It almost has to be something demonstrated, but let me cover a couple of areas where traveling occurs and it's missed a lot.

First of all, on the perimeter, and this happened in the Iowa game, the pivot foot was changed. I want you to imagine catching the basketball, and you are in motion, catching the basketball, you can, once the ball touches your hand, step with one foot. If both feet move after your hands have made contact with the basketball, without it being dribbled, that's a walking violation. That happens many times on the perimeter. I really believe that one of the great weaknesses in officiating is an official's understanding of not only what traveling is but how to look for it. I see this time and time again in everything that we do with our scouting of opponents and looking at tapes of other teams playing.

The second place a traveling violation occurs is when a drive is initiated. Let's say that you are making a fake with your right foot. You step with your right foot and you are going to cross over and come back to your left. If that left foot moves before the ball is on the way to the floor, in other words, the ball is still in your hands and you've crossed over with your right foot and slipped your left foot, that is a walking violation. That pivot foot that you have established after catching the ball must remain firmly planted on the floor until the ball is in the process of being dribbled and has in fact left the driver's hands.

Another area where traveling occurs an awful lot and is not detected is in the post area. The post man gets the ball and he gets a little bit crowded by the man guarding him, and also perhaps by help that slides into position. He slides one way, or fakes one way, rather, and then comes back the other way. Many, many times he will slide his pivot foot or make a small step with his pivot foot, and again there is a traveling violation that has gone unnoticed.

A travel that happened in the Iowa game that happened three or four times probably was one that a move had been made, a step and then a hop after the step. Now they're allowing the hop to take place, if it is followed right on the heels of a dribble, but the step and then the hop is a travel violation.

FISCHER: These next two questions are from Indianapolis. Based on the number of years you've coached in the Big Ten, what average number of losses can a team normally sustain and still win the Big Ten Conference title?

KNIGHT: Well, I think if you're going to say under most conditions what you would like to have as a record in the Big Ten, or what it would take to win the Big Ten, I think far more often than not you'd be safe with 15 and 3. I think that most coaches would on occasion be happy with a record of 14-4.

FISCHER: This fan wonders if the area on the east side of the floor, specifically the press seating area where tables are used, and also the wheelchair area are injury hazards to players?

KNIGHT: Well, you're going to have stands there. What we've done is take out a row or two of stands to provide on-the-court seating for people in wheelchairs. I don't think that becomes any more of a problem for the players than people sitting in the stands, if in fact we retained the row or two rows we have removed.

As far as the press is concerned, I think that we would have no problem in that regard putting the press up in the press box above the balcony. I think that would be an excellent place from which to watch games. They would be there where they've got the whole game in front of them. The panorama of the game would be good. There are enough people in the press that are not very athletic and no one would have to move his or her head so quick that maybe some kind of a whiplash injury could occur from being down on the floor. So, we do have a press box above the balcony and I would think that perhaps this year and certainly next year, Don, that's where we'll find the press in residence.

FISCHER: (Laughter.) This from question is from Evansville, Indiana. Could you detail the priorities in setting up your matchups with an opposing team using any of your most recent opponents as an example?

KNIGHT: If we take the Iowa game, we've got to have somebody with quickness and strength to play against Earl, and we immediately go with Matt Nover. You know he has the best combination of quickness and strength for us. Then Street, a very good rebounder, we've got to matchup with somebody that can rebound for us. That's going to be Alan Henderson. We'd look at their third starter in the front line, Winters is a player that plays both inside and outside as Cheaney does for us, so that becomes a natural matchup. Also we have matched fairly well with size and strength as we can against those three people.

Then in the back court, Iowa has a very, very good scorer in Barnes, and in our starting lineup then, we would like to have perhaps the most quickness we could have on Barnes, and that would have been with Chris Reynolds. Then we have a decision to make there. Do we want the kind of pressure Reynolds can exert on Barnes who's a scorer, or do we want it on Smith who is a ball handler? In that ballgame, I think, we opted to put the pressure on Smith who is a ball handler.

FISCHER: All right. Our next question is from Bloomington. What are the new rules on the number of players you can have on scholarship next year, and what are your thoughts on the new gender equity rules that are being instituted? Is gender equity an NCAA legislation or just a Big Ten pronouncement?

KNIGHT: Gender equity is a national problem, I think. I use the word, problem, because I really believe this. Until people in college administration recognize that everybody in athletics has a position in athletics because football and basketball are revenue producing sports, it will continue to be a problem. Until football and basketball are eliminated from all the rules and regulations, I think we're going to have major problems in the overall administration of college athletics. These two sports provide every opportunity basically that there is in college athletics around the country. Administrators, coaches, participants, be they men or women, everybody in athletics has a position because of football and basketball.

Now there are exceptions here and there, like with Wisconsin's hockey program, it's been a great hockey program. They make money, but rarely does a school have a third revenue producing sport such as Wisconsin has. Until it is recognized and established that we have to do what is necessary for basketball and football to be as good as possible, then we're not going to have the kind of situation for the other sports that we all would like to have.

FISCHER: Scholarships next year?

KNIGHT: There will be 13. One has been cut out of basketball. You don't need to cut any out of basketball; 14 scholarships is fine. We can get by with 14, but you get kids injured, a kid gets hurt or a kid leaves, or whatever, you get cut down to the point where you can't be as effective as you normally would. That's again why I say, until somebody just has enough gumption to get up and say, "Wait a minute. Football and basketball are providing every single opportunity there is in athletics, for men, for women, for participants, for coaches and for administrators. And let's treat these sports accordingly."

Once again Indiana faces a highly ranked and regarded team, the Michigan Wolverines, at Ann Arbor. Michigan comes into the game ranked second in the country and Indiana is ranked sixth. This is a battle for an early lead in the Big Ten, to be sure, but it is also another gritty test of Indiana's mental toughness. This also will be a measure of Indiana's ability to win a "big" game. Indiana had already lost to two top five rated teams, Kansas and Kentucky, and it will have to play well to beat Michigan on the road.

As in other pre-game shows, Knight begins with a review of the previous game against Penn State, and talks about the adjustment they will make to playing in the Big Ten. He talks again about the importance of effort, and finishes with an analysis of the Michigan team he faces. The Fab Five are sophomores now and they make Michigan one of the most talented teams in the country.

A part of the outcome of the Penn State game, I think, was a result of making their first trip away from home in the Big Ten. I mean, you're playing in much bigger arenas, for one thing, than Penn State has been used to playing in. It's going to take some getting used to for them. Playing in the Atlantic 10 conference that they've played in, the only really good sized arena that they play in anywhere is at West Virginia, and it seats about 14,000. You really only have a couple of large basketball arenas in the entire east region: Maryland, 15,000; Syracuse's big indoor stadium arena holds 30,000 or 32,000, and Seton Hall, playing in the Meadowlands, and Georgetown playing where the Bullets play. That's about it. You don't make a road trip in the East like you do here, where with the exception of Northwestern, all the arenas are 14,000 or bigger. And that's going to take a little adjustment.

I think that's probably why they were very comfortable at home. In their first game with Ohio State, they played a game that they could have easily won. Then coming into our place, a lot of factors were stacked up against them. We got off to a good start and then improved upon it. It will be a different story when we play Penn State at Penn State.

We got better effort. I don't think there's any question about that. Our effort improved. I think that we had effort all across the board, but that's not something that you can put on any kind of a graph. You've got to have it going upward all the time, I mean effort today should be better than it was yesterday, not 74% to 48% to 61%, it just can't be up and down.

Effort is one of those things that should be there. In basketball, the basket is the same height. It's going to be there, and that's not going to change. You don't have to come in and wonder, "oh, I wonder how high the basket will be today?" The basket is there.

You can't wonder about effort. I can't come into a game and say, "I wonder what kind of effort we're going to get today?" If we do, then we become an inconsistent team, and an inconsistent team doesn't win anything. The consistency of effort has got to be there, and it hasn't been there with this particular team. Until we have that, we will then be just what our effort is: inconsistent.

Leary and Reynolds both did an excellent job in the last two games, but it's not sufficient to stop there. I think all four of our guards have done well. Obviously, I couldn't have been too pleased with Bailey and Graham in the Kentucky game, and both of them have come back to play very well in these last two games.

The three-point shot is going to be there, and we took advantage of it in these games. We're going to get the three-point shot. I'm sure that we'll take it when it's there, but we've got to have some judgment in when we take it and at what point in the possession we take it.

The Michigan team we play tonight is a very talented team, and there have been some good things done with this team that help it play unselfishly. It plays up and down the floor well. It passes the ball very well, and even as talented as this team is, there are players that have roles, and they fulfill their roles. Howard is a very good poster. Webber combines excellent inside play with decent outside play. Rose drives the ball well and shoots it adequately, so that there are some things that they mix and match. All together, with their tremendous size and quickness, Michigan becomes a very, very difficult team for us or for anybody else to play against.

In order to play with this team, we've got to have some patience and we've got to work to get good shots. If we come down and take a bad shot, that's a turnover. We are not going to get a big, big number of offensive rebounds. Nobody is against this team. So your shot selection first of all has got to be good.

On the defensive end, you can't help a lot on this team, because the more you're forced to help, the more you jumble up your block out situation, and that's just one thing you can't afford to do with this team. Probably, Michigan's number one offensive point getter is offensive rebounding.

The matchups are going to be important. We've got to do a really good job keeping this team off the backboard.

Fischer then asks about lineup tonight. Knight, anxious to move to his final preparation for the game, responds:

I didn't think we were ever going to get to this question, because I know it signifies the end of the show. We'll go with a lineup that involves the same front line that we've been using, Cheaney, Henderson and Nover, with Graham and Bailey at the guards.

GAME SUMMARY

INDIANA 76   MICHIGAN 75

For many, Indiana's battle with Michigan will rate as one of the best college basketball games of the season. It had everything: great defense, great offense, big plays on both sides, and a knock-out punch at the end. Like most great games, it was tough on the nerves for those of us watching. Fortunately, it had an IU ending.

The game showcased perhaps the best sophomore talent in the country, the Fab Five of Michigan and a sophomore for Indiana who takes a back seat to no one. Alan Henderson was sensational, with a game high 22 points and pulling down 8 rebounds. He blocked 5 shots, including the potential game winner, from his more celebrated rival, Chris Webber, in the final seconds. Henderson, who had been in a shooting slump, was helped that morning, prior to the ballgame, by assistant coach Ron Felling with his shooting touch. Apparently the extra work paid off.

Meantime, accolades could be passed to every other player on the team as well, because each had a very important contribution to this win. They included Calbert Cheaney's 20 points and relentless movement without the ball. Damon Bailey had ten assists without a turnover and Greg Graham turned in excellent offensive play and aggressive defense during the entire game. Matt Nover also was effective battling inside on the boards against both Chris Webber and Juwan Howard. The solid relief stints by Todd Leary, Chris Reynolds, Brian Evans and Pat Knight, all helped Indiana win this important game.

Indiana shot 55 percent from the field while Michigan was held to 47 percent. From three-point range, Indiana hit on 7 of 17, Michigan connected on 7 or 20. From the free throw line, the Hoosiers converted just 5 out of 10, while Michigan went to the line just 6 times, converting 4. Indiana topped Michigan in rebounding 33 to 31, which is somewhat surprising, considering the height advantage of Michigan. Turnovers were minimal for both teams, with Indiana having 10 and Michigan 6.

This was the kind of win that Bob Knight had wanted for this team.

INDIANA

No.	Player		Total FG		3-point				Rebounds									
			FG	FGA	FG	FGA	FT	FTA	Off	Def	Tot	PF	TP	A	TO	Blk	S	Min
40	Cheaney, Calbert	f	9	19	1	5	1	2	0	3	3	2	20	3	4	0	0	39
44	Henderson, Alan	f	10	15	0	2	2	2	2	6	8	3	22	1	1	5	1	36
24	Nover, Matt	c	3	7	0	0	2	6	1	3	4	2	8	0	3	2	0	33
20	Graham, Greg	g	5	7	2	2	0	0	1	4	5	0	12	5	2	0	1	36
22	Bailey, Damon	g	2	5	2	4	0	0	1	2	3	1	6	10	0	0	0	32
32	Reynolds, Chris		0	0	0	0	0	0	0	2	2	0	0	2	0	0	0	6
30	Leary, Todd		1	1	0	0	0	0	0	2	2	1	2	0	0	0	0	6
34	Evans, Brian		2	4	2	4	0	0	0	2	2	0	6	1	0	0	0	11
25	Knight, Pat		0	0	0	0	0	0	0	0	0	0	0	0	0	0	0	1
	Team								3	1	4							
	TOTALS		32	58	7	17	5	10	8	25	33	10	76	22	10	7	2	200

Total FG%	1st Half .531(17/32)	2nd half .577(15/26)	Game .552(32/58)	Deadball	
3-Pt. FG%	1st Half .333(3/9)	2nd half .500(4/8)	Game .412(7/17)	Rebounds 3	
FT%	1st Half .000(0/2)	2nd half .625(5/8)	Game .500(5/10)		

MICHIGAN

No.	Player		Total FG		3-point				Rebounds									
			FG	FGA	FG	FGA	FT	FTA	Off	Def	Tot	PF	TP	A	TO	Blk	S	Min
4	Webber, Chris	f	8	17	1	4	1	3	1	5	6	4	18	0	2	3	0	33
32	Voskuil	f	3	7	2	5	0	0	0	4	4	2	8	3	0	0	0	24
25	Howard, Juwann	c	8	12	0	0	1	1	1	4	5	1	17	4	1	0	0	35
5	Rose, Jalen	g	9	18	1	2	0	0	3	1	4	3	19	4	1	0	2	37
24	King, Jimmy	g	4	8	3	7	0	0	0	2	2	2	11	5	1	0	1	38
14	Talley		0	0	0	0	0	0	0	0	0	0	0	0	0	0	0	3
3	Pelinka		0	3	0	1	0	0	2	1	3	1	0	1	0	0	0	13
42	Riley		0	2	0	0	2	2	1	2	3	1	2	1	1	0	0	12
11	Fife		0	1	0	1	0	0	0	1	1	1	0	1	0	0	0	5
	Team								3	0	3							
	TOTALS		32	68	7	20	4	6	11	20	31	15	75	19	6	3	3	200

Total FG%	1st Half .382(13/34)	2nd half .559(19.34)	Game .470(32/68)	Deadball	
3-Pt. FG%	1st Half .250(3/12)	2nd half .500(4/8)	Game .350(7/20)	Rebounds 2	
FT%	1st Half 1.00(2/2)	2nd half .500(2/4)	Game .667(4/6)		

Officials   Ed Hightower, Burr, Phil Bova
Technical Fouls
Attendance   13,562

Score by Periods	1	2	OT	OT	Final
Indiana	37	39			76
Michigan	31	44			75

There was no time for the Hoosiers to rest after the impressive win in Ann Arbor. This difficult road trip continued at Champaign against a talented Illinois team. The Illini would be up for this game, and one question in Knight's mind was would Indiana be able to focus on Illinois after the big win against Michigan?

Knight begins by talking about the Michigan game, and then gives his pre-game analysis of the Illinois team he faces today. Fischer refers to the Michigan game as a "great" game, however Knight reminds Don that "great" is reserved for very special games, NCAA championships.

In my career at Indiana, there have been just three "great" wins. There are good wins and games that have been important in seasons, but the word "great," there are only three of them.

There is a tendency in a situation like ours where there is so much interest in basketball, the players, and in everything that they do. After winning a game where people think it's such an outstanding accomplishment, that excitement occasionally carries over to the players, and they forget a little bit about the next game.

There isn't anything more important in the season than the next game, and getting ready for the next game. If you sit around after the last game, with people patting you on the back, that's the easiest thing to do. It is particularly hard in basketball, as opposed to football, because you've just maybe got a couple of days, and you're back playing again. And that's the case here with us. My hope is that we've got our attention focused on Illinois because there's a simple axiom for us in our remaining 15 games. We're going to have to play well to win.

The foundation, the basis of playing well, is mental preparation, individual mental preparation. Each kid being focused on what his responsibilities are in this specific game, not what he did in the last game or what we did as a team in the last game, but those things he has to do and we have to do in this game. I think that applies to any team, not just ours, or to any player, not just ours.

The biggest problem, after a game that was very satisfying and that everybody enjoyed winning, because it was against a very good team, is getting ready for the next game. In fact, it becomes of paramount importance. It's not all that difficult to get ready to play when you've played poorly, or to get ready to play after a loss. When you've got good kids and kids that want to do well and they slip up and maybe don't play as well as they can or as well as they should, in most cases they're going to bounce back. Their attention is going to be riveted on playing well the next chance that they have.

That usually becomes the difference between teams over the course of a season. It's that team that can get focused most quickly on the upcoming game and play the upcoming game to the best of its abilities. And that's what our question will be here tonight.

We will have to do that tonight, because the Illinois team has excellent experience. Kauffman has been in school for five years and Thomas has been in school four years. They are their two leading scorers. Thomas is as good a posting player as there is anywhere. He just works and works and takes advantage of openings and steps in. He is very, very difficult to play against inside. Kaufmann is a relentless offensive worker. He works an awful lot like Cheaney does, utilizing many of the same opportunities that we try to get for Calbert. So you start with two very good scorers, and you've got to do a good job on each of them.

Their supporting cast is very good. They've got good ball handlers. They shoot the ball well. They've got good size. They've got good bench strength. If we were to play reasonably well, and this team were to play well, this is a team that could beat us. It will not be a game that we can go into and play anyway other than as well as we can play, if we want to win the ballgame.

They're a team that plays a little bit better than we do defensively. They rely a lot on taking away the inside and jamming things up and making it tough for you to do anything going toward the basket. That necessitates your being able to shoot the ball from the outside, and I think the outside shot will be a very important factor in the game tonight for us.

Illinois is an excellent offensive rebounding team. Bennett and Thomas are very good offensive rebounders. That is part of Kauffman's play, too. I used the word "relentless worker" for Kauffman, and part of that is that he just goes to the offensive board. If you get careless because he's out on the perimeter and you think he's going to stay there, he's going to wind up getting a bucket against you, because he just charges the board.

Alan Henderson has not shot particularly well over three or four games, and yet he managed to score some, but not the way we want him to. He is a very good shooter, and his ability to step outside and hit the jump shot is important to our offense. I think people are probably a little bit reluctant to go out with him because that exposes the inside maybe to some of our quickness with Nover and Cheaney. So Alan going to the outside and hitting the shot certainly was instrumental in our being able to win last Tuesday against Michigan.

I think that our effort has been better in our last three ballgames than it was in that last non-conference game that we played against Kentucky. And effort again tonight will be very important. We have a very interesting thing here in the ballgame tonight. A big responsibility for how we play tonight will be the defensive play of our guards. And we've challenged them to see if that guard play can be a lot different for us tonight than it was the last time our guards had a real significant defensive role.

Not that it isn't always of significance, but sometimes it's more so, such as in the Michigan game, where you're trying to take away as much inside from them as you can. And the same thing against Iowa with Earl in the post. The guard play really hurt us in the Kentucky game, and I'm anxious to see a comparison between where we were then and where we are tonight with our guard defense.

GAME SUMMARY

INDIANA 83   ILLINOIS 79

The Hoosiers garnered another great performance from Calbert Cheaney who pumped in 30 points on 8 of 14 shooting from the field and 14 of 16 from the free throw line. Indiana also got excellent performances from freshman Brian Evans and junior Todd Leary. They came off the bench and were also major reasons behind the victory. Evans had his best game of his young career with 15 points, shooting 6 of 8 from the field and 3 for 3 in three-point shots. He also pulled down a team high 8 rebounds.

Leary added 12 points, including two from three-point range and had just one turnover. Greg Graham also played well, while Matt Nover and Alan Henderson struggled a bit in this game. Despite Illinois' best game and its best shot, the Hoosiers prevailed.

In the field goal shooting department, Indiana hit on 48 percent while Illinois hit 46 percent. In free throw shooting, the Hoosiers connected on 26 of 32 (81 percent), while Illinois hit on 12 of 18 from the stripe. Indiana was outrebounded by Illinois 36 to 31, and the Hoosiers had 13 turnovers to 17 by Illinois.

Indiana's record in Big Ten play stands at 4-0 and the Hoosiers hold a game and a half lead in the conference standings.

INDIANA

No.	Player		Total FG FG	FGA	3-point FG	FGA	FT	FTA	Rebounds Off	Def	Tot	PF	TP	A	TO	Blk	S	Min
40	Cheaney, Calbert	f	8	14	0	2	14	16	2	3	30	1	4	0	1			33
44	Henderson, Alan	f	2	8	0	0	2	5	6	4	6	1	0	1	0			26
24	Nover, Matt	c	0	2	0	0	0	0	4	4	0	1	4	0	1			23
20	Graham, Greg	g	3	5	2	3	7	8	4	1	15	4	1	0	1			33
22	Bailey, Damon	g	1	5	0	1	3	3	3	2	5	5	1	0	1			20
32	Reynolds, Chris		0	0	0	0	0	0	0	1	0	1	0	0	0			7
30	Leary, Todd		5	10	2	3	0	0	3	1	12	2	1	0	1			28
34	Evans, Brian		6	8	3	3	0	0	8	0	15	3	2	0	0			29
25	Knight, Pat		0	0	0	0	0	0	0	0	0	0	0	0	0			1
	Team										1							
	TOTALS		25	52	7	12	26	32	0	0	31	16	83	18	13	1	5	200

Total FG% 1st Half _____ 2nd half _____ Game .481(25/29) Deadball
3-Pt. FG% 1st Half _____ 2nd half _____ Game .840(7/12) Rebounds _____
FT% 1st Half _____ 2nd half _____ Game .813(26/32)

ILLINOIS

No.	Player		Total FG FG	FGA	3-point FG	FGA	FT	FTA	Rebounds Off	Def	Tot	PF	TP	A	TO	Blk	S	Min
34	Kauffman, Andy	f	5	14	2	4	2	3			7	4	14	2	5	0	0	28
30	Bennett, Robert	f	2	7	0	0	0	0			5	4	4	0	1	0	2	22
25	Thomas, Deon	c	8	12	0	0	7	10			9	1	23	1	2	2	2	36
11	Clemons, Rennie	g	2	6	0	0	2	2			6	2	6	3	3	0	0	25
24	Keene, Richard	g	5	11	3	6	1	3			4	3	14	1	1	0	2	25
4	Taylor, Brooks		1	1	0	0	0	0			3	5	2	3	2	0	1	15
32	Michael, Tom		1	1	1	1	0	0			1	1	3	1	0	0	0	15
44	Wheeler, T.J.		4	9	2	5	0	0			0	3	10	2	3	0	0	23
33	Davidson, Mark		0	0	0	0	0	0			0	1	0	1	0	0	1	6
3	Harris, Davin		1	1	1	1	0	0			0	0	3	0	0	0	0	1
	Cross		0	0	0	0	0	0			0	0	0	0	0	0	0	1
	Roth		0	0	0	0	0	0			0	0	0	0	0	0	0	1
	Griswold		0	0	0	0	0	0			0	0	0	0	0	0	0	1
	Rice		0	0	0	0	0	0			0	0	0	0	0	0	0	1
	Team										1							
	TOTALS		29	62	9	17	12	18	0	0	36	24	79	14	17	2	8	200

Total FG% 1st Half _____ 2nd half _____ Game .468(29/62) Deadball
3-Pt. FG% 1st Half _____ 2nd half _____ Game .529(9/17) Rebounds _____
FT% 1st Half _____ 2nd half _____ Game .667(12/18)

Officials _____
Technical Fouls _____
Attendance 16,299 _____

Score by Periods	1	2	OT	OT	Final
Indiana	31	52			83
Illinois	32	47			79

BOB KNIGHT TALK SHOW

January 18, 1993

Bob Knight is a student of history and he has great respect for leaders from older generations. He frequently expreses his admiration and esteem for former basketball coaches. These were the men Coach Knight looked up to and learned from when he was beginning his career as a college coach.

Bob uses this show to eulogize the late Henry "Hank" Iba, a man Knight considered an outstanding basketball coach, a mentor and a friend. There is a profound reverence in Coach Knight's comments about Coach Iba, who was the only person to coach three Olympic teams. The U. S. Basketball Writers Association named their Coach of the Year Award in his honor. Listeners who were not familiar with his accomplishments soon understood Iba's contribution to basketball and his influence on Coach Knight. These comments reveal a personal side of Bob Knight that is not seen very often.

FISCHER: Bob, talk about a man very special to you throughout your career in basketball, a man that I think you idolized, so to speak, Hank Iba.

KNIGHT: I don't think that anybody has had the effect on the coaching or the teaching of the game of basketball as did Henry Iba. There isn't a game played, at any level of play, that doesn't to some degree involve part of his teachings. And I'm sure that the vast majority of the coaches that are utilizing Coach Iba's thoughts, experimentations and work are really not even familiar with where they came from or in fact who the developer or the originator of some of these thoughts on basketball might be.

Coach Iba was recognized throughout his entire coaching career for his attention to defense. His defense was characteristically a sagging, sloughing defense that jammed up the middle, took away cuts and post play. He had different areas where he set up his defense, and he called it his "10, 20, 30, and 40." He divided the court into quarters like that. That's how far up and down the floor he moved his defense, depending upon what he thought he was going to be able to do against any specific opponent. Those thoughts, plus the help part of defense, whether it's zone or man-to-man, were some of his teachings.

Now Coach Iba spent a lifetime detesting zone defense, yet he had the best parts of zone defense in his defense—the help, the movement toward the ball, the recognition of the basketball, and where it was and what kind of position you had to have relative to where the basketball was located. Those thoughts are prevalent in every defensive play in basketball today.

I will never forget the first time I met him. It was in Akron, Ohio. I was coaching at the Military Academy and he had just come back from winning the second gold medal in the Olympics in 1968 in Mexico City. The following spring was the first time that I met him. And you want to talk about humility and a humble person. I'm this young coach from Army, kind of standing there hoping to get a chance to meet Coach Iba. While talking to a couple of friends of mine, there's a tap on my shoulder and I turn around and the man standing there says, "Son, my name is Henry Iba."

All I could do was what you just did, chuckle. I always kidded him, once I got to know him pretty well. I said, "Coach, you either are the most humble person in the world or you thought I was the dumbest coach you've ever known to have to introduce yourself to me." That's how my relationship with him started.

I first worked with him in 1972, at the Olympic trials. It was to be a tragic basketball Olympics and a tragic Olympics, period, because of the terrorist attack on the Israeli athletes. The basketball tournament was virtually stolen from the United States at the end of the game by the head of the International Association coming down and declaring that the Russians had the ball back out of bounds and that time was out. It was just an awful thing that happened to our basketball team, and really to Coach Iba. I don't think he ever quite got over that.

He was almost 70 at the time, and he coached two Olympic teams, and he really didn't want to coach the third one. He wanted somebody else to do it, but there were a lot of warring factions at that time in Olympic basketball—the AAU, the Armed Forces, the colleges, the NAIA and Coach Iba was the only person that they all could agree upon. So to eliminate the strife that would have occurred in selection, he decided to take it. He did a great job with the team.

I always regretted the fact that the best player available in the country, Bill Walton, decided not to participate in the Olympics. Walton, I think, would have made that a great Olympic team. There was an injury, or whatever, but there's no doubt in my mind that if Walton had wanted to, he could have competed in that Olympiad in 1972. That made Coach Iba's job all the more difficult, not having the best player available.

Well, then from there, he spent a lot of time helping coaches. I've never known him to ever turn down a request to help somebody. In kind of an interesting personal story on that, my wife, when she was coaching girls' high school basketball in Oklahoma, once called Mr. Iba. The girls in Oklahoma still play the old fashioned girls basketball that involved three on three on the offense and three on three on the defense, commonly referred to as six on six. And Karen called Coach Iba and asked him if he would mind helping her a little bit. And his reply was, "well, you know you play six on six. How can I be of help to you?" And she just simply said, "Well, I know you can, and I would like to talk to you about rebounding and some defensive things."

So here she is, this young woman going to see one of the great legends in basketball history, and she said nobody could have been more gracious or taken more time with her to answer questions than he did. So, she was always a great favorite of his, and Karen was inducted into the Oklahoma Basketball Coaches Hall of Fame after she retired from coaching, and it really tickled me that Coach Iba, Ralph Floyd, our Athletic Director, and I were all three able to be there for her induction.

Coach Iba was really happy to be there, and I think by that time considered her as one of his protégés. So we just had such a close association, not only between Henry and me, but between Coach Iba and Indiana basketball—the players, the coaches.

Every day that we were active in the 1984 Olympics trials, practice, games, travel, whatever, he was there and didn't miss a single day. I wanted him to have a last Olympic experience that was going to be much better than the one he had in Munich, because of the game being taken away from the United States, as I have discussed. At the end of our game with Spain for the gold medal, our players carried him off the floor, and that's one of the real highlights in my coaching career, seeing that happen and seeing how much it meant to our players. He was eighty years old, four days before we played for the gold medal, and that was a great thing.

The Oklahoma SID called me when Coach Iba died for comments on what Mr. Iba meant to basketball, and instead of going through a lengthy discourse as I have here; I said, "Just say, from my point of view, of all the shadows cast across the history of basketball, his was the biggest." And I say that because of the influence he has had on all the people that have taught the game.

He started coaching in 1930, and he was active as a coach of a team for the next 45 years. During that time, he coached state championship teams in high school in Oklahoma City. He coached two NCAA championship teams in 1945 and 1946. He had a lot to do with paving the way for the Big Ten in basketball. He coached the two Olympic championship teams in 1964 and 1968. Nobody has contributed to this game or the enjoyment that we all get teaching it more than Henry Iba did. A great, great loss to basketball, but even with that, the memories and association with him that I have had for the past 23 or 24 years are great and endless.

FISCHER: We need to add nothing more to that. We'll be back after this two-minute time out.

FISCHER: Bob, let's take a look at the two ballgames you played this week. The first being the Michigan ballgame. A terrific win for Indiana and a ballgame, I know, you felt this ball club was capable of winning as well.

KNIGHT: I don't think we ever play where there isn't some way that we are capable of winning. Now there may be different approaches that we have to use in some games, and we may have to play extremely well, but I think there's always a way that you can win.

As I have told our team, prior to each of the last two ballgames, we're not going to beat these teams without playing well. I mean these teams are going to give us their best shot. When they do that, they're all pretty decent basketball teams. They don't always give each other the best shot, but they certainly do to us, and that makes them, I think, pretty good teams. And if we aren't playing really well, we could be the position where we simply aren't going to be competitive in any given ballgame.

I thought that we played well at Michigan. Over the course of the game, we did a pretty good job at least playing even with Michigan inside, probably as strong an inside group of players as there is anywhere in the country. We got good scoring from Cheaney and from Henderson, and then good scoring contributions throughout the rest of our lineup. We played pretty even through most of the game; except we added to our halftime lead to go up by ten and then Michigan really spurted and caught us. But then we played—I think at 43—the next 32 or 33 points virtually even. And it came down to a point where we had to make plays from behind two or three times at the end of the ballgame, which we did.

That is something that we weren't able to do in our games with Kansas and Kentucky, and it was really kind of discouraging in those games that we weren't able to do what we did in the Michigan game at the end. I had to be pleased with both ends of the court. I think in the Michigan game we were able to do some things both offensively and defensively. We got to the free throw line a little bit. We hit some shots. Bailey did a really good job of moving the ball. He had 10 assists and no turnovers, which I think was excellent. That's one of the best single game performances we've probably had from a guard in a long time, and probably as close to being about as good as we have ever had.

I think that any team is at its absolute most vulnerable position when it is coming off a really good win against a good team, and is going away from home to play a good team like Illinois, which is just sitting there waiting for a crack at them. Plus, Illinois is very well put together, offensively and defensively. Now, the last couple of years they have not had quite the outside shooting to really be a good complement to the inside play of Deon Thomas, who I think is one of the really premier inside players in the country. I love watching the way the guy plays. He just plays hard, never complains about anything, works hard, takes great advantage of openings and opportunities that he has. He is able to complete the play when he has an opportunity to do so with an advantage, an opening, a step-in move at the post. He's got a variety of ways that he can score inside.

Kauffman is back this year. He was Illinois' leading scorer for two years, so he's a real addition. And then they've got a lineup they can put in that really doesn't hurt them in any way, and that spreads three other shooters around the court. If they want to get good penetration, they've got that in Clemons, so they have got a lot of things that enable them to play offensively all over the court rather than just relying on Thomas inside.

Illinois' shooting has improved enormously to go along with that inside game, and they're just a very tough team to defend against. We had some things set up that we thought were pretty good against them, yet at the same time, we didn't do a couple of things that we wanted to do, and they capitalized on them. They hurt us when we deviated from what we were trying to do.

Defensively, they've always been a tough team to get inside against. We're talking about Coach Iba's defense; they play it to the absolute hilt. They make it tough to get in the lane. You're not going to get much cutting against them. If your offense drops back against the base line, it's going to be difficult for you to get much, other than the outside shot.

We worked, I thought, particularly well in the second half with Cheaney getting to the free throw line. Finally, the free throw was a real asset to us. We hit 26 out of 32. Part of that was getting Cheaney to the foul line a lot. He shot 16 free throws, but he also did a very good job of inside movement and working to get the ball in position where Illinois was susceptible to the foul. We came back, not in such a way that we're going to dominate the game. We really maybe only were dominant in the first two or three minutes of the game. I think we were ahead 11 to 4 to start with, but Illinois soon got back into it. We did a really good job at the end of the first half, getting it back to a one-point deficit from a five-point deficit that looked like it was going to be 10 at any moment.

Then in the second half, we got started out well, but Illinois did too. I looked up at the scoreboard at one point mid-way through the second half, and I felt that we had played really well, and we were still one point behind. So Illinois obviously was playing well also. We went from there to chip away at a couple of small deficits and get a lead that enabled us to lead at the end of the ballgame. So after these two games, played as they were, back to back, with the problems I thought we were going to encounter with both teams—each would be difficult for different reasons, I felt pretty good about the basis of our play.

FISCHER: Bob, talking about players in these two ballgames, I guess the two that come to mind the quickest, of course, are the guys that came off the bench in the Illinois ballgame—Todd Leary and Brian Evans.

KNIGHT: You know we had some really good play, and knowing that you are usually at the upper echelon of media people understanding this game, I still figured that's where you would start from. But I think you've got to start in the Michigan game, because Leary and Evans both played well against Michigan. Each made a couple of baskets, some vital points, both did a good job in other aspects of the game, and they have each played well. I think all four of our kids on the bench have played well under different circumstances over the course of the first 16 or 17 games that we've now played. Coming into the game and scoring 27 points between them is obviously a big shot in the arm for us, so we really have to be extremely pleased about that.

Yet, going back to that Michigan game, we got a really good performance out of Alan Henderson, some very, very key baskets and good defensive play from Henderson and Nover. They slid a lot in the Illinois game. We didn't get nearly the kind of play out of them. I think if anybody really had some slippage going from Michigan to Illinois, it was those two kids. And we've got to come back with them being really consistent and reaching the level of their abilities, their capabilities, each time we go out to play.

Cheaney scored well in both games, scored 50 points in both games and really worked well, worked to get shots, worked to do things. Calbert has got that great offensive ability, and we've got to try to get as much out of that as we possibly can. So, all in all, I think from where we had to have it, I think we got some pretty good things going in the two ballgames. I was pretty pleased with our roster all the way through in the Michigan game, and as I said, we had a little slippage in the Illinois game. We've got to pick back up for these next 14 ballgames to the point where there is some real consistency in our play.

FISCHER: I don't think we mentioned anything last week about this basketball team's grades. I think you have to be pretty proud of the GPA these guys turned in.

KNIGHT: What we had was an awfully good grade average for our players. I think the average grade here on campus for male students is somewhere around a 2.3 or 2.4, and the average grade for the basketball team this past semester was over 2.95. Obviously, several of our players had over 3.0 grade averages to get that. We were very, very pleased with that, and I think it's just an indication that you can study, do well academically, and do well on the basketball floor.

At the same time, I think it's good to mention this because of kids out there that are starting to play basketball, that are in grade school or junior high school or even those in high school, although in some cases it's going to be too late for some of those in high school. The most important thing that a kid can get out of athletic competition, I think, is a willingness and an ability to compete in the classroom. When our guys do well in the classroom, it pleases me at least as much as when they do well on the basketball floor. And when we're doing well on the floor and in the classroom at the same time, nothing could be more pleasing to me as a coach than that. So obviously, we're very proud of what this team has done this past semester academically.

We tell them the same thing about class work that we say about a basketball game. We reach a level of performance in a game, maybe through most of the

Michigan game, say, or certainly in various parts of the Illinois game where I think we played very well. You've shown us what you could do on the basketball floor, now let's do it every time we play. It is the same thing in the classroom. Here's your grade point average. This is what you are capable of doing. You've got a 2.85 here. You've got a 3.4 here, whatever it is. Now, I don't want to see anything less than that. I want to see the best kind of performance from you in the classroom that you are capable of giving, because I know what you are capable of giving is right here. It is the same thing on the basketball floor. And when you can get those two things together, as I think we have to a great degree here, with our basketball team on the floor and in the classroom, obviously we're very pleased with it.

FISCHER: One other thing is Quinn Buckner being rumored to be the head basketball coach of an NBA club.

KNIGHT: Well, I don't think that anybody, just through intellect and understanding of basketball and what it takes to win is more qualified to do something like that than Quinn would be. You know, he had a 10 year career in the NBA, was an outstanding player, has played on a championship team at every single level—high school, college, the Olympics and the pros. He is very intelligent and competitive, and I think would be demanding as a coach. I think what he has to do is just simply decide what he would like for a life style. Does he want to have 100 basketball games on the horizon each year, or does he want to continue to do what he does with TV and what is pretty much his own leisure and his own choice.

Coaching, at any level, dictates an awful lot of choices for the coaches, and I don't mean by giving him a lot of choices but, instead, making a lot of choices for him. When you are at the professional level with 100 game days, and the preparation and the travel involved, you know it's not like there's a whole lot left over to do exactly what you're going to choose to do. That's a big reason why coaching in the pros has never held any interest for me.

FISCHER: Let's go to our letters now that we have received over this past week. This from Columbus, Coach. Aside from playing a more up tempo pace in recent years, have you changed your style of play or your philosophy on the way you want your teams to play since you began coaching at Army?

KNIGHT: We've changed our defensive thinking a couple of times, relative to point of pickup. I think the biggest difference in basketball now as opposed to when I started coaching is the number of kids playing who are excellent with the dribble, who change direction, who can go with either hand, who can penetrate and pass off the dribble. It is very difficult to guard. By the old physics principle, action is quicker than reaction. Reaction comes after action. And the offense always initiates the action. The really good dribbler, the kid who is very good with the basketball, creates a lot of problems for the defense. And I think you have to take that into consideration when you set up your defensive approach, either fundamentally or in a given game.

Offensively, you know people talk about our up-tempo and so forth and so on. Since we've been here, Johnny Orr's Michigan teams usually led the conference in scoring per game. I think there was a year or two when we slipped in there and were leading the conference in scoring on a per-game basis. Rarely was there a year that we weren't second in points scored, so we've always, I think, gotten the ball up and down the floor.

I think we've been thought of as a defensive team. Before the clock came into being, we obviously used to use a delay game at the end of the ballgame. I used to think, without the clock, if we were ahead with five minutes to play, it was going to be tough to beat us. We handled the ball well, we had good patience, and we took advantage of the free throw line, and cuts to the basket. With the advent of the clock, the delay game has been taken away from us. So we might get into a position to win a ballgame because of getting it down the floor and what our defense exerted. I don't think we've ever been or have even been thought of in any way as a slow team. With the exception of how we tried to utilize ball handling, passing and cutting, at the ends of games, when we were ahead.

FISCHER: This is from Danville, Indiana. How do referees differentiate between a block and charge, and why were so few fouls called in the Michigan game?

KNIGHT: In most cases I really believe that referees differentiate poorly between blocks and charges. We've got examples that we put on tape from as recently as the Illinois game where a call is made and later, almost an identical play, no call is made. Or a block is called on a play followed a few possessions later by a seemingly identical play where a charge is called. That's probably the hardest play in basketball to call, and it is really, in my opinion, not called all that well by most officials.

FISCHER: This is from Fort Wayne, Coach. Ernest Hemingway and John Volker were both renowned writers from Michigan and trout fishermen. First, do you enjoy their works? Which of the two more clearly reflects your viewpoints on fishing?

KNIGHT: Well, they were Eastern fishermen. They were Michigan and Pennsylvania fisherman. Hemingway was basically a deep sea fisherman, and I have never really entertained much thought or felt in any way that I enjoyed saltwater fishing, so Hemingway and I differ a great deal in that regard as far as fishing is concerned.

And that's the case with the Michigan writer also. I've not done a great deal of fishing in Michigan, but what I have done has been in Lake Michigan or the

St. Joe River, not really the fly fishing for trout that I enjoy in the Western states.

FISCHER: From Terre Haute, you were quoted in the paper regarding the free throws that Todd Leary was not allowed to shoot in the Michigan game as saying that the correct call was made but that the official didn't handle it well. Could you please explain?

KNIGHT: What I meant was I don't think the official made an incorrect call. I think the official felt that he was correct, but I don't think he saw the whole play. As nearly as we can put together from memory, and we don't have a tape that clearly shows what happened, but going by memory, it seems without reservation that before the ball was even handed to Todd Leary, he's telling Calbert Cheaney that I want to talk to him. Cheaney obviously would be turning and the official was giving the ball to Leary on the line, at the same time. We all feel, that Cheaney is moving off the line. The timing was really close in this.

It's the kind of situation that I think would be hard to see, but yet I did feel that it wasn't handled properly because the official has to see that. I don't think he had his head up. That was the first thing I say when I was looking toward Calbert, and this call was made. I didn't think the official was handing the ball to Todd while he was looking around the lane. Had he been, I think before he ever passed possession on to Todd he would have seen Cheaney move and could have withheld that possession until Cheaney had moved off the line.

The Hoosiers remained in sole possession of first place in the Big Ten and became the only unbeaten team in the conference by capturing a second straight road win with a hard fought victory over Illinois in Champaign. Indiana is now ranked second in the country, but there is no time to savor the recent wins or the high national ranking.

The Indiana-Purdue game is always very competitive because of the long-standing instate rivalry of these two schools. Purdue comes into the game ranked thirteenth, and this game has the added motivation of Purdue's big win last year at Lafayette, a game that cost Indiana a piece of the Big Ten Championship.

Knight plays down the revenge angle on any game; but to Hoosier fans, this game had a revenge factor. Knight begins by looking back to the Illinois and Michigan games, and then turns to the Purdue team he faces today.

The thing that was really good from our standpoint was that we didn't have a lot of time between Michigan and Illinois to get ready. We got back to school following the Michigan game, took our day off and started to work to get ready for the Illinois game. The players sit around campus and obviously everybody was excited because we had been able to beat Michigan up there and get a good start early in the conference season. I'm sure our players heard an awful lot of compliments during the next couple of days and how well they had played. That's always of concern to me.

Sometimes the hardest thing in the world to do is to come back and play well after having played well in a game, especially when you're playing a good team and playing that team on their own court. This is one of the great challenges, I think, in a basketball season. We had that challenge certainly in the Illinois game.

I think we played pretty well against Illinois. We got off to a good start. Illinois came right back, had a 5-point lead looking as though it might go on to ten points by the half. We were able to stick the breaks into the thing a little bit and came out of the halftime with just a 1-point deficit. So I thought we were in pretty good shape at the half. Then we played pretty evenly throughout the second half. We got a little lead, and then they had a little lead, back and forth. Then when we had to make the plays and when it came down to winning the ballgame, we made enough plays to win it.

We really only made one poor play at the end, a pass exchange that gave up a basket and took away an opportunity to have a 5-point lead. We wound up with a 1 point lead instead. So to come out of that game, as we did, and particularly to play in it as we did against a team that was ready to play, was well set up to play and played very well was pleasing. It certainly was just as pleasing to us as being able to go up and play a team as talented as Michigan in the kind of game we played up there.

Evans and Leary played well in the Illinois and the Michigan games, but both of those guys have played really well in important minutes throughout the course of the season. We look at our bench and sometimes we can't find it because we only have four kids there, but I think each in his own way has been a contributor. Chris Reynolds obviously is not a player who has always been a substitute player. Chris is a starting player. I always look at him as a starting player because he has specific roles for us that only he can handle, that he's the best at. Each of the other three kids, Brian, Todd and Patrick, have come in and fulfilled roles and played minutes that allowed other people to rest. They all have, for the most part, done the kind of job that a bench has to do if you are going to be successful over the course of a difficult season.

I think each played the entire second half, for example, against Illinois. So nowhere was their play more obvious, because of the length of their play, than in the Illinois game on Saturday night. Between the two of them, they scored 27 points and played very well in other aspects of the game.

Looking ahead to Purdue, I've not seen them play very much. They're obviously going to be a team that plays hard. They are one of those two perennially "young" teams in the league. They are always a "young" team. Regardless of how many years they've been in school, they remain a "young" team, which always kind of amuses me. They have excellent experience. Their bench has a lot of experience, guys that have played in their third and fourth years.

Their starting lineup is total in school two or three years behind ours, which certainly is no great gap. They've played well. They've gotten off to a good start this year. Robinson is a very, very good basketball player, surrounded by other good players. Like in our situation, Cheaney is a very, very good basketball player, surrounded by other good players.

So, the key thing that was said, "another important Big Ten game." Well, it's another Big Ten game, and it goes without saying that they are all important to contention. If you want to be a contender, every game you play is important.

Our situation, as long as I have been at Indiana, has been that we have no rivals. I mean that basketball is our biggest rival. If we play well, if we play the game well, if we do those things that we are capable of doing, then let the wins and losses fall as a result of how we have played. Getting into individual games, we couldn't keep up with all the people who think that we are their rivals. I mean we would go nuts trying to handle that one.

Basketball always has been and always will be our biggest rival. Our most important game of the season Saturday was the Illinois game. Before that, it was the Michigan game. Tonight it is the Purdue game, and on Sunday, it will be the Ohio State game. And our whole approach is a seasonal one, not an individual game approach. And I think in doing it that way, we have been able to enjoy a degree of success that would seem to indicate that we keep approaching it that way.

We have had more time at the free throw line, and what made us successful, going a little bit deeper, is that we had Cheaney shooting 16 free throws in the ballgame. And getting him to the foul line was important.

One of the things that really concerns me and has concerned me is the amount of pushing and holding that goes on as far as Cheaney is concerned. He is quick, he works hard, he is usually quicker than the people he is playing against, and so consequently there is a lot of hand action involved in defending Calbert. In the Illinois game, a lot of it was called, and consequently he got to the free throw line which is where he should be going. I mean, if opponents can't be fancy with footwork, then you are going to have to put him on the free throw line. That is an important part of our offense.

When he's taken out of the game because of holding or grabbing or jostling around, then it really reduces our effectiveness offensively, and those things are really not a part of basketball. It's like the same rule in football. One bump and then let the receiver go. I mean here there are no free bumps.

GAME SUMMARY

INDIANA 74   PURDUE 65

Indiana won its third straight game on the road in Big Ten Conference play, and its fifth overall without defeat in beating the Purdue Boilermakers at West Lafayette's Mackey Arena.

Calbert Cheaney led the Hoosiers with 33 points and continues to make a strong case for National Player of the Year honors. Cheaney got help from the rest of the Hoosiers as well, but credit goes to another strong performance from Brian Evans. The redshirt freshman from Terre Haute cut the heart out of the Boiler come back when he drilled a three-point field goal after Purdue had reduced the lead to four with just over five minutes left. Evans totaled 9 points and 6 rebounds in the contest.

Matt Nover had a fine game, hitting 5 of 7 from the field, also pulling down 8 rebounds and scoring 10 points total. The Hoosiers hit 51 percent from the field while Purdue was held to 40 percent shooting. Indiana converted 19 of 25 free throws while Purdue went to the line 28 times and hit 18.

Purdue won the battle of the boards 36 to 32. The Hoosiers had one less turnover than did Purdue, with 17 turnovers, Purdue with 18.

Indiana now stands 16-2 overall on the season.

INDIANA

No.	Player	Total FG		3-point				Rebounds									
		FG	FGA	FG	FGA	FT	FTA	Off	Def	Tot	PF	TP	A	TO	Blk	S	Min
40	Cheaney, Calbert	11	15	2	3	9	10	0	10	10	2	33	4	2	0	2	39
44	Henderson, Alan	2	7	0	0	2	4	1	1	2	4	6	1	2	0	5	29
24	Nover, Matt	5	7	0	0	0	2	4	4	8	2	10	1	6	0	0	26
20	Graham, Greg	2	6	0	1	4	4	0	1	1	4	8	4	1	0	2	27
22	Bailey, Damon	2	7	0	0	2	3	0	1	1	4	6	1	3	0	1	29
30	Leary, Todd	0	3	0	1	0	0	1	0	1	0	0	2	1	0	0	15
34	Evans, Brian	3	5	1	1	2	2	0	6	6	4	9	1	1	0	0	21
21	Reynolds, Chris	1	1	0	0	0	0	0	0	0	2	2	1	1	0	0	11
25	Knight, Pat	0	0	0	0	0	0	0	0	0	0	0	1	0	0	0	3
	Team							1	2	3							
	TOTALS	26	51	3	6	19	25	7	25	32	22	74	16	17	0	10	200

Total FG% 1st Half .429   2nd half .688   Game .510   Deadball
3-Pt. FG% 1st Half .500   2nd half .500   Game .500   Rebounds 3
FT% 1st Half .667   2nd half .789   Game .760

PURDUE

No.	Player	Total FG		3-point				Rebounds									
		FG	FGA	FG	FGA	FT	FTA	Off	Def	Tot	PF	TP	A	TO	Blk	S	Min
13	Robinson, Glenn	9	22	0	2	4	7	4	6	10	4	22	0	2	1	1	39
22	Martin, Cuonzo	4	7	0	0	5	6	2	2	4	3	13	0	1	0	0	34
34	Stanback, Ian	1	3	0	0	0	2	2	2	4	2	2	0	0	0	0	26
11	Waddell, Matt	2	10	0	1	5	5	1	4	5	2	9	5	5	0	3	32
12	Painter, Matt	4	7	1	2	1	2	1	2	3	3	10	3	4	0	2	31
00	Williams, Kenny	1	3	0	0	0	2	4	1	5	2	2	1	1	0	0	9
23	Roberts, Porter	1	5	0	2	0	0	0	0	0	2	2	0	4	0	1	10
30	Darner, Linc	0	0	0	0	0	0	0	0	0	2	0	0	0	0	0	8
21	Dove, Herb	1	1	0	0	1	2	0	1	1	2	3	0	0	0	0	6
35	McNary, Cornelius	0	0	0	0	0	0	0	1	1	0	0	0	0	0	0	1
33	Jennings, Justin	0	0	0	0	2	2	0	0	0	0	2	0	1	0	0	4
	Team							1	2	3							
	TOTALS	23	58	1	7	18	28	15	21	36	22	65	9	18	1	7	200

Total FG% 1st Half .241   2nd half .552   Game .397   Deadball
3-Pt. FG% 1st Half .167   2nd half .000   Game .143   Rebounds 5
FT% 1st Half .571   2nd half .714   Game .643

Officials   Tom Rucker, Jody Silvester, Ron Zetcher
Technical Fouls
Attendance   14,123

Score by Periods	1	2	OT	OT	Final
Indiana	36	38			74
Purdue	23	42			65

Indiana returned to Assembly Hall to play the Buckeyes of Ohio State. This is another rivalry that always produces a hard fought game. Losing the Big Ten Championship to Ohio State last year gave this game an added edge.

Bob Knight shares his sympathy for the tragic death of Chris Street of Iowa, and talks about the kind of influence college athletes can have on younger kids.

We got off to a really good start in the Purdue game. We were up, I think 25 to 10 at the start of the ballgame, and then proceeded to miss eight or ten shots in a row. We only had one bad shot and the rest of them were all good shots. We just couldn't get them down, or we would have had a tremendous start in the ballgame.

In most games, you're only going to get one chance, if in fact you ever get a chance. Sometimes the game just goes back and forth. You may only get one chance to put somebody away, and we had it there and let it slip away from us. So, that's the first thing that you think of. We would like to have continued our play through that really dead stretch that we had, but we didn't. Now the other guy comes back a little bit and takes advantage of the fact that you aren't scoring much, and they cut our lead down to 8, and then we are able to go back up to 13 by halftime.

We came back ourselves, after that dead stretch, and that was obviously a very good thing for us. Then, it happened that way again in the second half. We went along in fairly good shape, with an 8-point lead when we gave away a defensive rebound that resulted in a three-point play. So, instead of our having a chance to go up 10, we're now at just up by 5.

The next couple of possessions were very, very critical for us, because when you've got a 5-point lead, one basket and you're even, almost. The biggest basket for us in the game was Brian Evans' three-point basket with a 4-point lead that took us back to 7. From that point on, I thought that we played in such a way that we pretty much controlled the outcome of the game.

We have discussed many times, bench play doesn't necessarily have to involve scoring or long periods of play for the bench to be effective. In our game with Illinois as an example, Leary and Evans played the entire second half and between them scored 27 points in that ballgame. So there, our bench did play long periods of time and did score a lot of points. But the last couple of minutes of the Purdue game, we had three players who had started the ballgame on the bench. Our bench came in then and we went from 8 ahead to 13 ahead by the half in that 3 minute span. So our guys who came in and filled in spots, plugged up the dike, so to speak, really did a good job not only maintaining where we were, but improving our position. And that in the final analysis has to be a very key point in the ballgame.

Ohio State is 9-4 on the season, 2 and 2 in the Big Ten, and they are a very quick team. They've got four very interchangeable guards for three positions. They're very quick, they apply good pressure defensively. They're all very good with the basketball. They create problems for you with their ability on the ball, and then get rid of the ball.

We're going to have to have good perimeter defense in this ballgame. I think that will be the key for us in the game. If we don't have control of the perimeter at our defensive end, then we're going to be in all kinds of trouble and give up a lot of points, which I don't think we can afford to do in any ballgame, and certainly not in this one.

Ohio State has played very well for the most part over the course of this season. They have gone at it a couple of different ways with perhaps, at times, a conventional lineup rather than the three guard lineup that they have used the last couple of games. We just don't know how they will decide to start this game. As I said, I believe our key point will be our perimeter defense.

Don Fischer asked Coach Knight to comment about Calbert Cheaney being a "marked man" by other teams. Cheaney has a lot of defensive pressure, a lot of holding and grabbing.

This is a point of great irritation for me. I watch as carefully as I can during the course of the ballgame, and then we study tapes afterward. My job, or our job as coaches, is not to officiate. We're trying to look at positioning and movement, and yet it seems to me that the most acceptable way of defending against Cheaney is to grab him every chance you get. He's done a great job of fighting through all of that. It also gets to the point where that's not the way Cheaney should be defended. It should be Cheaney's ability to get open against the other guy's ability to keep him from getting open. It's not a hands-on, grab the jersey game.

In the game the other night, Cheaney made a cut off at the post and the guy guarding him grabbed him with both hands from behind, grabbed his jersey. That's something that I hope will be addressed. I've tried to make sure that it will be, and it's totally unfair to Calbert to have to play through that stuff.

I want to end this commentary saying something about Chris Street, the Iowa player who was killed in a tragic auto accident this week. We sometimes don't realize just how important kids in athletics are as role models for younger kids growing up. There are so many kids that are involved in Little League sports of one kind or another. Chris Street was a great example as a person, as a student and as a player, of what younger kids should be hoping they can grow into from Little League play.

Regardless of what the sport might be, he was one of my favorite players in the Big Ten because of how hard he went after things and how much he meant to his team. It's a tragedy, and yet, when I pause to think about Chris Street's future that will never be, I am immediately reminded of the same thing with other kids. You know, I get a letter almost every day from a kid that is suffering from a fatal illness of one kind or another. I think that there is no tragedy as great as that which befalls a kid, depriving him or her of a chance to see what life is all about, and that certainly is the case with Chris Street.

GAME SUMMARY

INDIANA 96   OHIO STATE 69

Indiana returned home after a three-game road trip, pounding out a big win over the Ohio State Buckeyes for a perfect 6-0 Big Ten record.

Calbert Cheaney continued his brilliant play with a 27 point, 11 rebound effort, while Coach Bob Knight continued to get excellent help from his bench that included a fourth consecutive strong performance from freshman Brian Evans and an inspiring effort from senior guard, Chris Reynolds. Reynolds' hustle and defensive play seemed to energize the Hoosiers in the second half runaway, while Evans' 14 points and 6 rebounds gave the front line depth where it appeared weakest in the early part of the season.

Alan Henderson also played well with 14 points and 9 boards. Greg Graham was also in double figures, with 11 points, and led the team in assists with 3. Indiana hit 51 percent from the field and connected on 28 of 33 free throws for 85 percent. Ohio State connected 47 percent from the field and hit 13 of 19 free throws. The Hoosiers out-rebounded Ohio State 40 to 30.

Indiana turned the ball over 12 times while the Buckeyes turned it over 19 times.

OHIO STATE

No.	Player		Total FG FG	FGA	3-point FG	FGA	FT	FTA	Rebounds Off	Def	Tot	PF	TP	A	TO	Blk	S	Min
34	Funderburke, L.	f	2	6	0	0	4	6	0	4	4	2	8	2	4	2	1	23
40	Dudley, Rickey	f	2	2	0	0	0	0	2	1	3	5	4	1	0	0	0	9
4	Etzler, Doug	c	0	1	0	1	0	0	0	2	2	0	0	0	0	0	0	8
15	Skelton, Jamie	g	4	10	0	3	2	2	0	1	1	2	10	1	3	0	0	25
20	Davis, Alex	g	4	6	1	1	0	0	0	0	0	4	9	1	1	0	2	25
41	Watson, Antonio		3	5	0	0	0	0	1	3	4	3	6	0	2	0	1	23
3	Simpson, Greg		6	15	1	4	2	3	0	3	3	3	15	2	6	0	2	32
23	Anderson, Derek		1	7	0	3	4	4	2	0	2	1	6	3	1	0	0	25
31	Brandewine, Tom		1	2	0	0	1	4	2	0	2	1	3	0	0	0	0	9
33	Macon, Charles		3	3	0	0	0	0	1	3	4	3	6	0	1	1	1	13
44	Wilbourne, Nate		0	0	0	0	0	0	1	1	2	1	0	0	1	0	0	5
42	Ratliff, Jimmy		1	1	0	0	0	0	0	0	0	0	2	0	0	0	0	3
	Team								2	1	3							
	TOTALS		27	58	2	12	13	19	11	19	30	25	69	10	19	3	7	200

Total FG%	1st Half .464(13/28)	2nd half .467(14/30)	Game .466(27/58)	Deadball	
3-Pt. FG%	1st Half .167(1/6)	2nd half .167(1/6)	Game .167(2/12)	Rebounds	2
FT%	1st Half .833(5/6)	2nd half .615(8/13)	Game .684(13/19)		

INDIANA

No.	Player		Total FG FG	FGA	3-point FG	FGA	FT	FTA	Rebounds Off	Def	Tot	PF	TP	A	TO	Blk	S	Min
40	Cheaney, Calbert	f	10	22	1	4	6	6	5	6	11	2	27	2	4	1	1	31
44	Henderson, Alan	f	5	9	0	0	4	5	4	5	9	3	14	0	1	0	1	24
24	Nover, Matt	c	3	6	0	0	2	4	2	4	6	3	8	0	2	0	0	25
20	Graham, Greg	g	4	7	0	2	3	3	1	0	1	1	11	3	3	0	3	29
22	Bailey, Damon	g	2	7	1	3	4	4	2	1	3	1	9	2	0	0	2	25
32	Reynolds, Chris		1	2	0	0	0	0	0	1	1	3	2	2	0	0	0	20
34	Evans, Brian		4	4	1	1	5	7	2	4	6	2	14	1	1	0	1	24
30	Leary, Todd		2	3	1	1	4	4	0	2	2	1	9	1	1	0	1	16
25	Knight, Pat		1	3	0	0	0	0	0	0	0	0	2	1	0	0	0	6
	Team								0	1	1							
	TOTALS		32	63	4	11	28	33	16	24	40	16	96	12	12	1	9	200

Total FG%	1st Half .375(12/32)	2nd half .645(20/31)	Game .508(32/63)	Deadball	
3-Pt. FG%	1st Half .400(2/5)	2nd half .333(2/6)	Game .364(4/11)	Rebounds	1
FT%	1st Half .737(14/19)	2nd half 1.00(14/14)	Game .848(28/33)		

Officials	Ed Hightower, Sam Lickliter, Jody Sylvester
Technical Fouls	1 - Ohio State 2nd Anderson
Attendance	17,007

Score by

Periods	1	2	OT	OT	Final
Ohio State	32	37			69
Indiana	40	56			96

BOB KNIGHT TALK SHOW
January 25, 1993

FISCHER: Before we get started, just a brief update: Indiana with a fine victory over the Purdue Boilermakers 74-65, and then winning yesterday over Ohio State, 96-69 at the Assembly Hall. That makes it 6 in a row in the Big Ten, a 6-0 record in the conference, and improving the Hoosier's mark to 17-2 for the season.

   Bob, let's talk for a moment about the two games this week, a good performance at Purdue and certainly a good performance yesterday at Assembly Hall against Ohio State.

KNIGHT: Yes, Don, they were.

FISCHER: Could you elaborate a little bit on the Purdue ballgame first, Coach, on Tuesday, which your ball club was able to win by 9?

KNIGHT: Good defense, good offense to start. Little offense and defense in the middle. Good defense, good offense to end.

FISCHER: And would that assessment hold fairly true for the Ohio State game yesterday?

KNIGHT: Fairly slow to start, good offense, defense from then on. We played really well at Purdue offensively and defensively to start with. Then, as I think will always be the case when you're playing against a good basketball team. They had a chance to come back at us and they did. The thing that you really have to think about, and sometimes I have a hard time doing this, is that when a team does come back at you, if you can neutralize that and then get things going back again your way, that's awfully important. There are going to be some times when you've got to be able to do that, and that was the case, Don, in our game against Purdue.

   In Sunday's game with Ohio State both teams came out pretty well offensively to start with, and then I thought we were able to get things going. Once again we had a little slip, but not a real major slip in what we were doing. Then came back from that, and Chris Reymolds did a great job in getting that game turned around for us and really going our way at both ends.

FISCHER: Coach, Calbert Cheaney's play throughout the entire Big Ten season, actually throughout the whole campaign to this point, has been exceptional, but his last four ballgames have just been phenomenal.

KNIGHT: Well, you know, "phenomenal" is a pretty big word, Don. Calbert has played awfully good basketball and has gone way beyond scoring, which many times isn't what happens with the really good scorers. Sometimes you're talking about a good scorer and not really doing much else, but that's not been the case with Calbert. He has handled the ball well, he's played very well defensively, and he's done a good job on the floor. I doubt that over these past four or five games there has been any player in the country that has played basketball in all of its facets better than Calbert Cheaney has.

FISCHER: Our first call is from Indianapolis, Coach. Do your assistant coaches specialize, such as on defense, or with centers, or with guards, forwards, or shooting? Do you hire assistant coaches with the thought that they will specialize in any particular area?

KNIGHT: No, not at all. We just simply try to get the absolute best basketball coaches that we can have. Basketball is of all things, a multi-dimensional sport. A coach, to be able to coach, has got to have an ability to teach in all of these dimensions, and that's something that has been necessary for our coaches from the very beginning. And, as you well know, we've been blessed with a great number of outstanding coaches, but never more so than those we have with us right now.

FISCHER: This is from Indianapolis. After the Purdue game, Coach Keady said to the effect, we played so awful, we made the other team play awful too. Aside from the black humor there, does an opponent's poor play ever detract from your team's intensity or effectiveness in playing the game?

KNIGHT: I don't think that it's poor play. I think sometimes teams can play really hard and with both of them playing hard, you see that effort most often at the defensive end. Anybody that's going to play with purpose and effort on defense is going to take some things away from the offense. When two teams are playing that way, it can become a tough game, one that is not exactly poetry in motion. It can be a game where points are hard to come by and patience is at a premium. Execution is all the more important, and I think that's what happens more often than not in a game like that.

FISCHER: From Elwood, this listener says, Brian Evans came off the bench and made such an outstanding contribution in scoring and rebounding in the last few ballgames. Could you please comment on his maturation into a much better player?

KNIGHT: Brian Evans was a pretty good player last year when he was redshirted. We felt that coming into this year he was going to have to do a really good job for us if we were going to be able to play effectively over the course of the year, and he has worked hard at what he can do and what he can't do. We've been very pleased with his development.

FISCHER: Here's a related question, Coach, from Lafayette. The caller would like to know if Brian Evans is in effect filling the role that Pat Graham would have filled.

KNIGHT: Well, not really. We could use Pat Graham probably in more ways going into a game than anybody that we've had in recent years, Don.

FISCHER: This from Indianapolis. If a player is fouled in the act of shooting a three-point shot and the shot goes through the basket, does that player get one free throw, making it a four-point possibility?

KNIGHT: Yes, he does.

FISCHER: I believe we saw that situation in the Purdue ballgame last Tuesday. In fact, Calbert Cheaney took a 3, hit the 3 and was fouled and went to the line, and I can't remember if he hit the free throw. I think he did.

At any rate, an Indianapolis caller asks why does Indiana have a Final Four banner for '73 but does not have one for last year? I don't think Indiana has a banner for '73 for the Final Four.

KNIGHT: Yeah, I think we do. I think that what we did was put it up at the north end of the building. I've got to think now. I'm out there every day. We've got a banner for an Associated Press Regular Season National Championship. We've got a banner for the 1973 Finals, the 1979 NIT Championship, and one for the 1983 Big Ten Championship. I think we have on order a banner for the '92 Finals. With the exception of that 1983 banner, we had decided when we came into this building that any banner we put up in the interior of Assembly Hall would be for something that had been done on a national level.

FISCHER: Coach, I think you might want to talk about that '83 Banner, why it's hanging there.

KNIGHT: We came into the last three games of the year, as you will recall, in 1983, and we had just lost to Michigan or Michigan State on a trip up there when Ted Kitchel sustained an injury that ended his college playing career. We went into those games 10-3 and came out 10-5. And we had three games left, all at home, with, in order, Purdue, Illinois and Ohio State to play.

The fan support was just absolutely tremendous throughout those three games, including the days leading up to and the days in between. I don't think I've ever seen anything quite like it. And we were able through great team effort and individual effort by Randy Wittman to win all three of those ballgames and finish up as the Big Ten Champion that year. Because it was such an effort on the part of fans, we put that 1983 banner up there to remind the fans of their contribution to Indiana basketball.

FISCHER: Our next caller from Bloomington would like to know, do you feel that your two losses were because of your team's laxity or because of the other team's effort?

KNIGHT: Well, I feel that any time you lose it's a combination of what both teams do.

FISCHER: This is from Vincennes. Please comment on Matt Nover's shooting slump at the free throw line and your thoughts on it.

KNIGHT: I've had a lot of thoughts on it. I'd like to know what to do also, but I honestly don't need any suggestions right now.

FISCHER: This is from Marietta, Georgia. My son is 6 1/2 years old and interested in basketball. What are your recommendations on getting him started properly on the fundamentals?

KNIGHT: Get him a basket that he can reach with his shots and a smaller ball and try and help him get the ball toward the basket. Get him to dribble with his right hand and his left hand, and then stay out of his way. Bake him cookies when he shoots well and don't give him any cookies when he doesn't shoot well. Put a little incentive in that kid.

FISCHER: A Kokomo caller, Coach, would like to know about shooting free throws. Should the shots come off the heel of your hand or off the finger tips?

KNIGHT: Off the fingertips.

FISCHER: Another call from Kokomo. Compare Scott May and Calbert Cheaney, their similarities in style and leadership and their dissimilarities as well.

KNIGHT: Well, the thing that I really like about Calbert at this point is that he is playing a total game. I think he's playing a total game better than at any point in his career, and by that I mean he is scoring. He has always been an outstanding scorer. He's playing the boards well. He played excellent defense as recently as yesterday's game, playing out on the perimeter. He's passed the ball well, although passing was not one of the things he did real well in yesterday's game.

I think that Scott was probably a stronger rebounder at both ends than Calbert. They both work really hard to get open. They have a real good sense and feel for how to get open. I think maybe of all the players I've had, Scott May had the best facility to read the defense and get open. Scott was a great player for us, and Calbert is becoming a great player for us.

FISCHER: This, Coach, is from Hilton Head Island, South Carolina. What do you feel the promise is for Todd Lindeman?

KNIGHT: I think that he's got a chance, when we get going next year, to be a very, very good basketball player. Nobody that we have ever had here has a better work ethic. Nobody ever has been more determined to get the most out of his size and ability than Todd. There really hasn't been a player that we've been more pleased with from the standpoint of effort he's put forth than Todd. And I think all that's going to pay off in a big way for him.

FISCHER: Our next caller of the evening, from Indianapolis, Coach, says, With few exceptions, you have recruited from Indiana, Illinois and Ohio, generally speaking. Next year two recruits will be from California (three from California are actually coming in). Are you beginning to recruit more nationally?

KNIGHT: Well, Jimmy Thomas was from Florida. Keith Smart was from Louisiana, Todd Jadlow was from Kansas, Todd Meyer was from Wisconsin, Dean Garrett was from California, Joe Hillman was from California. Have I missed anybody?

FISCHER: No, I think that pretty much covers it.

KNIGHT: We've had several kids from around the country. Yet it would be ludicrous for us to think that our basic recruiting area would be anywhere other than these three states where there are a total of around 32 million people living and where an awful lot of good high school basketball is being played.

FISCHER: That is right. This is from Georgetown, Coach. What kind of defensive skills does your team work on in practice?

KNIGHT: Most of the drills involve foot work, the use of the hands, individual defense, all the way through the most complicated aspects of team defense.

FISCHER: This is from Greenwood. How is Calbert Cheaney able to get open if he is being guarded in a box and one?

KNIGHT: Movement is the key, and there are also some really good possibilities for screening in a box and one. But the person being defended has just got to make up his mind that he's going to work hard enough to get open.

FISCHER: This is from Hamillville, Tennessee. Is the offense spread out more with Brian Evans in the ballgame?

KNIGHT: Oh, it can be, or we can play it tighter to the lane, depending upon what we're trying to do at any given moment.

FISCHER: This is from Jasper, Indiana. With the addition of a team to the Big Ten why can't we expand the schedule to 20 games?

KNIGHT: The coaches, really with the exception of my vote, would like to reduce it to as few as 14 or 16 games. It was decided that with an additional team and the prospect of playing against 10 Big Ten opponents, the 18 game schedule would be maintained.

FISCHER: This question is from Fort Wayne. Did any of the members of your very first team in Cuyahoga Falls, Ohio, go on to play in college, and do you ever hear from or keep in touch with any of those players?

KNIGHT: I do hear from them occasionally, and one of them, Gary Eber, in fact played for me at West Point. A kid named Bob Fort played at Wittenburg along with another boy, Buzz Appleby, and a third player, Skip Higley, played at the University of Florida.

FISCHER: Our next caller is from Whiting, Indiana. How much time do you actually spend in practice on defensive footwork and do you ever change those kinds of drills?

KNIGHT: We change them depending upon what the opponent is doing. We usually start out every practice with some thought on individual defense.

FISCHER: This is from Indianapolis. Will you explain what "setting a pick" means?

KNIGHT: Setting a pick is another word for "screen". I prefer the word "screen". That's a method by which one offensive player helps another to get open. You have a screener and a cutter. The screener is the man who positions his body in such a way as to make it difficult for the defensive man guarding the cutter to maintain a close guard position while the cutter is moving toward the ball or into a position to get open. The cutter tries to utilize the screen in such a way that he gets away from the man guarding him and has an opportunity to shoot the ball.

FISCHER: This is from Plainfield. Did Chris Reynolds play in the ballgame on Sunday give him the right to be a starter in your next ballgame on Wednesday?

KNIGHT: I think that we got a great effort and a great game out of Chris. We'll use Chris, whether it's off the bench or whatever way we think best. And you've got to understand that starting a game is no more important than starting after a time out or starting the second half or being in at the end of the game. We start five guys because the rules say that.

FISCHER: All right. This is from Clarksville. Why is the shot clock reset for a kicked ball and not for a ball knocked out of bounds by hand?

KNIGHT: Because the rule makers simply felt that kicking the ball could not be tolerated, and that the use of the hands in checking the ball were two entirely different things.

FISCHER: A caller from Wapakoneta, Ohio. Did you attempt at all to recruit Greg Simpson out of Lima (Don pronounced this LE ma)?

KNIGHT: It's Greg Simpson out of Lima (pronouncing it LI ma).

FISCHER: LI ma, Ohio, correct.

KNIGHT: "LE ma" is in Peru. Peru is somewhat south of the continental limits of the United States, which is an area that I really just read about. I long since have given up any desire to go down that way. We were involved in preliminary recruiting with Simpson. It wasn't long before he was pretty certain that he was going to go to Ohio State.

FISCHER: This is from North Vernon, Indiana. Coach, it's so hard to get tickets to home games. Have you got any suggestions?

KNIGHT: There are a couple of things people should understand about this situation. When we play and the students are on vacation, there are tickets available. You've got to get a request in early for them. There are always tickets available for our two tournament games. In fact, if you really want to see Indiana play basketball, we've got it set up so you can see at an absolute minimum seven games, two games in our tournament in Bloomington and two in the tournament in Indianapolis as well as the game that we play in the Hoosier Dome. That's in addition to tickets being available for the two preseason exhibition games that we always have. Then inquiring through our ticket office will probably enable you to pick up tickets for other games that are being played during the vacation period when there are no students on campus.

FISCHER: This is from Bloomington, Coach. Have you ever felt that any of your teams have peaked too early, or do you believe in that sort of thing at all?

KNIGHT: Well, no. Teams can play very well early in the season, that is everything coming together. Is the team peaked, or does the team happen to play poorly in a particular game? A team is capable of performances that cover a wide range of the spectrum relative to the potential abilities that any given team might have.

FISCHER: All right, Coach, I think we have time for one more question tonight. This is from Indianapolis. What is the reason behind the black and gold ribbons in yesterday's ballgame?

KNIGHT: We were wearing them, Don, simply to show the sympathy that everyone connected with Indiana basketball has for the tragic death of Chris Street. We wanted his family and teammates to know just how much we thought of Chris as a person and as a player. Matt Nover played with Chris on the Big Ten trip this summer and really got to know him well and enjoyed meeting him and liked him very much. We just thought that was perhaps all we could do to show his parents that everyone connected with Indiana basketball thought a great deal of their son.

Minnesota was another Big Ten opponent that Knight felt was very talented. His analysis proved to be very accurate as the Gophers gave Indiana a run for its money. Coach Knight began with a review of Indiana's win over Ohio State on Sunday, a 96-69 triumph.

We're like two for two, or two and two in Ohio State game. To start, both teams went back and forth a little bit, as is many times the case at the beginning of a ballgame. Then we gradually moved into a position where we were 12 points ahead and let that slide a little, so I felt we kind of came out of the first half like one and one.

Then, we go in at the half, and I'm kind of thinking, well we got things going our way pretty well and then we slipped a little bit. And that's why I say one and one because we didn't have the whole thing going our way the first half. I was really pleased with the start of the second half, because we went back up to a 15-point lead, which is a really good position for us to be in at that point in the game.

We made two bad plays on offense, not defensively, but on offense that led to our losing seven points from that lead. Now we're confronted with an eight point lead, whereas just moments before we had a 15-point lead and had the ball and it looked as though we were going to have some patience and work to get a 17 or 18-point lead out of it.

Here, as you well know, a couple of plays and the other guy is right back in the ballgame, from having been 15 down and right on the brink of elimination. At that point, we're one and two, and now we came back with really good effort and really good play from then on through the rest of the ballgame that brought us back to two and two within that same game.

What I'm saying is, there were four parts to that game, two of which were the long parts of the game where I thought we played pretty well. Yet there were two little, short parts in the game that were very negative for us, that took us out of what we were doing, that took us out of the way we were playing and eliminated some of the accomplishment that we had over considerable minutes of playing time.

I thought that we did a good job of containment on the perimeter, and I think that Ohio State offers you the quickest perimeter of any team in the conference to play against. Basically, I thought our positioning, our help and recovery were good. I had to be pretty pleased with what we were able to do from the standpoint of how we contained things on the perimeter of their offense.

Minnesota is now 11-4 on the season and 3-3 in the Big Ten, Coach Knight shares his thoughts on today's game.

I think Minnesota overall has the second best collection of talent of the other 10 teams that we play in the Big Ten. They are very strong, big, and deep. They've got a really good player that I've liked since he went there. Whether he would have been interested in coming to Indiana or not, I don't know. And that's Nate Tubbs from Fort Wayne. I'd love to have Tubbs playing for us.

When we were in the midst of recruiting that year, that was the same year that we were recruiting Cheaney, Greg Graham and Pat Graham, and we just really didn't have a lot of room for another kid 6-4. The Minnesota coaches have obviously done an excellent job with him in his development while he has been there. I really like him as a player. He and Walton, who is a player very similar in size to Tubbs, afford them a really good link between perimeter and inside play. They are both left-handed and they are 6-5 or so, strong, can play inside/outside, and then they've got four or five inside players.

Carter and Kolander are the starters, and they are backed up by Washington, Jackson and Nzigamasabo. Then they've got guards. One can come in to replace either Leonard or McDonald. They've got a whole combination of things that they can do. They have a lineup that can be quick or a lineup that can be strong, a smaller, a bigger lineup, inside play/outside play, excellent rebounding at both ends. Because of this team's physical equipment, of greatest concern to us is all the different kinds of teams that they can put together.

From our standpoint defensively, we've got to do a good job with post defense. We've got to be able to take away some cuts, we've got to be able to help on the post, and we've got to wind that up by being able to block out and play at least evenly with them on the boards.

From an offensive standpoint, when you get a kid like Calbert, who is a good scorer, who can shoot the ball, who can get it in the basket in a variety of ways, drive it, tip it, shoot it, go outside and shoot it, then the thing that kid has to be able to do to take advantage of his scoring ability. To me, that is his play without the basketball. I think Cheaney has done an excellent job of developing his abilities and his instincts to play without the basketball during the time that he has been with us. He has developed into a truly very, very effective scorer.

Again, our bench gave us good play in the game before the Ohio State game and, as I said, we don't have a big bench in either context of the word "big." They have done an excellent job for us, and they're going to have to continue to do so as the season progresses.

FISCHER: Lineup wise tonight?

KNIGHT: We'll go with the same lineup, Don, that you have been wanting us to use over these last couple of games.

FISCHER: Best of luck in tonight's ballgame, Coach.

KNIGHT: Thank you, Don. It's nice to have you still rooting for us.

GAME SUMMARY

INDIANA 61   MINNESOTA 57

In what seems to be more the rule than the exception, Indiana took the best shot of an opposing team again and came out the winner with an excellent perform- ance in the clutch. If you were told that Bob Knight's club was out shot from the field 55 to 44 percent, and from the free throw line 78 to 74 percent, outrebounded 26 to 21, and had only 4 assists to 13 against the second most physically talented team in the Big Ten, you would think that the Hoosiers lost. But before one of the more vocal crowds of the year, Indiana pulled itself from defeat and captured an- other important win.

On a night when top scorer Calbert Cheaney couldn't find his shot, IU never led until just over four minutes remained, when Damon Bailey drove the lane for a lay-up, was fouled and converted a three-point play. Bailey's 17 points led the Hoosiers, but it was his toughness in the second half that Bob Knight was most impressed with when the game was on the line. Alan Henderson added 16, Greg Graham 12, and Cheaney hit for 11, including the two insurance free throws that iced the ballgame with one second to go.

The key to this triumph was defense and the will to win. Once again in Big Ten play, Indiana found a way to win, and that's an asset Knight has wanted for a cou- ple of years from this group of young men.

Indiana now has improved to 18-2 overall and a perfect 7-0 in Big Ten play.

This is the first Hoosier squad to accomplish such a strong start since 1987 when the Hoosiers were Big Ten and National Champions.

MINNESOTA

No.	Player		Total FG		3-point				Rebounds									
			FG	FGA	FG	FGA	FT	FTA	Off	Def	Tot	PF	TP	A	TO	Blk	S	Min
32	Walton, Jayson	f	6	9	0	0	2	2	1	7	8	5	14	2	1	0	0	29
34	Carter, Randy	f	3	6	0	0	0	0	2	1	3	5	6	3	1	0	0	32
51	Kolander, Chad	c	1	2	0	0	3	4	0	3	3	4	5	0	2	1	0	25
10	McDonald, Arriel	g	6	10	0	2	2	2	0	0	0	1	14	2	5	0	1	34
21	Leonard, Vashon	g	4	9	0	1	0	0	0	3	3	5	8	4	3	0	1	22
4	Tubbs, Nate		0	0	0	0	0	0	0	2	2	3	0	0	1	0	0	12
23	Orr, Townsend		2	3	2	3	1	2	1	0	1	1	7	1	1	0	2	20
25	Jackson, Dana		0	1	0	0	3	4	2	2	4	0	3	1	1	2	0	24
40	Washington, David		0	0	0	0	0	0	0	0	0	0	0	0	0	0	0	1
3	Wolf, Ryan		0	0	0	0	0	0	0	0	0	0	0	0	0	0	0	1
	Team								1	1	2							
	TOTALS		22	40	2	6	11	14	7	19	26	24	57	13	15	3	4	200

Total FG%	1st Half .619(13./21)	2nd half .474(9/19)	Game .550(22/40)	Deadball	
3-Pt. FG%	1st Half .500(1/2)	2nd half .250(1/4)	Game .333(2/6)	Rebounds	3
FT%	1st Half .800(8/10)	2nd half .750(3/4)	Game .786(11/14)		

INDIANA

No.	Player		Total FG		3-point				Rebounds									
			FG	FGA	FG	FGA	FT	FTA	Off	Def	Tot	PF	TP	A	TO	Blk	S	Min
40	Cheaney, Calbert	f	2	9	0	1	7	8	3	2	5	1	11	2	3	0	0	39
44	Henderson, Alan	f	6	10	0	0	4	5	1	2	3	3	16	0	0	1	4	32
24	Nover, Matt	c	1	3	0	0	0	0	1	1	2	1	2	0	0	1	0	28
20	Graham, Greg	g	5	7	2	4	0	0	1	0	1	1	12	1	3	0	1	37
22	Bailey, Damon	g	4	10	1	2	8	11	1	3	4	4	17	1	0	0	0	31
32	Reynolds, Chris		0	0	0	0	0	0	0	0	0	2	0	0	1	0	0	9
34	Evans, Brian		1	3	0	2	1	3	1	1	2	2	3	0	1	1	2	20
30	Leary, Todd		0	1	0	0	0	0	0	0	0	0	0	0	0	0	0	3
25	Knight, Pat		0	0	0	0	0	0	0	0	0	0	0	0	0	0	0	1
	Team								2	2	4							
	TOTALS		19	43	3	9	20	27	10	11	21	14	61	4	8	3	7	200

Total FG%	1st Half .423(11/26)	2nd half .471(8/17)	Game .442(19/43)	Deadball	
3-Pt. FG%	1st Half .333(2/6)	2nd half .333(1/3)	Game .333(3/9)	Rebounds	2
FT%	1st Half .857(6/7)	2nd half .700(14/20)	Game .741(20/27)		

Officials   Art McDonald, Tom O'Neill, Sid Rodeheffer

Technical Fouls

Attendance   15,696

Score by Periods	1	2	OT	OT	Final
Minnesota	35	22			57
Indiana	30	31			61

Northwestern often plays before a lot of empty seats, but with the large IU alumni and fan base in the Chicago area, Welsh-Ryan Arena was packed with red and white. Knight first talks about his team's play against Minnesota, and then covered the strengths of the Northwestern team.

We were a little slow coming out of the blocks to start with, and Minnesota was not playing at the same pace we were. They were playing kind of an accelerated pace, and they played very well. They were, I thought, extremely aggressive on the offensive end, taking advantage, right off the bat, of a drive that was made on the right side of the basket for their first bucket. And before we realized that the game was on, I think we were down by 10, and it then became an all-night affair for us to just get back into the ballgame.

We had a really good chance. We missed an open 15 footer at 20 to 18 that would have tied it. Then we gave up, I believe, 10 straight points at that juncture of the game.

We got back to the half at 32-30, and Minnesota hit a three right at the buzzer that put us down by 5. I felt really good about the halftime situation, as I was look- ing at a 32 to 30 score on the board where just moments before it had been 30 to 18. So I felt we would be able to go off the floor in pretty good shape, if we could keep them from scoring on that final possession. We didn't. Instead of the 2 point deficit, we now had a 5 point deficit.

We started out the second half and scored immediately Then Minnesota came right back and took the lead back to a 9 point lead. Now, we again had a chance, after a time out at about 53-50, to make a couple of plays and get back in the ball- game. I told the team at the time out, "this is the last chance we're going to have. They got away from us at 20-18, they got away from us again at 32-30, and now here we are at 53-50 and unless we get it back, I feel that we will have a very, very difficult time winning the ballgame."

The other way, it might have been impossible. We did get the lead at 56-55, and then we made some plays and misfired on a couple of plays also. When you get to that point, I'd like to be able to say that we were able to make each play that was vital to the outcome of the ballgame. We had a couple of plays that we made defensively that we turned into mistakes at the other end of the floor and weren't able to capitalize on from the standpoint of points scored.

With Minnesota having possession of the ball with plenty of time to get a shot, we were really lucky to escape as we did. But yet, we had to do some things to get into a position to win and then win the ballgame.

I thought Minnesota played very well. They were set up well to play the ballgame. They executed what they wanted to do without a great deal of interference from us, and took the ballgame right down into position where they had a chance to win it.

I think that we did a pretty good job defensively. In fact, as the game moved on, our defense got a little better as the game progressed. We hope that from the standpoint of our defense, individual defense, we can build a little bit on this game.

Northwestern is a team that has struggled to 5-9 on the year, and they have not won a game in the Big Ten this season.

The thing that you've got to do when you look at Northwestern is just disregard what's happened, scores, or anything else, and just look at players. Let's start on top. They've got a kid in Baldwin who's a very good ball handler, very quick with the ball. You're not going to take it away from him. Maybe you will force him into some mistakes, but you're not going to take the ball away from him. With the ball in his hands a lot, Northwestern is going to be able to move and maneuver and manipulate the defense in such a way that they are going to get some good opportunities to score.

They complement Baldwin around the perimeter with two 6-5 kids who are very good athletes, Lee and Neloms, both around 190, 195 pounds. They can drive the ball. Lee particularly is a very good outside shooter. You go inside, there is Rankin, who I really like.

We've talked about Rankin a lot before. He's 6-11, probably weighs 255 pounds. Howell is 6-10, probably 230, so they've got two big kids inside, who matchup in terms of physical ability and size almost identically, and they are maybe even a little bit bigger inside, certainly as far as Matt is concerned, than our own kids. It becomes a matter of our intensity and our positioning and our execution. We're not going to come out here and beat this team, nor is anybody, really, in the Big Ten going to come out and beat them because you're so much better physically than they are. That's just not the case.

We will have a lot of IU fans here tonight and it pleases me to see this kind of support from the Chicago area. Illinois had been averaging a little over 11,000. We had a really big, surprisingly big, crowd from Indiana that had been able to pick up tickets to the game with Illinois. Over all the years that we've been coming up here to play, with so many Indiana people in the greater Chicago area, there has always been good Indiana crowd and one that we have always been pleased to have.

I thought that Damon started out rather shakily defensively. There were four baskets scored by Minnesota in the first 7 or 8 minutes of the game, all of which involved Damon's defensive play. But then I thought his game progressed. And I mentioned this just a moment ago. Our defense got better, and Damon's defense got better. And then, at the same time, as he was working hard defensively, he made some very, very key plays for us offensively and particularly ones involving his taking the ball to the bucket, and either getting the basket or drawing a foul and scoring from the free throw line. I think he was probably instrumental, along with Henderson, who kept us in the game in some key spots, in putting us in a position where we had a chance to win at the end.

GAME SUMMARY

INDIANA 93   NORTHWESTERN 71

Indiana raised its overall mark to 19-2 and a perfect 8-0 in Big Ten Conference play. That gave the Hoosiers a two-game lead in the loss column because Michigan fell to Iowa on Sunday.

In this workman-like effort for IU, the Hoosiers had a number of players in double figures, including Calbert Cheaney with 22 points, Greg Graham with 21, Brian Evans with 11, and 10 each for Matt Nover and Todd Leary. Indiana's 39 to 37 edge in rebounding was spread over a number of players with Evans having 6, 5 each for Cheaney, Henderson, and Greg Graham. The top assist man of the contest was Chris Reynolds with 5.

The Hoosiers hit 48 percent from the field, holding Northwestern to 40 percent, and Indiana managed to get to the free throw line 41 times, connecting on 35 of those for an 85 percent performance. Northwestern hit 84 percent from the line, but had only 19 attempts, connecting on 16. The Wildcats had 15 turnovers, as did IU.

INDIANA

No.	Player		Total FG FG	FGA	3-point FG	FGA	FT	FTA	Rebounds Off	Def	Tot	PF	TP	A	TO	Blk	S	Min
40	Cheaney, Calbert	f	7	15	0	2	8	9	2	3	5	2	22	0	2	1	2	32
44	Henderson, Alan	f	2	6	0	0	0	0	1	4	5	1	4	1	0	1	1	12
24	Nover, Matt	c	1	2	0	0	8	12	2	2	4	2	10	1	4	3	0	35
20	Graham, Greg	g	6	11	1	2	8	8	3	2	5	0	21	2	1	0	2	30
22	Bailey, Damon	g	1	5	0	2	5	6	0	0	0	2	7	2	2	0	1	20
32	Reynolds, Chris		1	1	0	0	2	2	0	2	2	2	4	5	3	0	1	27
25	Knight, Pat		2	2	0	0	0	0	0	1	1	0	4	1	1	0	0	7
30	Leary, Todd		3	5	2	4	2	2	0	3	3	1	10	0	0	0	0	13
34	Evans, Brian		4	9	1	3	2	2	3	3	6	2	11	1	2	1	0	24
	Team								1	7	8							
	TOTALS		27	56	4	13	35	41	12	27	39	12	93	13	15	6	7	200

Total FG%	1st Half .382(13/34)	2nd half .636(14/22)	Game .482(27/56)	Deadball
3-Pt. FG%	1st Half .222(2/9)	2nd half .500(2/4)	Game .308(4/13)	Rebounds __2__
FT%	1st Half .929(13/14)	2nd half .815(22/27)	Game .854(35/41)	

NORTHWESTERN

No.	Player		Total FG FG	FGA	3-point FG	FGA	FT	FTA	Rebounds Off	Def	Tot	PF	TP	A	TO	Blk	S	Min
4	Neloms, Cedric	f	9	25	1	2	1	2	3	2	5	2	20	1	6	1	1	38
40	Howell, Charles	f	4	6	0	0	3	4	2	0	2	3	11	0	2	0	1	25
55	Rankin, Kevin	c	3	7	0	0	6	6	5	5	10	2	12	4	1	2	2	35
23	Baldwin, Patrick	g	7	13	0	1	5	5	1	1	2	4	19	4	2	0	4	37
24	Lee, Dion	g	1	4	0	2	1	2	1	3	4	5	3	3	2	0	0	16
3	Purdy, Matt		1	2	0	1	0	0	1	0	1	3	2	0	0	0	0	9
22	Simpson, Eric		0	0	0	0	0	0	0	0	0	1	0	0	0	0	0	4
30	Kirkpatrick, Kip		1	7	0	3	0	0	1	2	3	4	2	3	0	0	1	21
33	Yonke, Bret		0	2	0	1	0	0	0	1	1	1	0	0	1	0	0	4
34	Rayford, T.J.		0	1	0	0	0	0	0	0	0	0	0	0	0	0	0	4
44	Williams, Dewey		1	1	0	0	0	0	1	3	4	0	2	1	1	0	0	7
	Team								1	4	5							
	TOTALS		27	68	1	10	16	19	16	21	37	25	71	16	15	3	9	200

Total FG%	1st Half .379(11/29)	2nd half .410(16/39)	Game .397(27/68)	Deadball
3-Pt. FG%	1st Half .000(0/2)	2nd half .125(1/8)	Game .100(1/10)	Rebounds __1__
FT%	1st Half .875(7/8)	2nd half .818(9/11)	Game .842(16/19)	

Officials   Phil Bova, Randy Drury, Verl Sell
Technical Fouls
Attendance   8,117

Score by Periods	1	2	OT	OT	Final
Indiana	41	52			93
Northwestern	29	42			71

IVAN RENKO

".... A REAL COUNTER TO THIS IDEA OF ONLY 13 SCHOLARSHIPS."

BOB KNIGHT TALK SHOW
February 1, 1993

The Hoosiers were ranked first in the USA Today *CNN poll, and for the first time since 1983, they hold the top spot in the Associated Press Poll. Indiana has now gone through the first round of Big Ten play with a perfect 8-0 record. The team will soon begin the rematch games in the Big Ten and the games that Indiana plays on the road are always challenging.*

When Knight's teams are performing well, he is often playful and mischievous. This season Knight has some fun with the NCAA's new limit of 13 scholarships for college basketball and the recruiting rating services that he has criticized before. Knight creates European basketball star "Ivan Renko," and in the process, sends the media and recruiting services on a frenzied chase across Europe to find this mythical athlete. In the end, Knight gets a good laugh out of these antics, and coaches, players and fans from coast to coast join in the fun.

Coach Knight uses this show to give an update on the progress of the real high school basketball recruits who have signed with Indiana.

FISCHER: Coach, if you would, talk a little about the two ballgames this past week. Your team had a very close game against Minnesota at home and a solid victory over Northwestern on the road.

KNIGHT: If we start with the Minnesota game on Wednesday night, we're talking about a very, very tough and a difficult ballgame from our standpoint. We got into the game with a deficit to overcome right off the bat. I think we were down by as much as 10 before we had even scored 10 points. We had three chances to get back in that game. One, I think we were down 16 to 6 and we got it to 20 to 18 and missed the shot. That would have tied it. Then from there, Minnesota scored 10 straight points, and we went down 12.

We got it to 32 to 30. They made a very big three-pointer at the buzzer at the half to go up 5. I felt that if we could get in the locker room with that 2 point deficit at the half, we would really be in good shape, but it wasn't to be. Instead, we were down 5.

Then in the second half, we really weren't able to do much with that deficit for a long time. We scored the first bucket and got it down to 3. We may have had it at 3 a couple of times, but then they went up as much as 9. The score was 53-50 with about six minutes to go in the game.

At a time out, I told our guys that this was really going to be our last chance to get back in the ballgame. If we didn't take advantage of it then, this game could get away from us. We wouldn't be able to get back in it. Well, at that point, I thought we'd played very well in terms of making the plays that we had to make, both offensively and defensively. We made some free throws, we got a couple of buckets, and we made some very good defensive plays in the ball-game from then on.

FISCHER: Then you took on Northwestern on Saturday in a road ballgame in which Indiana again filled the house with 8,117. This was a complete sellout at Northwestern's Welsh-Ryan Arena and a solid victory in the ballgame. I know you felt very strongly that this Northwestern team was one of those teams that's a lot better than their record would indicate.

KNIGHT: Northwestern again got off to a good start. They played well. We got into a situation where in the early 20's we had a tie ballgame. From there, we took it to a 12-point lead by the end of the half, and we had some good play by a lot of people. I thought we got really good play from Greg Graham through-out the entire first half.

   We got some pretty good play down the stretch where we went from 1 down to 12 ahead. We had good play from Alan Henderson, particularly on the defensive end of the floor. Then our four guys on the bench all came off and contributed really well during that last 6 or 7 minutes of the first half, which put us in a position where we were in fairly good control of the game from that point on. We couldn't quite get it out of the woods until some time in the third five minutes of the second half.

FISCHER: Coach, on the basis of defense alone, were you pleased with that part of their play this week?

KNIGHT: I think our defensive play was pretty good. I think that we did a good job in the Minnesota game, although we weren't doing a lot of things well offensively. We did a good job in not letting the game get away from us to the point we were going to have an impossible time of getting back into the ball-game. Our defense from that point when the score was 23-22, with us down 1, over maybe the next 15 minutes of game play was really pretty good.

   We were able to create offensive opportunities with our defense. I thought we made it relatively difficult for Northwestern to score during that period, which is basically what defensive play has got to be about.

FISCHER: Before we go to phone calls this evening Coach, would you give us a progress report, an update, of the basketball recruits that have already signed with Indiana next season and how they're doing this year?

KNIGHT: Let's start with the kids farthest away, the three kids in California. I think probably most important there is that Richard Mandeville had a fracture in the small bone in his leg and has been out of action for about three weeks, but hopefully will get back in time to play before the end of the season, but that's somewhat doubtful. He had been playing very well until then, averaging a little over 20 points a game, and 12 or 14 rebounds a game.

Robert Foster is from Fairfax High School in Los Angeles. The Los Angeles City Schools have a three-week period where they're not in school and don't play games. Robert got off to a little bit of a slow start and then picked up considerably with his play. He's had a lot of games where he's had 11 assists in ballgames, probably averaging, maybe, from a point standpoint, around 16 or 17 points a game. He's been a very good leader for his team. In talking with his coach, Harvey Campanni, Harvey seems to be very, very pleased with Robert's progress.

Then there's Monty Marcaccini who's from Notre Dame High School in Sherman Oaks. Monty was the most valuable player in December in a very large tournament there, in fact, a tournament that Mandeville's team also played in. He's had some games where he has scored extremely well, in 30 point range, with a number of rebounds, 16 or 17, and maybe as many as 8 or 10 assists.

All three got off to a very good start, and their teams are playing well. They are looking forward to the competition as it goes right down through the end of the season into their tournament play.

Robbie Eggers of Cuyahoga Falls, our 6-10 kid from Ohio, has had some ankle problems. He came over to see our game with Ohio State. The night before the ballgame, Eggers came off the bench, not thinking that he would be able to play, and sparked his team to a win in a game against Barberton, always a tough team from Akron. Robbie has had good success throughout the course of the year. He's probably averaging 22 or 23 points a game, always in double figures in rebounding.

There are two Indiana kids that we've had. Steve Hart who is at Hampton, a prep school in New Hampshire, has had some really good games recently. In his last two games, he even scored 51 and 48 points and has had several games where he has scored over 30 playing in the best competition that New England has to offer.

The other one is Sherron Wilkerson from Jeffersonville. I think that fans here are very familiar with the kind of season that Jeffersonville has had. They've been in and out of the number one ranked spot in Indiana high school basketball and have been very close to the top spot all year long, and Sherron Wilkerson has had a big role in the success of the Jeffersonville team to this point. As this season has unfolded, these six kids have, I think, all enjoyed very good and very productive senior years.

FISCHER: Yesterday, Coach, you mentioned on your TV show to Chuck Marlowe, the possibility of another recruit at Indiana. I guess you learned about him from a European clinic that you spoke at last year, and obviously his name was brought up to you. At any rate, let's talk a little bit about the fellow you mentioned yesterday from Yugoslavia.

KNIGHT: Well, the boy's name is Ivan Renko, and obviously as I indicated yesterday, he's a kid that we hope to have here at Indiana. The NCAA rules on recruiting really preclude me from saying anything else about the kid. But as you indicated, and as I believe I said yesterday, this boy was brought to my attention by coaches at a clinic where I spoke in Europe last summer.

Actually, one of the coaches, and sometimes these things come about in interesting ways, but one of the coaches that approached me about this particular kid is a guy that I had met the very first time I went to Europe with basketball. That was when I did a clinic in Spain, the first summer that I was here in Indiana, in 1971. You never are quite sure when things are going to come back to help you. Little did I know in 1971 that I would have met a guy that over twenty years later was going to be involved in steering us toward a player who could be at some point a very, very good player.

FISCHER: Coach, my question here is somewhat of a concern in that the scholarship limit next year goes to 13. You will be full with the six kids that are coming in with 13 scholarships next year. How can you add him?

KNIGHT: He doesn't necessarily have to be an added scholarship now, and that's a point that is kind of interesting. At the recent NCAA Convention, there were two proposals by the Basketball Coaches Association, the NABC that were voted down. One, almost unanimously which was the addition of a third full-time assistant coach for basketball, and the second one, defeated by a fairly narrow margin, was renewing the scholarship level to a total of 14, rather than the 13 that would go into effect next year. While that was defeated by a narrow margin, it nevertheless was defeated.

Now, we've had some success with a couple of foreign players in the past. Ewe Blab was a very good player for us, playing an awful lot of minutes while he was here, and Magnus Pelkowski, from Colombia, helped us in a lot of situations. A lot of players from foreign countries are involved in playing for clubs or playing for teams sponsored by corporations in the leagues in their own countries, playing at the national level or the junior national level, or whatever it might be. In the case of many of these players, there is funding available to send these kids to school, whether it be in their own countries or abroad.

The foreign player could be an excellent source and a real counter to this idea of only 13 scholarships. I, along with most coaches, just don't feel that 13 scholarships are enough. By the time you have injuries, or a kid transfers because he isn't getting to play enough, you are where we are right now, down to 9 players and redshirting Todd Lindeman. The foreign player, particularly the foreign player with access to funds that would enable him to go to school without the use of a scholarship, I think, is going to be a more and more important part of recruiting in the future, if the limit stays at 13.

And then we're exploring other areas at the same time. A really interesting area for me, and I've thought a lot about this for some time, is recruiting kids out of the armed services. Do you remember a player from Minnesota, Richard Coffey? Richard Coffey was, I think, a paratrooper. I think he came out of Ft. Bragg, North Carolina. He was about 20 or 21 years old when he started playing at the University of Minnesota. Here was obviously a very well put together kid emotionally, competitively and in every conceivable way possible. He knew what he wanted to do, a very, very mature kid. I thought he was a tremendous asset to Minnesota while he was there. He came out after a couple of years in the military.

I've got so many contacts in the military because of my associations at West Point, that we started looking around the military a little bit at that time. In this past year, we have been far more serious about it simply because of this 13 limit in scholarships. There are a lot of things available to people coming out of the military similar to the G.I. Bill for furthering their education. They enable ex-service personnel to go on to college without needing the benefits of a scholarship. We have spent a lot of time in that area.

A few years ago, you'll remember, we spent a lot of time working in the junior college area when it was necessary for us to do so. We've been very, very pleased with some of the results we've gotten out of looking at the military, and I think that is going to be a productive area, not just for us but for other people as it was for Minnesota a couple of years ago. As I said, it has been something that already has proved beneficial to us.

FISCHER: Coach, our first caller is from South Bend. Do you feel you're a better coach now than when you were at Army, or are you the same coach with just better material?

KNIGHT: Well, I hope I'm better. I mean I would hope that 20 years later I've learned a little bit more than I knew 20 years ago. I'd hate to think that I haven't unproved any over that time.

FISCHER: This is from Bloomington. It has been reported that you shot a 76 on the IU golf course last year. Were you playing from the white or the blue tees, and he would like to know if you took any Mulligans?

KNIGHT: We were playing kind of midway between the whites and the blues, and I did not take any Mulligans. I was playing with three guys that just simply wouldn't let me do that.

FISCHER: This is from Fortville, Coach. Do you believe the death of Chris Street will continue to motivate the Iowa basketball team?

KNIGHT: I don't think that something like that, Don, is a source of motivation. I think that kids, particularly in a case of somebody who was as outstanding a person as Chris Street, mourn and grieve for the loss of a teammate. I think that Iowa played very, very hard with Chris, and I think they would continue to play very hard without Chris. I think that those players directly responsible for taking Chris' place on the team could feel that they have an obligation to play as Chris did, which is about as hard as a kid could possibly play. I'm sure that the Iowa team has always played hard, and I'm sure it will continue that throughout the rest of the season.

FISCHER: This is from Indianapolis, Coach. In spite of the fact that Matt Nover isn't scoring a lot of points lately, is he still playing well?

KNIGHT: Yeah. Matt has done a good job for us defensively. He's done a good job keeping people off the boards. I think we've had some improvement in his free throw shooting. He got to the line 12 times against Northwestern, which was very good for us. He has worked hard, as Matt always works, which makes his contribution a very good one for us.

FISCHER: This next caller is from Greenwood. Since there's no round robin in the Big Ten, how is it determined that you only play some teams one time. How is it that Wisconsin and Michigan State would be your selections this year?"

KNIGHT: Well, without getting into the mathematics of the thing, let me say that over a period of years, with eleven teams, you can work out a schedule where, over a two year period, you have two of your ten opponents that you play just once each. So that works out to playing each team at your place once each year and their place the next year.

Now, our situation this year is that we play Wisconsin at Madison and Michigan State at Bloomington. Next year we'll play Wisconsin at Bloomington, and Michigan State at East Lansing. Then, in the '95 season, we will have two new teams that we'll do the same thing with for two years. We'll have two other teams, one of which we'll play at home, one of which we'll play on the road. That's in keeping with the idea of maintaining an 18 game schedule. The coaches probably felt, given their preference, perhaps everyone but me, that they would prefer playing a 16 or 14 game schedule.

I've been very pleased, at least to this point. The presidents making the final decision have felt that we need to maintain the 18 game schedule that we have had since, I think, 1975.

FISCHER: A caller from Clarksville would like you to comment on the three-point line distance. Is it far enough?

KNIGHT: Well, is it far enough for what?

FISCHER: I guess I'm assuming. . . .

KNIGHT: No, I ask that question not for you to answer. Is it far enough for what? The three-point line is probably a 35% shooting line. Do you want to move it out further and shoot 25% from the three-point line? Do you want to leave it where it is, and hopefully a team can make 40% of the shots or 43%, or whatever? I think that what you are trying to accomplish with it will determine where the line is set. If you want people to be able to hit the shot with some degree of consistency, then it should be left where it is. If you want to make it a shot that is only rarely hit, and therefore perhaps only rarely used, then move it out another three feet.

Don, before you ask the next question, can I ask you a question?

FISCHER: Sure.

KNIGHT: Before we come back from a commercial break, when you give me that command, "Stand by," is there any problem with you if I just keep sitting where I am?

FISCHER: Yes you may. You haven't been standing up all this time, have you?

KNIGHT: Well, yeah, I have been. Over all these years, Don, when you say, "Stand by!" I immediately come to attention.

FISCHER: It must be that West Point training.

KNIGHT: Well, probably, or my own military training when I was protecting you and people like you. Let me say, though, that I'm getting to a point where all this standing up is beginning to wear on me a little bit, and I wondered if it would be within protocol, in your part of the media profession, for me to just try to be as alert as possible, but to continue to sit.

FISCHER: That would be just fine.

KNIGHT: Thank you, Don.

FISCHER: At ease. Let's go to a listener from Georgetown, Coach, who would like to know . . .

KNIGHT: At ease. At ease. The following will be named for latrine duty today. Fischer, you head the list. How would you have liked for me to have been your NCO in basic training?

FISCHER: Does AWOL say anything?

KNIGHT: Fischer, I would have caught you before you could have gotten off the base

FISCHER: Several callers want to know, Coach, if you're going to have the autograph session again this year after the season?

KNIGHT: Much to the chagrin of a few and I think to the delight of many, we will once again cancel the basketball banquet. I know that you had volunteered to be a waiter this year, but we'll put that on hold for another time. We once again have canceled the basketball banquet.

I'm sure that will probably launch an investigation by at least the Indiana Office of the Central Intelligence Agency as to why we have done that for a second consecutive year. There really is nothing subversive about it. There has been no communist influence whatsoever in our canceling the banquet for a second time. It is not retribution at all for Calbert Cheaney having missed a free throw in the first half of the Northwestern game. We simply have canceled the basketball banquet.

It will, however, at a date to be announced Don, be replaced by an autograph session attended by our players and as many people who would like to come into Assembly Hall for the two hour period that we'll set it up.

BIG TEN—REMATCH GAMES

"EXERCISE PATIENCE"

Iowa
Penn State
Michigan
Illinois
Purdue
Ohio State
Minnesota
Northwestern

Indiana vs. Iowa
February 6, 1993
Iowa City
Pre-game Show

Indiana travels to Iowa City for the rematch game with the talented Iowa team that is ranked ninth this week. No matter what happens in the first game with an opponent in the Big Ten season, the rematch is often a completely different outcome. It is as if you play two different basketball teams. Last year, for example, Indiana won by over 40 points against both Minnesota and Purdue at Assembly Hall, only to lose to those two teams on the road visits to Minneapolis and West Lafayette. Mental preparation is again foremost to Knight.

Understandably, Carver-Hawkeye arena was filled with sadness over the death of the outstanding Iowa player Chris Street. Iowa would retire Street's jersey in an emotional ceremony prior to the game. The crowd was very emotional for this game and so was the Iowa team.

Knight talks about preparation for the game and how the loss of Chris Street will influence the game.

There is a little bit of a misconception, I think, in getting ready to play a game with a week between games. Our preparation was not aimed at Iowa nearly as much as our preparation was aimed at our own team.

We didn't practice on Sunday and Monday at all, which is an indication that I think this break came at a very good time for us. I think our team was tired. We'd had a long go at it, 21 games without much of a break with several of those games coming right on the heels of another one. The two day break from basketball was very good for us. Then we came back on Tuesday, Wednesday, Thursday and Friday, and probably averaged, in those four days, maybe at the most an hour and twenty minutes of practice.

Sunday, the coaches went through our games up until that time, looking at what had given us the most difficulty whether it was something that the other guy did or something that we did. There are two things that you always try to look at when you're having problems. Sometimes problems in basketball are not a result of what the other guy did. They're self-inflicted. When that's the case, then you simply try to improve those areas where you've been deficient or where you have created your own problem. If the problem has been something that the other guy has done offensively or defensively, then you study it to see how we could handle it better or how we could set up better, or how we could move better against it, so that when we encounter it again, we will be able to do a better job against it.

I really believe that over the long haul most of the problems that we have or that any team has are a result of its own inefficient play in whatever the area might be. Let's just take the block out as an example. If a team is giving up a lot of offensive rebound baskets, that can be a result of two things. Usually it might not be big enough and strong enough; or, and I think often this is the case, it just isn't doing a good job blocking out. Most teams at this level are going to have kids that are strong enough and capable enough to block people off the board. It's just that they don't do it. So you've got to improve upon that, or you're going to be in a real hole in terms of the opportunities that the other guy has to score against you.

So basically, we spent these four days trying to work on things both offensively and defensively that we felt we weren't as good as we should be, or we could be, or we had to be. Then we also put in our preparation for the game with Iowa. But we really didn't spend any more time preparing for Iowa as such than we would have if we had played the game on Wednesday or Thursday and then be playing this game again on Saturday night. Our work was to prepare Indiana to play as well as we possibly can play.

Looking to Iowa, first, you are not ever going to be able to replace a kid like Street. You just do what you can when you go into an unfortunate situation like that. We've said many times relative to the tragedy of that accident that here was a kid who not only was an outstanding example for younger kids on the basketball floor but off the floor as well.

Iowa is a team, just purely from a basketball standpoint, that has had as one of its strengths, depth and a lot of people playing. They call upon that depth now to replace Chris Street, and they are still, I think, the same kind of team. They are a very, very strong rebounding team. They are an aggressive team. They pound the backboards with Barnes and Smith. They have the kind of quickness and speed that can get the ball up the floor in a hurry, get it in position to score very quickly. At the same time, adding Murray, they apply pressure in their full-court setup with the various presses that they try to use. So it's a basketball team that's just as strong as it's ever been and one that I think is among the better teams in the country.

In looking back to our first game against Iowa, we have to do a better job around the basket than we did. We gave up points around the basket that we can't afford to give up. We allowed people to drive against us, from a defensive standpoint that we just can't have happen, if we are going to do a solid job defensively.

Offensively, I think probably with the exception of the start that we had in the first ballgame; we created some pretty good things for ourselves offensively. We had pretty good movement, we shot the ball from the outside, we got some points inside, we had good balance in what we were doing, and we were able to go up and down the floor with the basketball and handle it in such a way that we got a lot of good shots in our running game. So those things, all added together, indicated to us as we studied the game that offensively we may have been a little bit ahead of where we were defensively in the first game we played Iowa.

At Northwestern last Saturday, we played real well to start with, and we went into the low 20's, going back and forth on the score board. Then we were able to move it out from there to a 12-point lead at the half. I thought we played well in doing so. I don't think that we were playing poorly. We made a couple of mistakes, obviously, as I am sure Northwestern also did in the early stages of that game when it was, I think, a Northwestern lead at 23-22.

Then in the second half, for the most part, we were able to maintain a comfortable distance and then gradually, the last 7 or 8 minutes, pull away so that the game was totally out of Northwestern's reach. I thought that we had perhaps more individual good play at times in the game than overall good play as a team.

GAME SUMMARY

Indiana 73   Iowa 66

The Hoosiers picked up another key victory, this time over an emotionally charged Iowa Hawkeye squad that prior to tip-off retired the number of their deceased starting forward, Chris Street.

Iowa jumped to a 10-point lead early in the ballgame, but Indiana held its composure, came back and led by 1 at the half, 38-37. In the second half, Indiana never really lost control of the ballgame. When the Hoosiers had to make the plays in the final few minutes of the contest, they did exactly that.

This was a brilliant performance from senior, All-American Calbert Cheaney. He hit 12 of 15 field goals, led the team in rebounding with 9, and was 3 for 3 from three-point range as he regained his three-point shot. Indiana had one other player in double figures, Greg Graham with 15 points. Alan Henderson did a good job on the boards, pulling down 8 rebounds. The Hoosiers outrebounded Iowa 36 to 33 on a night when Indiana's field goal shooting was just 46 percent while Iowa shot 46 percent.

From the free throw line, the Hoosiers converted 15 of 24 for 62 percent. Iowa was 11 of 15 for 73 percent. The victory moved Indiana to a perfect 9 and 0 record at the halfway mark of the Big Ten season and gave the Hoosiers a 2-game lead in the conference standings.

The Hoosiers overall now stand 20-2 for the year.

INDIANA

No.	Player		Total FG		3-point		FT	FTA	Rebounds			PF	TP	A	TO	Blk	S	Min
			FG	FGA	FG	FGA	FT	FTA	Off	Def	Tot	PF	TP	A	TO	Blk	S	Min
40	Cheaney, Calbert	f	12	15	3	3	0	0	2	7	9	2	27	3	2	0	2	38
44	Henderson, Alan	f	4	11	0	0	1	2	4	4	8	2	9	1	2	2	2	33
24	Nover, Matt	c	2	5	0	0	1	2	2	3	5	3	5	0	2	1	0	20
20	Graham, Greg	g	3	8	1	4	8	10	0	4	4	2	15	4	0	0	3	38
22	Bailey, Damon	g	1	7	1	5	5	8	1	2	3	2	8	3	1	0	0	30
32	Reynolds, Chris		1	3	0	0	0	0	0	1	1	2	2	2	1	0	1	15
34	Evans, Brian		1	2	0	1	0	2	1	0	1	1	2	1	1	0	0	7
25	Knight, Pat		0	0	0	0	0	0	0	0	0	0	0	0	1	0	0	4
30	Leary, Todd		2	6	1	3	0	0	0	1	1	2	5	4	0	0	0	15
	Team								1	3	4				2			
	TOTALS		26	57	6	16	15	24	11	25	36	16	73	18	12	3	8	200

Total FG% 1st Half .484(15/31) 2nd half .423(11/26) Game .456(26/57) Deadball
3-Pt. FG% 1st Half .400(4/10) 2nd half .333(2/6) Game .375(6/16) Rebounds __4__
FT% 1st Half .400(4/10) 2nd half .786(11/14) Game .625(15/24)

IOWA

No.	Player		Total FG		3-point		FT	FTA	Rebounds			PF	TP	A	TO	Blk	S	Min
			FG	FGA	FG	FGA	FT	FTA	Off	Def	Tot	PF	TP	A	TO	Blk	S	Min
23	Winters, James	f	1	3	0	0	2	4	1	3	4	3	4	5	3	0	2	24
34	Lookingbill, Wade	f	3	7	1	5	1	2	0	1	1	2	8	1	0	1	1	18
55	Earl, Acie	c	8	11	0	0	0	1	1	3	4	2	16	1	5	3	2	35
10	Smith, Kevin	g	3	7	1	2	4	4	0	6	6	2	11	5	2	0	0	25
20	Barnes, Val	g	5	16	0	4	0	0	1	4	5	2	10	2	1	0	0	34
42	Webb, Jay		2	3	0	0	0	0	0	2	2	3	4	0	1	1	0	9
52	Millard, Russ		1	5	0	1	4	4	2	2	4	1	6	0	0	3	0	19
13	Glasper, Mon'ter		1	2	1	1	0	0	0	1	1	1	3	4	0	0	0	15
44	Bartels, Jim		0	0	0	0	0	0	0	1	1	0	0	1	0	0	0	6
3	Murray, Kenyon		2	2	0	0	0	0	0	2	2	5	4	0	0	0	1	15
	Team								2	1	3							
	TOTALS		26	56	3	13	11	15	7	26	33	21	66	19	12	8	6	200

Total FG% 1st Half .533(16/30) 2nd half .385(10/26) Game .464(26/56) Deadball
3-Pt. FG% 1st Half .400(2/5) 2nd half .125(1/8) Game .231(3/13) Rebounds __1__
FT% 1st Half .600(3/5) 2nd half .800(8/10) Game .733(11/15)

Officials Ted Hillary, Ron Zetcher, Rick Wulkow
Technical Fouls
Attendance 15,500

Score by

Periods	1	2	OT	OT	Final
Indiana	38	35			73
Iowa	37	29			66

Bob Knight Talk Show
February 8, 1993

Knight describes the various stages of the Iowa game in a way that almost makes you feel like you are sitting on the bench or in the locker room at halftime. Fischer does an excellent job of leading Knight through an appraisal of his team's strengths and weaknesses at the halfway point in the Conference schedule.

Indiana is ranked number one in the country and Knight shares his interesting perspective on team rankings. He also discussed the inconsistencies of recruiting reports and player ratings.

FISCHER: Coach, let's briefly talk a little bit about this ballgame that was played on Saturday night, a victory over the Iowa Hawkeyes, 73 to 67. Your ball club played exceptionally well, it seemed, considering the amount of emotion that the Iowa team played with.

KNIGHT: We got off to a good start. We had two good drives to the basket and got fouled on one and got a point out of that. We got a bucket out of Bailey and Graham. We were off to a start doing a little of what we wanted to do. Before long, we got down to a point where we were down by 7, 10, 11 points. At the 10 minute mark we were very close to being in a bind, not just because of our play but because of what Iowa was doing. We were very close to being in a situation where we were going to have a very difficult time digging ourselves out of the hole that we were in.

I think that as the first half moved on, we settled down a little bit. We knew that the game was going to be a very emotional one for the Iowa team, and we had to play with some emotion ourselves. Our start maybe had us a little bit too pumped up, and we got going then as the half wound down. We went from a 10 point deficit to a point where we actually had, I think, a 5-point lead toward the end of the first half but were unable to maintain it.

We led by just one point at the half. At least we had reduced the game then to a 20-minute game where we started out virtually even, rather than 20 minutes to try to catch up.

It was important that we start the half of that game in such a way that we didn't get back into a catch-up position again. We had to be, I feel, pretty pleased with our effort as well as what we were able to accomplish in the second half of the ballgame. I don't think we ever got behind, maybe only one time were we behind by 2 points. Other than that, I think that we were either ahead or even. When it came down to it at the end of the ballgame, we maintained a lead that even gave us a little bit of a margin for error. We had to be pretty pleased with the way the game went down to the final stages for us.

FISCHER: Both of these teams like to get to the free throw line a lot. It didn't seem that the officials were going to allow that to happen. They weren't calling a tight ballgame. Talk a little bit about that, and is there adjustment to make for your team as well as Iowa?

KNIGHT: I thought the game was officiated pretty tightly, Don. I disagree with you on that. When we got down into the last 5 or 6 minutes, when we were kind of delaying things and trying to run time off the clock, I had no complaints whatsoever about contact being allowed that should have been called as fouls. We got to the free throw line.

We said at the halftime that one of the keys in the ballgame would be which team could do the best job getting to the free throw line. By virtue of our having a little bit of a lead, by some good movement in taking the ball to the basket, I think we were able to do that. I felt that we were able to work with the way that the game was going and able to take advantage of that.

FISCHER: One guy who didn't go to the line, you said it was a bit of a miracle, was Calbert Cheaney.

KNIGHT: We are getting to a point now where Cheaney is just being held and grabbed so much in games that it impedes what we do offensively. No, I don't mind people switching hard and taking away his cut. That's part of basketball, but not holding on with both hands, sometimes. To some degree it's being called, but I don't think nearly to the extent that it happens.

Cheaney is very quick, he's strong, he's very tough to guard. That's what makes him such a good player. You reduce his abilities if you can play with your hands and grab and hold. That's not what basketball is meant to be.

FISCHER: Talk a little about your basketball team. Give them a grade, so to speak, as far as the Big Ten season is concerned, at the half-way mark in which you have reached a 9 and 0 record.

KNIGHT: I think that we've tried to develop a better mentality and a tougher mentality to play, and basically since the end of the non-conference portion of our schedule, that's happened. We were able to slow down and exercise some patience in the game yesterday. There were two stretches in the game Saturday night, during the first 10 minutes and then part in the second half, when we went ahead 2 or 3 points, and then, all of a sudden, we tried to shoot our way quickly into a big lead. We're not a team that is particularly good at that.

The way we can get things going is at the defensive end of the floor, if we can create some problems, get the ball loose, get it out, and get it down the floor. But coming down and shooting quickly in half-court offense has not really been a particularly good thing for us.

What we have to do is exercise patience, get in the half-court play, work and maneuver until we can get the kind of shot that we can hit, or have the opportunity to take the ball to the basket. Throughout much of that game, I thought we did just that, and then we had some pretty good complementary defensive play to that offensive play. I think our defense, in the conference, has been more consistent and better than it was during the non-conference portion of our schedule.

In our rebounding, Henderson is a real key factor. As he rebounds, so does our team. In the Iowa game, Cheaney had 9 rebounds, and he has been a 4 rebound average guy during all the time he's been here. When he gets 9 or 10 rebounds, it really helps us and becomes a big factor for us on the floor. Iowa is a very good rebounding team. In fact I think Iowa had the leading margin for rebounding in the country going into this game. We were at least able to neutralize their rebounding and rebound even with them. When we can do that, it makes us all the more effective.

FISCHER: I thought one of the most impressive statistics coming off the stat sheet after the ballgame was the fact that Acie Earl, who is listed at 6-10, he may be the biggest 6-10 player I've ever seen, had only 4 boards in that game.

KNIGHT: He's big, Don. He has such long arms, and attached to the ends of his arms are great hands. He has tremendous hands on the ball, getting the ball away, knocking the ball away, and tipping the ball. He has as good hands for a big kid as I've seen or we've ever played against.

We did a pretty good job in keeping him off the boards, I thought Alan did a very good job in defending against him in the last 5 or 6 minutes of the ballgame. Not only in defending against Earl, but we've been working hard with Alan in coming off the man and getting into position to help. In one situation, Henderson makes a great block coming off Earl, and then makes the block on one of the other Iowa players that Nover does a good job coming up with. It was a very big defensive play for us.

FISCHER: Bob, let's talk for a couple of moments about some players on your basketball team and their progress, one being Damon Bailey. One of the things I know you've always felt Damon had to improve on is continuing to play well in other areas when he is not shooting the ball well. Has he improved in that?

KNIGHT: I thought he did a good job, again in our most recent game, the Iowa game. I thought he did an excellent job in getting the ball into position where it could go to people who were open. I thought he ran our offense really well. He hit just 1 out of 5 or 6 shots and was 1 for 7 in the ballgame. Yet, we need him shooting well. He's a good shooter. He's been a pretty consistent 50% shooter on threes over the course of the year. We need him to combine his scoring with other things that he's able to do for us. That will enable the team to do some things that are beneficial in the long run.

In Saturday night's game, I think that the last 5 or 6 minutes, he had a real determination. I could sense it in his face, the way he came down the floor. He seemed to be saying, "We're going to find a way to score on every possession. We're going to get fouled. We're going to get the ball in the post, and we're not going to lose the ball." He handled the ball well.

Greg Graham did a really good job of getting the ball to people. When we played Northwestern, I didn't think that we got the ball to people who were open very well. We said there were at least a dozen times when we had guys open and were taking the ball away from them. I thought Greg did a much better job than he has been doing of exercising a little patience, hanging on to the ball for a count longer, looking for people that were open and then taking the ball to those people who were open. I thought he did an excellent job of that in the game.

FISCHER: Coach, Calbert Cheaney hit 12 of 15 from the field in the Iowa ballgame. He had nine straight shots at one point, 12 of 13 at one point in the ballgame. The rest seemed to do him a lot of good that you had last week.

KNIGHT: His three-point shooting has been way below standard for him. It was 5 for 26 in the Big Ten going into that game. Prior to the Big Ten season, he was shooting around 45% for the threes, which is basically where he has been over the years. He really didn't have the same kind of concentration, he wasn't getting into the shot nearly as well as he was before the conference started, and yet he was still doing a good job of scoring. He scored in the 30's a time or two without getting a three.

Saturday night he seemed to have much better action in setting up for the shot and he worked pretty well. I told him before practice, Sunday, that he just really did a good job moving around in the zone that Iowa played. He got into position where he was open, and he made a couple of really good passes for baskets in addition to the baskets that he himself scored. We have to have Cheaney be very productive offensively, and we've also got to be able to play off of Cheaney. He's like a really good running back that you use as a decoy a lot. You bring him into the line and then go around the end with somebody else, or vice versa. I think that deception with a really good player, be it a scorer in basketball or a ball carrier in football, is just as important as what you're getting out of the player himself in terms of yards gained or baskets scored.

FISCHER: Chris Reynolds didn't play a lot of minutes prior to the Northwestern ballgame. In those two ballgames he got a lot more minutes and seemed to be performing pretty well.

KNIGHT: Now if you'll check, Chris is probably fifth or sixth in minutes played, so he's playing a lot of minutes. You've made a couple of statements in this show that I happen to take exception to. Have you not gotten a lot of sleep, or what's the story here?

FISCHER: Well, you know we didn't get much sleep. I'm not saying that he hasn't played a lot of minutes this year, but in the games prior to the last two, he wasn't getting as many as he normally had this year.

KNIGHT: Well, yeah, we dropped his minutes back a little bit. I think that he picked up considerably, and, as I said, I think he's got to be fifth or sixth on the team in minutes played. Chris's defensive pressure has been very important in both of these ballgames, in both the Northwestern and the Iowa games. He was very instrumental in our picking up the tempo in our offensive pace and getting the ball out and getting it down. Plus the fact, as I indicated, he created some problems for the other team relative to what they were trying to do offensively. That gives us added opportunities to score, and it's very important, as we've indicated many times, that our defense is able to create some points for us.

FISCHER: Going to the front-line people, Matt Nover, Alan Henderson and Brian Evans. Coach, give us your synopsis of their play to this point.

KNIGHT: The front line people have done a pretty good job defensively and on the boards. I hope that we'll have some improvement in this area as the season goes on. By the same token, I've got to be kind of pleased with just what we have here in terms of the rebounding that we've had against some very good rebounding teams and the defense that we've been able to play against some good inside scorers.

Matt Nover's scoring has dropped off in conference play, and we'd like to see that pick up drastically and get him back to the point where he's scoring like he did. You know, if we can get 12 or 14 points out of Matt, that's a big help. He's been very solid defensively. He's helped well, he's blocked out, he's done a lot of very good things for us defensively, usually playing at a considerable size disadvantage in defending a lot of post people he's had to defend.

FISCHER: Coach, one other note about Todd Leary. Todd, of course, has given you some productive minutes, especially in the scoring department, but he's also been doing a better job of handling the basketball, hasn't he?

KNIGHT: Well not just that, I think Todd has become a very good player. I think we can use him in all kinds of situations and circumstances. He's a constant threat with the three; he's a very good free throw shooter. I think that he has moved himself into a position where he just plays basketball pretty well and has been consistent as a game-by-game contributor to what we're doing.

FISCHER: Coach, let's touch on an area we haven't talked much about in the last couple of years. I think a lot of fans who have not listened to this program recently might be interested in knowing your feelings and your philosophy on the rating system. Obviously, Indiana's ranked number one right now in the country, but I know that you've never put a lot of stock in that situation. I think just an explanation, if you would, as to how you look at ratings. Coaches have to deal with a very tough situation with their players, in making sure that they keep their feet on the ground all the time.

KNIGHT: We have a couple of rating systems with which we deal. The one you're talking about is the ranking of teams. In the past six or seven years, there has come into being another rating system, and that's the rating of recruitable players, or potential players. Let me deal first of all with the ranking system of teams.

I have always refused to be included on any ranking board that involves coaches simply because I've had coaches call me and say, "do you want me to vote for you high, or do you want me to vote for you low?" Well, you know if they're calling me and asking me, they are certainly calling other coaches. "Is it better for you to have a high ranking or a lower ranking? It's down to you and a couple of other schools to be number one. If you want to be number one, I'll vote for you number one. If not, I'll vote for you number 10." So, how much validity is there in that approach?

The preseason ranking has always amazed me. I think the most detrimental thing to the development of a team is the preseason ranking, particularly those with higher rankings, regardless of which team it is. Unless it is a team that knows it is going to play well, such as Duke's team last year. Duke was coming back from having won the NCAA Championship. They had everybody back except one or two non-starters, and so they are going to be good. They know they're going to be good. Everybody knows they're going to be good, and being ranked high in that situation should not make any difference to a team. And in Duke's case, it just didn't. Mike did a really good job with that team. The players did a good job with themselves, and they maintained that position all year long.

The other scenario is a team that somebody has picked to be high, because they think that maybe they have a lot of players back. Maybe they finished strong, yet maybe they lost a really key player. Maybe they lost a guard that didn't score many points but made sure everybody else did. Maybe they lost an inside guy who again wasn't a great scorer but rebounded well and defended well against the other team's best player. That's really hurt the chemistry of a team. If they have been given a ranking that's far above what they should have and what they are capable of fulfilling, that can hurt them. I think it can hurt players too at the beginning of a season.

As the season goes on, you get to the point where you just say to your team, "hey, that's something you can look back on and at some point in your life really enjoy. We were ranked number one this past week, and I just say that at some point down the way, you're going to look back and think that was really great. I played on a number one ranked team. That doesn't mean that we're the best team in the country, but people apparently have thought that we were, at least for that week, or the next day or two, or whatever. So, it's something that you can be pleased with."

But just keep in mind that the number one ranking that we're trying to get is when there are no more games left to be played. That's the greatest one of all. I've shown our players that here we've had 40 some players that are able to think back and claim that distinction-being ranked number one when the season is all over and there are no games left to play. Yet now, if somebody thinks that we are really a good team, well let's try to show them that we are. Let's take some pride, as we hope we always do, in the kind of team that we have. Let's just see how long we can stay where we are.

I've always said that the rankings are interesting for the fans. Fans can argue, "my team should be ranked higher than your team, or your team isn't that good and my team is, or I don't understand why these people can't understand how good we are." It's one of those things that I'm not really big on, as you know. I'm not big on the three-point shot, but then I'm not the only person that enjoys and watches basketball; so there are a lot of people that I'm sure really enjoy the rankings of teams just as they enjoy the three-point shot.

FISCHER: Bob, let's go to the other rating system that you mentioned, and that is the ranking of recruits, kids coming out of high school rated by recruiting services.

KNIGHT: You have to put a couple of things together in this whole recruiting picture. You put these recruiting services together, and I happen to be very close to the guy that I think started the whole recruiting business for basketball. It is a business. Recruiting services are paid by institutions to provide them with information about players all across the country. A recruiting service might be from Chicago or Washington, D.C., or New York City. I would imagine there are probably 50 of them available that you could subscribe to and they provide you periodic information on players. They rate players.

I used to buy a scouting report on Indiana. Until television tape almost made scouting obsolete, there were scouting services across the country that would scout teams for you when it was out of your budget or when it was impossible for you to make a trip. They would scout teams and then compile reports that you could buy. I used to buy the scouting report on Indiana, every year, usually at the conclusion of the year, just to see how people were looking at us. Occasionally I would buy them during the year. Sometimes I wondered if these people had ever seen Indiana play, after I read the scouting report. They had us doing things on offense that we absolutely never did. I mean they weren't even remotely close to things that we did. They had us in and out of things defensively that I've never played. Occasionally there would be pretty decent scouting reports on us. But it amazed me, the inaccuracy that was being sent out to people that would probably be playing against us and using these services to help set up the scouting of Indiana.

Well, it's the same thing with the recruiting services. Now, the founding father of all of this is a guy from New York named Howard Garfinkel, who is a real basketball junkie. He's a really good guy. He's a guy that first and foremost has the interest of kids at heart. This was not something that he was in for the money. He was not a guy making a buck off of something that he had seen. He had a real interest in helping kids. I've seen Howard work just as hard to get a kid in a Division III school as he would work to get a kid at one of the top basketball schools in Division I in the country. I always respected him for that.

He was early into the camp business. I set up the format that he still follows from my camp way back in the '60's when I was at Army. It was the second year he was in the camp business. He had a thing that he compiled by reading newspapers and talking to people all over the country, called *HSBI*. Now Howard is a very bright guy and always has some flowery phrases to all that he does. *HSBI* was High School Basketball Institute and he had a one through five star rating. The five-star rating was supposedly the top level that a player could reach as a potential college player. Well, Howard has missed on some five-star players. He also missed on some four-star players that he actually watched play several times. And he's as good as anybody I've seen in evaluating talent, and I still will needle him about some of his five-star mistakes.

We played South Carolina one year in the NIT, and South Carolina was a team loaded with five-star rated high school players coming out of the New York City area. We had them down by 27 points at one point in the second half. This was when I was coaching at Army. We had players that were just as good as South Carolina's players, and obviously just as effective playing as a team as these five-star players that South Carolina had. We ended up winning the game 59 to 45. They only scored 45 points against us, and "Garf" came down to the locker room and walked out of the Garden with me that night. I often laugh about this. He turned to me, and he said, "Knight, let me tell you something. You just shoved it up every five-star player in America as well as my bleeping magazine this evening." Well, I've laughed about that ever since, because what we had were two or three kids that were pretty good, yet had not received any notoriety coming out of high school. Blended together with all we had, we had a team that was very capable of beating this South Carolina team.

You get into these ratings, and it's in the eye of the beholder, the people that rate players. Every college market now has some kind of a newspaper, whether it is Indiana, or Kentucky, or North Carolina, or Notre Dame. Dan Dakich likes to read this to keep up with what is humorous about recruiting. And then some of it isn't very humorous, because these people, regardless of what school it is, these people can come out with some things like, "Indiana is recruiting so and so, so and so, and so and so." Well, I haven't said that, nor has anybody on our staff said that. Now we're talking about strictly hearsay or gossip.

As we got into this a little bit, and Dakich kept me posted on this, there were people that we were supposed to be recruiting listed in this paper that we hadn't ever even contacted, let alone recruited. There were kids that we were really recruiting hard that subscribers are being told, "Well, this is like Indiana's fourth choice or third choice." That kind of thing has a real bearing on your recruiting. Much of it is just totally inaccurate, because none of it comes from me. I mean, if you want to know who Indiana is recruiting, if you want to know who we're going to give a scholarship to, then you ask me because I'm the only one that can tell you. Nobody else can tell you until we have actually offered the scholarship to a kid. So, you get into this whole thing where these papers and these recruiting experts, all in quotes, talk about recruiting classes. How ridiculous is that?

The best recruiting class ever brought to Indiana University included two guys that nobody ever heard about, Dean Garrett and Keith Smart. We won the National Championship the next year with those two guys, and nobody ever even thought about that "recruiting class." A school like Indiana recruits a kid, a school like North Carolina recruits a kid, and immediately that kid jumps way up in the ratings.

Cheaney is a perfect example. Dakich, in kind of pulling the chain of one of these rating experts, wanted to know where he had rated Cheaney when he graduated from high school. The guy said, "Oh, we moved Cheaney way up and we . . . ." Well, Dakich had the reports that this guy had sent out, and he hadn't paid any attention to Cheaney. The guy honestly didn't know that Cheaney had gotten hurt before the end of his senior year in high school. He did not know that, and this is a nationally recognized recruiting expert.

So, you get these ratings on players, or who's recruiting what kid or to what extent; but, at least in our case, the only person that knows is me. And I've reached the point where I'm a little bit tired of hearing or seeing who we are supposed to be recruiting or not recruiting. As I've said, so much of this is just . . . well the terms that I use to describe this, Don, have to be used later at night, after our show is broadcast.

You get into the rankings of teams, you get into the ratings of potential players and some of this is basically being done by people who have neither seen the teams play that they are ranking nor watched the players play that they are rating.

After the first game with Penn State, Knight cautioned, "It will be a different story when we play Penn State at Penn State," and once again his concern was fore-telling. As all Big Ten opponents, Penn State was emotionally charged for a chance to upset Indiana, the number 1 ranked team in the county and avenge the embar-rassing loss at Bloomington earlier in the season.

Knight is often feisty after a big win and he begins by taking Fischer to task about Don's opening question. This book is about Bob Knight, but we see the skill and re-silience that Don Fischer has in dealing with a jousting Knight. We include Fischer's questions in this pre-game show to give you some idea of the challenges of an announcer interviewing a coach.

FISCHER: Could we discuss the Iowa ballgame this past weekend and your 73 to 66 victory on the road in a very tough place to play. Obviously your kids played with composure.

KNIGHT: Why do you say that this place or that place is a very tough place to play? I've had our team play at Assembly Hall when it was a tough place to play for us. I mean, the playground is a tough place to play. The hoop on the garage is a tough place to play. Every place is a tough place to play. This isn't an easy game. There are no easy places. What's the old song? "There is no easy road." I mean there are no easy places to play, so indicating that one place is "tough" always amazes me about all of you timid souls who verbalize or write about a game that none of you have ever taken part in yourselves.

FISCHER: Obviously, this basketball team played well in this ballgame against Iowa, though.

KNIGHT: I think they did play well in this game against Iowa. It was a tough game, and Iowa was a very tough opponent. I would hope that Indiana in that game, or in any game that we play, is a tough opponent for the other guy as well.

FISCHER: Coach, your basketball team, I thought, held their composure quite well at the beginning of the contest when there was a lot of emotion as far as Iowa was concerned.

KNIGHT: Let me say one thing for you, Fischer. There are a lot of people in your profession that by this time would have taken a commercial break. You, however, are to be congratulated, admired and respected for your perseverance at trying to hang in there in the face of stiff opposition.

Our team did play in a situation that was emotionally charged, tragically so because of the death of Chris Street. Chris was a kid who, I think, everybody who saw him play, liked as a player. Those who had a chance to ever meet him really appreciated him as a person. Yet, that game, without the added thought of Chris Street's absence, would have been a very emotionally charged game, as any game is in this conference, played between two teams that have hopes or aspirations of contending for the conference championship.

FISCHER: Coach, just a note on Calbert Cheaney's performance in this game. The rest really did him a lot of good.

KNIGHT: Well, I think that what was far better than anything else was simply the fact that Calbert's overall play was back where it had been two or three games ago. He rebounded, he passed, he worked to get shots. And in the process of all that, he hit three threes. What we've tried to do is get him to understand that that's just an accessory to his total arsenal of weapons that he brings to a ballgame. His movement is far more important than the three-point shot. His ability to draw people to him and then subsequent ability to pass the ball to open people is far more important than the three-point shot.

Sometimes I think that Calbert gets into a game where he wants to hit the three. That's the danger of the three-point shot. Every kid, I think, that hits the three-point shot gets a little bigger kick out of it, a little bigger internal thrill out of the three-point shot going in than any other thing that he can do on the floor. So that sometimes creates a little bit of a problem when the three-point shot, from a particular player, or at a given moment in a ballgame, is not exactly what you need.

FISCHER: Bob, you play for the first time here at University Park, on Penn State's home floor. This is the first time Indiana has paid a Big Ten visit here. Share with us your thoughts on this basketball team. You beat them by 48 in your first meeting. I know that a previous ballgame means absolutely nothing to you at this point.

KNIGHT: All we have to do is go back last year to a couple of games where we won by very big margins at home, and then turned right around and lost away. There are a lot of teams that play very differently on the road than they play at home. You're playing against two different basketball teams almost every time that you play, Don. You play against one on the road; you play another one at home.

This is reflected, I think, over the years and for all the years that I've been in Bloomington. I think we have won close to 65% of our games on the road, which is more than most of the teams in our league have won in total, in conference play. The closest team to us in playing on the road is, I don't think is even at a 40% level. And yet, there have been a lot of times when these teams have been very, very difficult, if not impossible, for us to beat when we played them on the road, because of both their approach to the game and our own approach to the game.

So we have tried to work with our team since last year in playing the game that's scheduled. We don't care who it's scheduled against or where. The game is simply scheduled, so it deserves the absolute best we can give it. If we did that and if the other team is good enough to beat us at our best, then they deserve to win. The thing that we want to try to avoid is helping the other guy.

FISCHER: Coach, their two best players, Amechi and DeRon Hayes, or at least what appear to be their best players, were pretty well neutralized by your ball club in the first meeting.

KNIGHT: Amechi got into a lot of foul trouble and only played 13 or 15 minutes in the ballgame. We did a good job defensively with Hayes, but tonight's another ballgame and another situation.

You talked about Cheaney's play. On 15 shots, Cheaney scores 27 points against Iowa, which is exceptionally good. Yet, that's the same kid that was just able to come up with 2 rebound baskets against Minnesota. So, on a different night, in a different game, we have different situations entirely.

FISCHER: Bob, just as a final note before you play this ballgame tonight with Penn State. The last three ballgames you've shot under 50%. Might a part of this maturation process these kids have gone through over the years be that they are able to win when not shooting the basketball particularly well?

KNIGHT: It's always important that you play well, regardless of how you're shooting. We've talked about that over the years. There are two really different aspects of playing the game of basketball. One is shooting the basketball and the other is playing the game. I think that if we can play the total game and then work to get good shots and then take them, I think things will go well enough our way.

One thing about not shooting well, it can always be the fact that you're not getting good shots, or you're not taking good shots. When that's the case, then you're going to have all kinds of problems, regardless of how you're playing in other areas of the game.

GAME SUMMARY

DOUBLE OVERTIME

Indiana 88   Penn State 84

Playing at University Park for the first time in the school's history, Indiana avoided a major upset by the Nittany Lions who played their best basketball game of the season. The Hoosiers must have been thinking it was a replay from last season, when Indiana won by over 40 points against both Minnesota and Purdue at Assembly Hall, only to lose to those two teams on the road visits to Minneapolis and West Lafayette.

Indiana's 48-point victory in Assembly Hall in January played no factor in this contest other than to motivate the Nittany Lions. Penn State, playing with nothing to lose, performed as well as it could and gave Indiana trouble at both ends of the floor. But the biggest struggle for Indiana in this contest was at the offensive end where it was able to hit just 45 percent from the field and never seemed to get into its offense. The Hoosiers began standing around against the Penn State zone and struggled to hit their shots until it really counted.

Calbert Cheaney scored 24 points in this game to lead IU. Greg Graham had 18, 16 from Alan Henderson and 13 from Damon Bailey. Henderson also led the Hoosiers in rebounding with 17.

A couple of bizarre plays at the end of regulation saved the Hoosiers. First, the controversial lack of call against Chris Reynolds and a foul on Greg Bartram gave Indiana the basketball with 17 seconds to go. Greg Graham threw up a three-point shot with almost no time left on the clock. The shot never came close but Bartram fouled him and it gave Graham an opportunity to go to the free throw line to win the game. He missed the first free throw, but despite the incredible pressure, Graham canned the next two, sending the game into overtime with the score tied at 68.

In the first overtime, Indiana got down by 6 points, but three-point baskets by Todd Leary, Calbert Cheaney and Damon Bailey offset Penn State's scores and sent the game into second overtime.

In the second overtime, Indiana again fell behind, this time by 4, 83-79. Calbert Cheaney sank a three-point field goal with 1:15 left, and Cheaney drove for another basket that put Indiana up 84-83 with 36 seconds to go. A Penn State free throw tied it at 84. Then Brian Evans rebounded the missed second free throw by Penn State and came down the floor. As Indiana worked time off the clock, Evans got the basketball and hit a driving jump shot with about 6 seconds to go in the game. Penn State's last ditch effort fell short into the hands of Damon Bailey on a long pass down court. The Nittany Lions fouled Bailey, who added two free throws for insurance, and Indiana came away with the double-overtime triumph.

INDIANA

No.	Player	Total FG FG	FGA	3-point FG	FGA	FT	FTA	Rebounds Off	Def	Tot	PF	TP	A	TO	Blk	S	Min
40	Cheaney, Calbert	11	23	2	5	0	0	2	6	8	2	24	3	4	0	0	50
44	Henderson, Alan	7	15	0	0	2	2	6	11	17	5	16	1	2	2	0	33
24	Nover, Matt	3	6	0	0	1	2	2	1	3	5	7	0	1	1	0	27
20	Graham, Greg	4	12	3	9	2	2	4	0	4	4	13	4	3	0	0	45
22	Bailey, Damon	5	12	3	6	5	8	1	1	2	4	18	3	2	0	1	41
32	Reynolds, Chris	1	1	0	0	0	0	0	2	2	2	2	3	1	0	0	14
34	Evans, Brian	1	2	0	0	0	0	0	2	2	1	2	0	0	0	0	12
30	Leary, Todd	2	5	2	4	0	0	0	1	1	0	6	6	0	0	1	28
	Team							3	2	5							
	TOTALS	34	76	10	24	10	14	18	26	44	23	88	20	13	3	2	250

Total FG%	1st Half .441	2nd half .444	OT .467	Game .447	Deadball
3-Pt. FG%	1st Half .167	2nd half .455	OT .571	Game .417	Rebounds___1
FT%	1st Half .750	2nd half .625	OT 1.00	Game .714	

PENN STATE

No.	Player	Total FG FG	FGA	3-point FG	FGA	FT	FTA	Rebounds Off	Def	Tot	PF	TP	A	TO	Blk	S	Min
24	Hayes, DeRon	8	16	0	0	0	0	2	4	6	0	16	6	1	0	0	46
30	Carr, Eric	1	4	0	0	0	0	1	1	2	3	2	2	0	0	1	29
13	Amechi, John	4	8	0	3	11	16	2	7	9	1	19	0	1	3	2	48
22	Bartram, Grag	4	9	1	3	0	0	1	2	3	3	9	3	1	0	2	38
00	Jennings, Michael	8	13	2	3	4	7	1	9	10	0	22	7	2	0	1	41
15	Carlton, Rashaan	5	7	2	2	2	2	1	1	2	3	14	0	2	0	0	16
20	Wydman, Steve	0	1	0	1	0	0	0	1	1	1	0	2	0	0	0	9
45	Joseph, Michael	0	1	0	0	0	0	1	0	1	0	0	0	1	0	0	4
4	Carter, Elton	1	5	0	0	0	0	2	2	4	4	2	0	1	0	0	19
	Team							1	0	1				2			
	TOTALS	31	64	5	12	17	25	12	27	39	15	84	20	11	3	6	250

Total FG%	1st Half .484	2nd half .440	OT .625	Game .484	Deadball
3-Pt. FG%	1st Half .333	2nd half .600	OT .000	Game .417	Rebounds___3
FT%	1st Half .000	2nd half .846	OT .500	Game .680	

Officials	G. Monje, S. Lickliter, D. Chrisman
Technical Fouls	
Attendance	7,540

Score by Periods	1	2	OT	OT	Final
Indiana	34	34	9	11	88
Penn State	32	36	9	7	84

Michigan vs. Indiana
February 14, 1993
Bloomington
Pre-game Show

Once again Indiana faced the talented Michigan team which was ranked fourth at the time and was looking to offset Indiana's 1-point win at Ann Arbor. Again, a national television audience is on hand for an Indiana game.

Knight uses this show to vent some of his anger for a poor performance at Penn State before talking about the Michigan team he will face.

We got started early in the game not having the kind of movement or penetration against the zone that we have to have in order to be effective in our zone offense. That carried over throughout the entire ballgame. We eventually made some shots. I'd rather say our offense eventually started to create things for us, but I'm not sure that was the case. We just happened to make shots the second half that enabled us to get back in the ballgame.

Defensively we made a lot of errors in terms of the fouls that we committed, the position on the floor in which we committed the fouls, our lack of help, just a lot of things that we weren't alert to. Penn State, certainly to their credit, took advantage of our lapses and our mistakes. That's what basketball comes down to. It's a game of mistakes, and the sign that we have in our locker room is "Victory favors the team making the fewest mistakes." When the other team is able to capitalize on mistakes that are made, then you are giving them some opportunities that they should not have. Any mistake you make that creates an opportunity for the other guy is something that you have given them, and if they can take advantage of it, then you are going to have a difficult time beating them.

The only team that can play with a big margin of error, in terms of mistakes, is an extremely physical team that can take somebody right out of the play on the boards; that's quick enough, and strong enough to be able to dominate and create problems. That's the only kind of team that can play well at this game and still make mistakes in doing so.

Ours is not a team that can play well with a lot of mistakes. I think we play pretty well when we don't make mistakes, but we don't play well when we do make mistakes. That's the whole essence in whether or not we are a tough team to play against.

You can say I should be pleased that we came back and won in two overtimes.

Well, why do I have to be pleased with anything? I don't think there is anything to be pleased with that happened out there.

We came back and made some plays that we had to make. In fact, we probably made a bunch of plays that we had to make. The down side of that coin, however, is that there are times when you shouldn't be in that position in the first place. Just like Penn State at the end of the ballgame committed a foul on a three-point attempt and allowed us to get back in the ballgame, and Greg Graham makes two of the free throws.

I was kind of mesmerized by the fact that you have on a white sweater and a red shirt. What a unique color combination to wear to an Indiana game on Valentine's Day.

Michigan is an extremely talented team. I think that their coach, Steve Fisher, has done an excellent job in putting them together as a team that enjoys playing together. They seem to have a really good mix with one another as the game is being played. The thing that nobody talks a whole lot about is that Howard may very well be the best offensive center in the Big Ten, if you look upon him as a center. He can do things other than just what the position of center may indicate he can do.

I'm not so sure that Riley isn't one of the top three or four centers in the Big Ten, and he's their back up center. He makes it very, very tough to play Michigan because they have a quality seven foot player that they bring into the ballgame to replace either Webber or Howard. That enables them to continue at almost the same pace, even if in fact they've got somebody in some degree of foul trouble.

FISCHER: Coach, what are your priorities for your basketball team today in this game?

KNIGHT: Just getting Dakich dressed well is my first priority. He's got a tag on his sport coat I see there that we probably have to get off the left sleeve or he'll go out there with that tag on his sleeve.

FISCHER: Coach, what are the two top things you want to see out of your basketball team today?

KNIGHT: I'd really like to see them play the best basketball game that an Indiana team has ever played. I'd like to them shoot 94% from the floor and 98% from the foul line. I'd like to see us outrebound Michigan by 20 rebounds, have absolutely no turnovers, and block 11 shots.

FISCHER: Lineup-wise today, Coach?

KNIGHT: Same lineup that you've used with varying degrees of success, Don, since you started using it.

FISCHER: Best of luck in today's ballgame, Coach.

KNIGHT: Thanks, Don. Again, it touches me deeply that on this Valentine's Day, you would still be opening up your heart to root for the Hoosiers.

GAME SUMMARY

INDIANA 93   MICHIGAN 92

In another game that was decided in the closing moments, after trailing at the half by 2 points, Indiana pulled ahead of Michigan at the end to win by a point and keep its Big Ten record perfect. Indiana did not lead in the game until six minutes remained.

Calbert Cheaney and Matt Nover each had 20 points, followed by 17 from Brian Evans and 16 from Greg Graham. Michigan's Fab Five were all in double figures, led by Chris Webber with 23.

Indiana led in rebounds 38 to 30 for Michigan, and nailed 23 of 38 free throw attempts while Michigan hit on 14 of 23. Indiana was able to draw 29 personal fouls on the Wolverines and forced Michigan into 14 turnovers, while committing only nine turnovers.

MICHIGAN

No.	Player		Total FG FG	FGA	3-point FG	FGA	FT	FTA	Rebounds Off	Def	Tot	PF	TP	A	TO	Blk	S	Min
	Webber	f	8	14	3	5	4	11			11	3	23	6	5	1	2	33
	Jackson	f	6	10	0	1	1	3			2	5	13	2	0	1	0	21
	Howard	c	5	8	0	1	5	5			5	4	15	0	0	0	0	32
	Rose	g	4	9	2	4	4	4			2	5	14	3	3	0	1	31
	King	g	6	9	4	6	0	0			4	1	16	6	2	1	0	35
	Pelinka		2	3	2	3	0	0			2	4	6	1	0	0	0	18
	Voskuil		1	1	1	1	0	0			0	3	3	1	1	0	0	10
	Riley		1	2	0	0	0	0			3	3	2	1	2	0	0	14
	Talley		0	1	0	1	0	0			0	0	0	1	1	0	0	5
	Fife		0	0	0	0	0	0			0	1	0	0	0	0	0	1
	Team										1							
	TOTALS		33	57	12	22	14	23	0	0	30	29	92	21	14	3	3	200

Total FG% 1st Half _____ 2nd half _____ Game .579(33/57)   Deadball
3-Pt. FG% 1st Half _____ 2nd half _____ Game .545(12/22)   Rebounds _____
FT% 1st Half _____ 2nd half _____ Game .609(14/23)

INDIANA

No.	Player		Total FG FG	FGA	3-point FG	FGA	FT	FTA	Rebounds Off	Def	Tot	PF	TP	A	TO	Blk	S	Min
40	Cheaney, Calbert	f	7	17	1	2	5	7			9	2	20	4	2	0	0	36
44	Henderson, Alan	f	4	11	0	1	4	7			8	1	12	0	2	0	0	29
24	Nover, Matt	c	8	11	0	0	4	5			8	2	20	0	2	0	0	33
20	Graham, Greg	g	6	9	2	3	0	2			2	4	16	2	0	1	1	29
22	Bailey, Damon	g	0	2	0	0	4	6			3	2	4	2	1	0	0	21
32	Reynolds, Chris		0	0	0	0	0	1			2	2	0	3	1	0	1	18
34	Evans, Brian		4	11	3	6	6	10			2	3	17	1	1	0	2	28
30	Leary, Todd		2	3	0	0	0	0			0	1	4	1	0	0	0	4
25	Knight, Pat		0	0	0	0	0	0			0	0	0	0	0	0	0	2
	Team										4							
	TOTALS		31	64	6	12	23	38	0	0	38	17	93	13	9	1	4	200

Total FG% 1st Half _____ 2nd half _____ Game .484(31/64)   Deadball
3-Pt. FG% 1st Half _____ 2nd half _____ Game .500(6/12)   Rebounds _____
FT% 1st Half _____ 2nd half _____ Game .605(23/38)

Officials _____
Technical Fouls _____
Attendance 11,269 _____

Score by Periods	1	2	OT	OT	Final
Michigan	46	46			92
Indiana	44	49			93

Bob Knight Talk Show
February 15, 1993

Indiana beat Michigan again by just one point to take a commanding lead in the Big Ten race with a 11-0 record. The Hoosiers were ranked first in the national polls, and were playing extremely well as a team.

FISCHER: We want to point out that Indiana's basketball team this past week won two ballgames, a double overtime 88-84 victory over Penn State on Tuesday and the Hoosiers winning yesterday over Michigan 93-92 at Assembly Hall.

Coach, if you might, just talk for a moment about these two ballgames this week. First the Penn State contest in which it took double overtime to defeat a ball club that played one of their best basketball games.

KNIGHT: They played very well against us Don, but we had some fairly decent spots in the game ourselves. We got into a situation where the club that we were playing was going to do all it can to use the game, that moment in the spotlight, to capitalize on as much as it possibly could.

In that first half, we have a 7-point lead, make a steal and miss a lay up. That was a big point for us and would have put us up nine. Then we have a chance to take the lead over into double digits. We didn't do it. There are only a couple of opportunities that you are ever going to have in a game to do what has to be done, and we just didn't get it done in the two chances we had in the first half. Consequently, we wound up in a situation where we had to really struggle in the second half. Penn State probably played a little better in the second half than they did in the first half.

FISCHER: When you talk about Penn State's play, Coach, the one guy that seemed to play so much better than he did the first time you played against him was John Amechi.

KNIGHT: They all played better, Don, and we've talked about this before. A team comes in here to play for the first time, after having played pretty well prior to that, with the exception of the Kentucky game, and it is a little apprehensive. Then, we got off to a good start which creates some more problems for them. Yet we see a lot of teams that just have a very appreciable difference in playing at home compared to on the road. Penn State was a much more comfortable team, more comfortable with what it was doing, much more into what it had to do, in playing at home than it was at Bloomington. Not only have players obviously improved, it was a different team. A different setting created a different Penn State team.

FISCHER: Coach, if we can, just talk a minute about the Michigan ballgame yesterday, a 93-92 win over the Wolverines at Assembly Hall. You had to be pleased with your ball club's play in that contest.

KNIGHT: Well, you know, John. Is it Don or John?

FISCHER: I think it's Don.

KNIGHT: You know, I was writing a letter here to John, and I'm at a point in my life where I can't remember when I talk to two people whose names rhyme which it is. So, fill me in one more time, Don or John?

FISCHER: It's Don.

KNIGHT: OK, thanks, Don. Well, I tell you what "John," you've got to be pleased with the fact that we won the ballgame. That, I think, comes first and foremost in thoughts on that game. Michigan is obviously a very, very difficult basketball team to play against and all the more so when they are shooting as they did in the game yesterday. There are other things involved too. We didn't really get off to a very good start. We didn't get things going the way we wanted to at the beginning. Also, we just didn't have really good patience. We got so impatient that we were pretty lucky with that start that we had that we were able to get back into the game. Once we overcame that and got back into the game, it was a lot better for us for the most part.

FISCHER: You got off to a tough start in the first half. You had the same problem occur in the second half, after you got it down to a two-point lead at the end of the first half. Again, Michigan played awfully well.

KNIGHT: I don't think there's any question about that, plus their shooting was better than their average has been over the course of the year. When they are shooting really well to go along with the inside game they have, they become extremely tough to play against

FISCHER: Were you pleased with your team's patience in the second half?

KNIGHT: Well, I think it got to be a little bit better. We were able to do some things and get into a position offensively with the basketball that enabled us to be a better offensive team than we were in the first half. We got that at the end of the first half. We had some better passing and some better movement in the last five minutes of the first half than we had up to that point. I think that got us back into a position in the game where we were at least able to come out in the second half and not have to fight from the 12 or 14-point deficit that looked like might be the case.

FISCHER: Let's go to the phones, Coach. First questioner is from Indianapolis. Please explain an intentional foul. In the last seconds of a close game, the trailing team blatantly fouls to gain possession of the ball, but it seems like it is very seldom called.

KNIGHT: We have to eliminate the word 'blatant' first of all, and let's stick with intentional. The interpretation of an intentional foul is a foul that's committed almost invariably by the defensive player. If it's not committed by the defensive player, it is probably something that involves fighting to a degree, then it becomes a flagrant foul and ejection is a possibility.

An intentional foul is defined as a foul committed when a player has no chance to get the basketball or makes no effort to get the basketball. Now, in my opinion, we had three fouls like that committed in the last minute or so of the game yesterday, none of which was called.

FISCHER: This is an 11 year-old from Indianapolis. Will you be at Indiana in 2000? If you are, I plan on being there.

KNIGHT: Well, we're just going to have to wait and see on that one. Just make sure, youngster that you are working to be the very best student you can possibly be between now and 2000, so you will have the kinds of opportunities that you want to have when you get to that point.

FISCHER: This from Indianapolis. Do you enjoy your fans? Are they important to you?

KNIGHT: The kind of fan that we have had over the years has meant a great deal to us. I think Indiana fans are the greatest there are anywhere, and we have thoroughly enjoyed the support of thousands and thousands of great fans throughout the country. That has always meant a great deal to us.

FISCHER: Our next questioner this evening is from Indianapolis. Why do you look so mad during ballgames?

KNIGHT: Well, we've got kind of a problem. We've got a broken chair and it pinches when I sit in it the wrong way. We just haven't yet been able to replace the chair because it's bolted to the floor. We've had a real problem with that. I have been after the University to get me a new chair, but they constantly refuse to do so, so I guess I continue to get pinched when I sit down. Why don't you and I exchange seats at the next game, and you'll see how mad you do get.

FISCHER: Well I can tell you this. I have a pad on mine. I bring it to every ballgame. This is from Indianapolis. Why does the team seem to be doing better in the second half of ballgames and not getting off to as good a start as they were earlier?

KNIGHT: Each time that we go out, we have somebody playing extremely hard against us. I think there's a lot of emotion at the beginning of a ballgame. We have just not been able to get off to a good start, and I think that is to a great extent the responsibility of the teams that we have been playing.

FISCHER: This is from Indianapolis. How can we get information about your basketball camp?

KNIGHT: Anybody interested in our summer basketball camp can just drop a note to me in care of the Athletic Department here at the University. The zip code is 47405. Just send a note requesting information on our summer basketball camp. I'll see that it's forthcoming.

FISCHER: Again from Indianapolis, Coach. Do you like the nickname, "The General?"

KNIGHT: I've never given that much thought. I'm not inclined to think much about nicknames. I've usually referred to people by their given name or, in some cases, by phrases that could never be mistaken for nicknames.

FISCHER: This is from Unionville. Have you changed your mind about how fans can or cannot react during opponents' free throw shooting?

KNIGHT: We've had a lot of waving and a lot of things in Assembly Hall in the last couple of ballgames, and it was brought to my attention. I didn't notice it at first. We had some chants start in the Michigan game that we just won't tolerate there. In fact, I made the comment that I would clear out the whole bleachers unless we stopped the chanting, and the chanting did stop.

FISCHER: A Fort Wayne listener asks, do you consider it a miracle that Calbert Cheaney played 50 minutes against Penn State and didn't shoot a foul shot?

KNIGHT: It's hard for me to imagine as much movement as Cheaney goes through that he doesn't get a free throw. Anything is possible, I suppose.

FISCHER: This is from Indianapolis. What problems did Penn State's 2-3 zone cause you?

KNIGHT: Our biggest problem at Penn State was defensively, not offensively. We scored enough points and got enough shots to win the ballgame, but we didn't guard anybody. Our defense was very, very poor. Penn State played well defensively. They covered well. If the other guy is doing a pretty good job defensively, you're not going to score as many points as if he isn't. They scored against us because we weren't doing a good job on defense.

FISCHER: This is from Noblesville, Coach. Was Ivan Renko at the Michigan game?

KNIGHT: Ivan has been to a couple of games on a trip here, but this was not one of them.

FISCHER: This is from Carmel, Indiana. Please give an update on the status of Pat Graham.

KNIGHT: Well, Pat's getting to be a little more active now. He's running a little bit, doing some shooting. Whether he's going to get back in a position where he can play is still something that we just don't know.

FISCHER: This is from Fort Wayne. Could you explain what constitutes the over-and-back call? And could you comment on the way this call was made in the Minnesota game?

KNIGHT: It comes into play anytime the ball is brought completely across mid court, either on the pass or the dribble. If it's brought across the line on the dribble, then both feet of the player dribbling the basketball must cross the 10 second line. Once it's across, it cannot go back into the back court or back across the 10 second line unless the defensive team gains possession of it and is responsible for it going back. The offensive team can then chase it down and bring it back. The offensive team can chase down a deflection by the defense into the back court and bring it down. But if the offensive team is responsible for the ball, without the defensive team gaining possession of it, then, in chasing it down, commits the over-and-back violation.

FISCHER: Any reaction, Coach, to the way the officials called it in the Minnesota game?

KNIGHT: As the rules go, that was called correctly.

FISCHER: This is from Evansville. How many redshirt players can a team have at one time, including a medical ? Is there a limit?

KNIGHT: No, there is no limit.

FISCHER: Why did you use the one-guard offense at the beginning of the second half yesterday, and did you feel that it worked?

KNIGHT: Well, we used it because we thought it would work. We felt that we got some pretty good things out of it. It wasn't necessarily a one-guard offense because we were able to use Cheaney in a way that got him outside a little bit.

FISCHER: This is from Zionsville. The Michigan players seemed to concede the Big Ten Championship in their comments in the papers after the ballgame yesterday to the Hoosiers as the "silver medal." Do you consider the NCAA the "gold medal" and the Big Ten the "silver?"

KNIGHT: No. I have never felt that way, and I would certainly feel a lot better about it if Michigan could get the other nine teams to concede the championship to Indiana. There's an awful lot of basketball to be played before this championship is decided, and I think it has become convenient since only one team is ever going to win a league championship, for teams that don't or certainly don't very often win, to bypass the league championship in their own minds thinking that playing in the NCAA Tournament is the most important accomplishment a team can have. Here, our first and foremost objective will always be to win the Big Ten Championship.

FISCHER: This is from Danville, Indiana. I noticed you are wearing a large ring on your TV show. Is this an NCAA Championship ring? If so, when and which team is it for?

KNIGHT: It's the championship ring from the 1976 season.

FISCHER: All right. This is from Jasper, Indiana. Do you think it's a distraction for a team to play non-conference teams during the Big Ten season? Is that why Indiana does not?

KNIGHT: Absolutely.

FISCHER: This is from Danville. In the past you have talked about your defense being off balance or out of position. Do you mean that on an individual player basis or on the team as a whole basis?

KNIGHT: Well, when individual players are out of position, that puts the total team defense in a position other than what you want.

FISCHER: This is from Indianapolis. What is your reaction to the Big Ten supervisor of officials indicating that the referee blew the call on Chris Reynolds in the Penn State game?

KNIGHT: I think that is an unfortunate choice of words because I think the referee called the play as he saw it. Without belaboring the point, there was a play at the end of the first half when the ball went out of bounds right in front of us and we all thought absolutely off a Penn State player. Chris Reynolds forced the play. The ball went off his hands, then off the Penn State player's hand, and then out of bounds. The ball was given to Penn State.

They subsequently, on that possession, scored a three-point basket at the buzzer. Had that call been made, at least as we felt it should have been made, then that would have not been a three-point addition to Penn State's score, which you can imagine makes a big, big difference at the end of the ballgame.

It's not always a call that isn't seen or missed at the end of the game that is the most important call in a game. Calls at other times are just as important to the outcome of a game.

FISCHER: Our next caller, Coach is from Berne, Indiana. Why did Michigan play man to man against Indiana when Penn State's zone seemed to work so well?

KNIGHT: Again, I go back to what I said a little while ago, Don. I think that our biggest problem in the ballgame with Penn State was with our defense. That means that our problem was with Penn State's offense, not quite so much with its defense.

FISCHER: This question is from Bloomington. You used to have a policy where current team members would talk to potential recruits and they might decide that a recruit would not fit into the program. With the present policy of allowing recruits to sign letters of intent in their junior and early senior years, will your present team members still have any input?

KNIGHT: We do the same thing that we've always done in that regard.

FISCHER: In other words, when the kids come to visit, they are taken over by the members of the team?

KNIGHT: Yes.

FISCHER: The second part of his question. Will there be a banner in Assembly Hall for winning the Preseason NIT?

KNIGHT: I'm not sure. That's an interesting question. We've given that a little thought, and in all probability, we will. The criterion on placing banners in Assembly Hall was that they be related to national championship competition. We don't necessarily mean NCAA competition, but a tournament that would involve teams from all over the country. Since that is exactly what the Preseason NIT is, we probably will get a banner worked up for that, Don. Is it Don or John?

FISCHER: It's still Don, Coach. This question is from Crawfordsville. Is there any way that we can get copies of your comments on these coach's shows?

KNIGHT: I don't think so at this point, but it is interesting that you would bring that up because the eminent Mr. Fischer and I are, at some point, going to make up a tape on Indiana basketball using cuts on things that we've discussed and on some things we have discussed that you haven't heard.

FISCHER: (Laughter)

KNIGHT: Every once in a while, Fischer makes some off-color remark or gets a little bit upset with one of my answers, and we have to delete what he says. I've saved those tapes over the years, and at some point we may put all of those together and make sure that it is distributed in such a way that it is for adults only. That will provide you with a greater insight into Don Fischer.

FISCHER: (Laughter) This question is from Versailles. What is the toughest arena to play in the Big Ten?

KNIGHT: Well, I hope it is Assembly Hall.

FISCHER: This is from Fort Wayne. What did you think about Penn State's fans standing right at court side?

KNIGHT: I thought that their seats must be pretty hard.

FISCHER: Coach, a guy asked me if anybody lost the hair off their legs. Was anybody pulling out hair as they were standing there to pass the ball in? It was pretty close, to say the least.

Coach Knight did not answer the question, but the players said that there was a lot of contact with fans on the sidelines when they would put the ball into play.

This is from Indianapolis. What do you do to keep the team focused after a big win like Michigan?

KNIGHT: As an example, last night after the Michigan game, we went out and built a bonfire on the intramural field here behind Assembly Hall. The team and all the coaches met there at midnight and we have a chant. We circle the bonfire and hold hands in this circle, and then we chant things. "Keep focused, keep focused. Pay attention, pay attention. Be intense, be intense." Last night at the end of our "be intense" chant, several members of our circle started chanting, "We're cold, we're cold."

Then one member in our group, after that chant, started chanting, "So what, so what, so what." The answer to that chant, then, became, "It matters to us, it matters to us."

Then the response was, "You're only cold if you think you're cold, you're only cold if you think you're cold." And the response then was, "We think we're cold, we think we're cold, we think we're cold." With all that, I thought we were able, hopefully to refocus ourselves.

Just as it did in the first half of the Big Ten season, the Illinois game came right on the heels of Michigan; so there was very little time to recover and prepare for an aggressive Illini team. Illinois which was 8-2 in conference play and in sole possession of second place saw an opportunity to close the gap behind league leading Indiana. Knight began by talking about the Michigan game and then the Illinois team he will face tonight.

The Michigan game was a little bit different than the one we had up at Ann Arbor. At Ann Arbor there were actually several stretches in the game that we controlled, I think we had a 5 or 6 point lead at the half, and were ahead for a good portion of the second part of the first half, as much as 10 points. Then Michigan came back and got in the lead by a point or two here and there, then we took the lead back. Never in the first game, were we very far away from the lead. The game went back and forth, and I would imagine, over the course of the 40 minutes at Ann Arbor, we probably led more than we were behind.

Here Sunday, I don't think we were ever in the lead until we went ahead 79-78 which was with maybe 6 minutes to go in the ballgame. We were 13 down early and on the verge of being knocked out of the game, but then we fought hard to get back in the game by the half. Then we went down again in the second half very much like in the Minnesota game. The pattern was almost identical, although I thought in the last maybe 8 minutes of the game Sunday, we probably played about as well as we have played any time all year.

Matt Nover has done an outstanding job of battling the big guys for us, keeping guys off the board, beating people defensively, game in and game out. He has had to give up size in both height and weight and he's just done a great job for us doing what he has to do at our defensive end. Then he has, on occasion, been a real contributor offensively, probably never more so than in the Michigan game Sunday. It would be to our advantage if Matt could continue offensively as he played on Sunday.

I'm not sure who all we had in the ballgame at the end of the first half. I think we had Evans, Reynolds, Matt, Patrick and Alan. Greg Graham then came in the last minute. We were once 10 down and they were able to get us within 2 at the half which obviously made it a lot easier for us to start the second half than if we had to start from a 10-point deficit.

The game, I think, as much as anything because of the way we played the whole 40 minutes, was a real team effort and all 9 kids had a part in the winning the ballgame. And that's the thing that I think becomes most pleasing with this team.

Illinois at 8-2 has not surprised me at all. They're a team that has everybody back from last year. They are a team that didn't lose anybody and then added Kauffman to it, who had been their leading scorer the two previous years. This is a team that has good all-around scoring and has an outstanding offensive player in the post in Deon Thomas. He maybe is as good as there is in the Big Ten. This is a team that I think figured to be a very good basketball team this year, and they certainly have been.

You start with the fact that they play a little bit differently defensively than most teams do. Michigan State plays a lot like they do. They play a very soft defense, and soft in terms of not really pressuring much on the perimeter, not going out and trying to stop passes or choke off passing lanes. But what they're doing is trying to make it very, very tough, which they do, for you to get anything inside against them. They try to protect 15 to 17 feet away from the basket, and they do a very good job of that.

It will be important for us tonight to generate some offense out of our defense, so that we can get some baskets from the defensive end, and beat their defense down the floor. Then, we are also going to have to do some shooting over the top of the defense throughout the course of the ballgame.

On offense, I mentioned Thomas. They start with a very, very tough inside game in Thomas. He is a very, very good scorer inside and probably can score in more ways than anybody in the Big Ten inside the lane. Then that is complemented with four or five very good three-point shooters. So they are a good team that, from an offensive standpoint, can do everything, beginning with the inside game right out through the three-point shot.

What we have to do in tonight's game is get off to a good start, have better patience on the offensive end, and have a better hold on things on the defensive end. We just have not gotten the kind of play early in a ballgame, particularly on the offensive end, with our patience, that we have to have to play the teams that we are playing.

GAME SUMMARY

INDIANA 93   ILLINOIS 72

Indiana improved its Big Ten record to 12-0 with an impressive win over Illinois. Calbert Cheaney made another statement for his Player of the Year bid scoring 29 points, hitting 10 for 20 from the field and 4 for 5 from three-point range. He also hit 10 of 20 free throws and pulled down 9 boards. Four other Indiana players scored in double figures with Greg Graham scoring 18, Alan Henderson and Damon Bailey had 14 and Matt Nover ended the game with 12.

Indiana forced 22 turnovers on the Illini, and held them to only 9 assists.

Indiana gave Coach Knight a strong first half and led at the break 54-33. The Hoosiers played Illinois even in the second half at 39 each.

Indiana now gets ready for instate rival Purdue.

ILLINOIS

No.	Player		FG	FGA	FG	FGA	FT	FTA	Off	Def	Tot	PF	TP	A	TO	Blk	S	Min
			Total FG		**3-point**				**Rebounds**									
30	Bennett, Robert	f	3	5	0	0	0	0	2	2	4	3	6	1	3	0	1	26
34	Kauffman, Andy	f	2	7	0	1	8	11	2	0	2	3	12	1	5	0	0	21
25	Thomas, Deon	c	6	13	0	0	2	2	3	2	5	1	14	1	2	4	0	39
11	Clemons, Rennie	g	3	6	0	0	2	4	0	3	3	2	8	2	4	0	2	32
24	Keene, Richard	g	5	11	1	5	0	0	0	1	1	4	11	1	3	0	1	27
44	Wheeler, T.J.		4	5	0	0	6	6	1	2	3	5	14	1	2	0	0	18
33	Davidson, Mark		1	2	0	0	1	2	1	0	1	2	3	0	1	0	0	15
4	Taylor, Brooks		1	1	0	0	2	2	0	1	1	3	4	1	2	2	0	10
3	Harris, Davin		0	0	0	0	0	0	0	1	1	0	0	0	0	0	0	5
32	Michael, Tom		0	0	0	0	0	0	0	0	0	0	0	1	0	0	0	7
	Team								1	4	5							
	TOTALS		25	50	1	6	21	27	10	16	26	23	72	9	22	6	4	200

Total FG%   1st Half .400(10/25)   2nd half .600(15/25)   Game .500(25/50)   Deadball
3-Pt. FG%   1st Half .000(0/2)   2nd half .250(1/4)   Game .167(1/6)   Rebounds   3
FT%   1st Half .722(13/18)   2nd half .889(8/9)   Game .778(21/27)

INDIANA

No.	Player		FG	FGA	FG	FGA	FT	FTA	Off	Def	Tot	PF	TP	A	TO	Blk	S	Min
			Total FG		**3-point**				**Rebounds**									
40	Cheaney, Calbert	f	10	20	4	5	5	7	3	6	9	3	29	0	1	0	3	34
44	Henderson, Alan	f	5	9	0	0	4	7	4	2	6	3	14	0	6	2	0	25
24	Nover, Matt	c	6	9	0	0	0	0	2	1	3	3	12	1	2	1	0	30
20	Graham, Greg	g	6	8	1	3	5	8	1	1	2	2	18	4	1	0	3	36
32	Reynolds, Chris	g	1	5	0	0	1	2	2	3	5	5	3	4	0	0	1	22
22	Bailey, Damon		5	7	1	2	3	5	1	1	2	1	14	5	3	0	1	28
30	Leary, Todd		1	1	1	1	0	0	0	1	1	3	3	2	0	0	0	13
34	Evans, Brian		0	2	0	2	0	0	0	2	2	0	0	1	1	0	0	6
25	Knight, Pat		0	0	0	0	0	0	0	0	0	0	0	2	1	0	0	6
	Team								2	1	3							
	TOTALS		34	61	7	13	18	29	15	18	33	20	93	19	15	3	8	200

Total FG%   1st Half .633(19/30)   2nd half .484(15/31)   Game .557(34/61)   Deadball
3-Pt. FG%   1st Half .667(4/6)   2nd half .429(3/7)   Game .538(7/13)   Rebounds   7
FT%   1st Half .667(12/18)   2nd half .545(6/11)   Game .621(18/29)

Officials   Tom Rucker, Tom O'Neill, Sid Rodeheffer
Technical Fouls   4 (Indiana 2, Illinois 2)
Attendance   16,336

Score by
Periods	1	2	OT	OT	Final
Illinois	33	39			72
Indiana	54	39			93

After an impressive string of wins in critical games, and reaching the number one ranking among major college polls, the IU basketball program received a setback when Alan Henderson injured his knee in practice Friday. This is the second player to have to sit out due to injury this season. The most important question is how serious is the talented sophomore's injury.

While doctors are examining the injury, coaches and fans are pondering how the team will perform without Henderson, what the lineup will be, and will it be able to redo its setup. When Scotty May was injured late in the 1975 season, Coach Knight told me privately that it was difficult to refocus an offense that was centered on a player like May. Now we were wondering if Indiana would be able to adjust to the loss of Alan Henderson.

Those IU fans that were old enough to remember Scotty May's injury, which ironically occurred in a Purdue game, are distraught over the loss of this outstanding sophomore. The subject has become the heart of conversation for IU faithful. To give you an idea of how top of mind Henderson's injury was in Indiana; shortly after the injury, Don Fischer was driving a little faster than usual from his Indianapolis home to Bloomington, and was pulled over by a sheriff. When the sheriff saw Don's name on the drivers license, the first words out of his mouth were, "How is Henderson?" That is the way it is in Indiana.

The tough mindedness of the Indiana basketball team comes from its coach. Though the loss of Henderson was disturbing to fans, Knight pressed ahead with his game plan and "business as usual" attitude. Later in the season he talks about how pivotal this period is to the team.

He begins his show talking about the Illinois game and then talks about Henderson and the Purdue game today.

One of the things that we stressed in getting ready for the Illinois game, after our game with Michigan, was the kind of start that we wanted to have. We did not get off to a good start in the Michigan game and we found ourselves 13 points behind. At 13 behind, we were on the verge of getting knocked right out of the game. The start wasn't just how well Michigan played, it involved some things that we did not do well.

One thing about basketball that you've always got to keep in mind is this, as the game ends, you have had the ball as many times as the other team has. Now, you may not have had as many shots as the other team had or you may not have as many free throws as they had, but you have the ball the exact same number of times. So, at that point, Michigan had done more with the ball than we had while we had it.

Basketball is different from baseball in that regard. In baseball, because of the game, you may have 40 at bats in the game, and the other team may only get 31 at bats. So you have had nine more chances to create something in baseball. Baseball is always uneven because of the way the game is played in terms of offensive opportunities. Basketball isn't. It is a matter of doing with your opportunities something more than the other team does. Michigan did that at the start of the ballgame to put us in a position where we were almost out of the ballgame before halftime. So the key in that game was our getting from an eventual 10-point deficit to a 2-point deficit by the half.

Then the same thing almost happened to us at the beginning of the second half when we got 9 down, and we got out of that and went on to win.

In the Illinois game, because of our slow starts over the five previous games, we really emphasized the kind of start we thought we had to have at both ends of the floor. We got a very good start. I think we were ahead 22-8, or so.

What we've tried to do in this ballgame today is to put an equal emphasis on the kind of start that we want in the first half as well as the kind of start that we want in the second half. We'll just have to see. We got that start against Illinois, and we need to have that kind of start today and to have it carry over into the second half.

A lot of people want to know about Alan Henderson's knee injury, and this will just be an ongoing thing. We are going to try to do whatever we can to get him back playing whenever it's possible for him to do so, if in fact that possibility does develop. We'll just have to wait and see what kind of progress is made relative to the swelling in the knee so we can make a determination.

As far as today's game is concerned, we will just handle things like we always handle things. We are reduced by one very good player and we've got other good players that just have to come in, not individually, but collectively, and make up for the absence of a very good player.

Today we want to get a really good start as I have said. Any time you are playing a team with a really outstanding player like Glenn Robinson, you have got to be able to do some things to limit what he can do against you. If Robinson runs wild against us, that becomes something that may be insurmountable for us. I think that we've got to be able to take advantage, in some cases, of our quickness, both offensively and defensively. If we don't utilize that, then we may be wasting the thing that should give us the best advantage in the game.

We have had a lot of questions about Pat Graham's status, and I think there's a definite possibility that he could help us yet this season. I think there's a chance that Pat could come back and play, and we just kind of look at that day-by-day.

Knight finishes the show with his own lighthearted question about something that everyone is wondering.

KNIGHT: Don, who are you going to start today?

FISCHER: Well, I'm not going to start anybody, but who are you going to start?

KNIGHT: Well, you know I rely on you for that, Don, so I guess we're kind of at an impasse on today's starting lineup.

GAME SUMMARY

INDIANA 93   PURDUE 78

Indiana won its 13th Big Ten game without a loss and in the process swept its rival Purdue. The victory was accomplished despite the absence of Alan Henderson, who suffered a knee injury, and would be a question mark for the rest of the season. Add in the foul trouble that limited Calbert Cheaney to just 25 minutes and 14 points, and it would have been very easy for the Hoosiers to fold.

Fortunately, this IU squad has matured, and it has become mentally tough like its coach. Knight's toughness seems to have been inbred into his players and the team personality.

Keying the triumph were Greg Graham's relentless drives and constant motion that had Purdue's players grabbing and hacking all day long. Graham ended the day with a career high 32 points, with 26 of those coming from the foul line, setting Indiana, Big Ten, and Purdue opponent records. IU was aided by freshman Brian Evans who came off the bench with 20 points and 7 rebounds, while Matt Nover contributed 12 points and a team high 9 boards.

Like most Hoosier performances this year, every member of the squad contributed, and this included the return of junior Pat Graham, whose foot injury has kept him sidelined since the Florida State game in November. He played nine minutes and scored 4 points in a short stint, but his presence inspired this team and the fans.

Indiana hit 50 percent from the field to Purdue's 49 percent. The Hoosiers hit 7 of 15 three-point shots for 47 percent, Purdue 4 of 14 for 28 percent. From the line, the Hoosiers were 34 of 40 for 85 percent, and Purdue hit 14 of 17 attempts for an 82 percent performance.

In the rebound department, the Hoosiers were out rebounded for the first time in a number of games by a 34 to 29 count. Indiana had 12 turnovers and Purdue had 16.

The Hoosiers now have a 24-2 overall record for the season. They remain in sole possession of first place in the Big Ten.

PURDUE

No.	Player	Total FG		3-point		FT	FTA	Rebounds			PF	TP	A	TO	Blk	S	Min
		FG	FGA	FG	FGA			Off	Def	Tot							
13	Robinson, Glenn f	9	22	1	3	5	7	3	11	14	5	24	2	4	0	2	38
22	Martin, Cuonzo f	12	15	0	0	8	8	3	1	4	4	32	1	2	0	1	36
34	Stanback, Ian c	2	3	0	0	0	0	1	6	7	5	4	1	2	0	1	29
11	Waddell, Matt g	0	4	0	2	0	0	0	2	2	2	0	2	3	0	0	21
12	Painter, Matt g	5	9	2	5	1	2	0	1	1	4	13	7	1	0	1	36
22	Dove, Herb	1	2	0	0	0	0	1	0	1	2	2	0	1	0	1	4
30	Darner, Linc	1	4	1	4	0	0	0	0	0	2	3	0	0	0	0	19
35	McNary, Cornelius	0	1	0	0	0	0	0	1	1	3	0	2	0	0	0	5
23	Roberts, Porter	0	1	0	0	0	0	0	0	0	2	0	0	1	0	0	9
00	Dove, Herb	0	0	0	0	0	0	0	0	0	1	0	0	0	0	0	2
20	Foster, Todd	0	0	0	0	0	0	0	0	0	0	0	0	0	0	0	1
	Team							3	1	4							
	TOTALS	30	61	4	14	14	17	11	23	34	30	78	13	16	0	6	200

Total FG%   1st Half .519(14/27)   2nd half .471(16/34)   Game .492(30/61)   Deadball
3-Pt. FG%   1st Half .400(2/5)   2nd half .222(2/9)   Game .286(4/14)   Rebounds   1
FT%   1st Half .750(6/8)   2nd half .889(8/9)   Game .824(14/17)

INDIANA

No.	Player	Total FG		3-point		FT	FTA	Rebounds			PF	TP	A	TO	Blk	S	Min
		FG	FGA	FG	FGA			Off	Def	Tot							
22	Bailey, Damon f	3	8	1	3	0	0	2	3	5	4	7	6	3	0	2	29
40	Cheaney, Calbert f	6	8	1	2	1	2	0	2	2	5	14	3	1	1	1	25
24	Nover, Matt c	5	7	0	0	2	2	3	6	9	2	12	0	4	0	1	39
20	Graham, Greg g	2	7	2	3	26	28	0	3	3	2	32	2	2	0	2	40
21	Reynolds, Chris g	0	1	0	0	0	0	0	1	1	0	0	1	0	0	1	8
34	Evans, Brian	7	16	3	7	3	6	2	5	7	3	20	4	1	1	2	35
30	Leary, Todd	0	1	0	0	2	2	0	1	1	4	2	1	0	0	0	14
33	Graham, Pat	2	3	0	0	0	0	0	1	1	1	4	0	1	0	0	9
25	Knight, Pat	1	1	0	0	0	0	0	0	0	0	2	0	0	0	0	1
	Team							0	0	0							
	TOTALS	26	52	7	15	34	40	7	22	29	21	93	17	12	2	9	200

Total FG%   1st Half .464(13/28)   2nd half .542(13/24)   Game .500(26/52)   Deadball
3-Pt. FG%   1st Half .667(6/9)   2nd half .167(1/6)   Game .467(7/15)   Rebounds   2
FT%   1st Half 1.00(12/12)   2nd half .786(22/28)   Game .850(34/40)

Officials   Jim Burr, Jerry Petro, Dan Chrisman
Technical Fouls   2 (Purdue 2)
Attendance   16,842

Score by Periods	1	2	OT	OT	Final
Purdue	36	42			78
Indiana	44	49			93

Bob Knight Talk Show
February 22, 1993

This talk show really stands out to me because Knight pays tribute to his team and recognizes the way they regrouped to play without Alan Henderson.

FISCHER: We will not be able to use telephones because of Indiana's travel plans and their trip to Ohio State for tomorrow night's ballgame in Columbus. Therefore, we have prerecorded our program this evening and will not be taking phone calls tonight.

Coach, please talk just for a moment about the Illinois ballgame, a 93-72 win on Wednesday night. How do you feel your ball club performed?

KNIGHT: We have talked about not getting a good start, going all the way back to the Minnesota game, five ballgames, actually, where we had not gotten off to a real good start. We had not been able to exert any control over the ballgame early in the game, and our primary concern going into the game with Illinois last Wednesday night was to get off to a good start at both ends of the floor. I was really pleased at our being able to do that. Any time you set up an objective that you are trying to obtain in a ballgame and you meet that objective, you've got to be pretty pleased with it.

We got off to a good start at both ends. I think we were ahead 22 to 8 in the ballgame early, and from that point on, we were never really in serious trouble as far as the outcome of the game was concerned.

Illinois did come back a little in the second half. That was a really good point for us, particularly because of what had transpired beginning with the Minnesota game. Although those were games that we won, we'd get behind by 10 or 12 points and then have to dig our way out. We just needed to be on top, and we got a really good game and movement out of Cheaney. He scored, I think, 29 points in the game, rebounded well, and led our team in assists, which was a little bit different than the game he played against Purdue yesterday.

Our all-around play was pretty good. Our defensive play was good against Illinois. We took that out to a 22-point lead in the first half and led at the halftime by 21, 53-32. We had scored over 50 and held the other guy below 35, and that's a pretty good margin. It says something good about your team both on the offensive end and defensive end. So we were really pleased with that.

You know, we had a lot of emotion after that Michigan game a week ago. We've talked about this a lot, that this is not the greatest place in the world when you win a big game. Your players may have a hard time keeping their heads where they belong and their feet on the ground. They hear so much about what a great job they did, and so forth and so on. That is what pleased me all the more about the start of the Illinois game. I felt in the first half of the game with Illinois we played as good basketball as we have played at any time this year.

I probably got a little lax at the half and didn't make the kind of demands on the team in the second half that maybe I should have. We just didn't have the same kind of intensity and therefore the same kind of quality play in the second half against Illinois that we had in the first half.

FISCHER: Coach, you talk about the emotional situation. You had identical scenarios earlier in conference play, when you played Michigan, Illinois, and Purdue all on the road. Then you came back in the same situation, the same three games, in line, once again in the second half of this season, but this time at Assembly Hall. When you talk about having an emotional drain, that happens throughout the season, does it not?

KNIGHT: Well, I think that the drain a team encounters is part of a season. Being able to foresee it, being able to understand it, being able to talk about it, being able to bring it to the attention of the players is important. From our standpoint the length of practices is very important. I think how long we practice, how long we are going to work is very important. We really need to constantly evaluate not if we are practicing long enough but are we practicing too long, particularly with the number of kids we have this year. An hour and a half practice with 10 kids might be over two hours practice by comparison with 12 or 13 kids.

FISCHER: Coach, let's talk a little about the Purdue ballgame yesterday. The Boilermakers are a very physical basketball team coming in. It's always a physical game when these two clubs meet.

KNIGHT: Purdue looked a lot bigger to me than they did the first time we played them. I looked at their front line as their lineup was introduced, and I thought, are we playing Purdue, or are we playing Michigan? Part of that, I'm sure, was because of Alan's absence.

They have always been a very physical team. Gene has been a very tough and demanding coach for them, and tough and demanding coaches basically do an awfully good job getting their kids to play hard and to play well. He's been as good as anybody at getting that done with his teams over the years. I think it is a tribute to both teams that they played this game, a very tough game, without any instance of guys jostling each other when they are playing. We've never had a flare up in an Indiana-Purdue game, which has always pleased me and I'm sure it has pleased Coach Keady as well.

FISCHER: Coach, you felt this Purdue basketball team had improved going into this ballgame over the first time that you met them?

KNIGHT: I don't think it was so much that I felt they had improved as they felt they had improved. They are around their team every day, they are there all the time, and I think they definitely felt they were a better team than they were the first time we had played them.

FISCHER: Coach, you go into this game without a player who has been a starter all season long, Alan Henderson. What does that do to your team psychologically?

KNIGHT: We were talking a moment ago about the psychology of play and all that's involved in understanding that. An injury is a part of that psychology. Rarely are you going to get through a season without somebody being out for a game or several games. Pat Graham has been out the last two years, and it was really nice to see him back in there playing. I think as he plays and gains a little bit more confidence on his foot that he's going to be better and better for us. So I'm really happy that Pat is back. We've just got to wait and see where we are with Henderson.

FISCHER: Bob, did you feel good about the way your ball club played in the Purdue game?

KNIGHT: We had to get off to a good start again. We spent some time talking about the start of the Illinois game, and I felt in the Purdue game we did get off to a good start. We actually got off to a pretty decent start in the second half, but we missed some opportunities that we had, and Purdue played very well at the start of the second half and the conclusion of the first half. For us to take the ballgame from a start where we actually were behind a little bit to a point where we had a 15-point lead in the first half was pretty good basketball on our part.

Then Purdue played well when they were the dominating team for maybe the last 5 minutes of the first half and the first five or six minutes of the second half. Then we got the thing going back our way, and I think once we got it up to a 10-point lead, I don't think it went back below that.

FISCHER: One other note about this ballgame. The play of Calbert Cheaney you mentioned earlier, and yet, you weren't really pleased with it.

KNIGHT: Calbert made some good plays. He made a really big bucket in the second half, but he wasn't as sharp and he wasn't into the game as I would have liked to have seen him, particularly under the circumstances. Without Henderson, we really had to get some things out of Cheaney. We really had to rely on his doing some things in this ballgame. He fouled out.

I'm not sure that he has ever fouled out of a game before, certainly not in one that he only plays 25 minutes of the ballgame. He made some careless fouls, he allowed himself to get into some situations that are just very un-Cheaney like.

On the other side of the coin, though, I felt that we would have to have a really good game from Cheaney, very similar to the game he played at Purdue. He scored 34 points and got 9 or 10 rebounds and had 4 or 5 assists. I felt that was what we'd have to have from him in this ballgame. We didn't get anything close to that, and yet we still scored 93 points, which is 21 more than we scored in the first game. We wanted to get to the free throw line, and we got there and made free throws.

FISCHER: Greg Graham made 26 free throws, and that sets a new Indiana and Big Ten record.

KNIGHT: I'm not sure that I've ever heard of a kid scoring 32 points on two baskets.

FISCHER: Yes, he had two three-point field goals, he had 32 points. It was just an amazing performance.

KNIGHT: And he did a good job in a lot of other areas, too. Greg played very well.

FISCHER: Brian Evans?

KNIGHT: Don, you can go down right through the roster. We got good play from everybody that was in the ballgame. As far as Evans is concerned, I feel pretty good about him not taking any bad shots anymore when we are in our delay offense.

FISCHER: Coach, the saddest part of any coach's schedule is when a kid gets hurt, and Alan Henderson, of course, injured a knee in Friday's practice session.

KNIGHT: Any time that you have a kid, particularly a kid who has worked as hard and has been as good a kid as Henderson has been, who has any kind of a health problem, and has to miss play, it is just a shame, you know. It is a big, big part of the kid's life to play games and to be here to compete in the games that are really important games. And yet injuries and illness have been a part of basketball as long as the game has been played and will continue to be. There just isn't any way you are going to get around the injury factor in this sport. There's too much running, jumping, jostling, and moving for you ever to think that people aren't occasionally going to get hurt playing basketball.

We have two things that have to happen now, following Alan's injury. The rest of the team has to come together and say, "Hey, here we are. We've got eight guys and we're able to add Pat Graham to that and we're back at nine, but we've just got to go play. And we've got to play and play well, and if we do what we are capable of doing, we'll do all right."

The second thing is that the kid who is injured, Alan in this case, has just got to do everything he can to get back to playing as quickly as he can. That's where you are after any injury, and certainly this injury is no different.

FISCHER: Coach, can you talk about what the injury involves?

KNIGHT: We don't really know yet. They are going to further examine the injury tomorrow, Don, and then we will have an absolute concrete idea of what is there, what has to be done, what steps have to be taken, and what the future is.

FISCHER: As far as injuries are concerned, you mentioned Pat Graham coming back. You got some valuable minutes from him.

KNIGHT: It was good that Pat got in and played. He only made the first shot that he took and then got another little chippy at the end of the ballgame. He seemed to move well, and we should have dressed him for the Illinois game, but he had only practiced once prior to that. We wanted him to get him a little more play in practice so he'd feel more comfortable about playing.

FISCHER: Is building up stamina the biggest problem he has now?

KNIGHT: I don't think there's any question about that. I've watched him shoot, and he still shoots really well. He has to have a little confidence in being able to play on that foot and doing all the things that are required of a kid playing at both ends of the floor.

FISCHER: Coach, Calbert Cheaney has been listed on the ballot for the U.S. Basketball Writers Association for the National Player of the Year award. There is a lot of talk about this. Obviously, he has to be very proud of that. I know you are, but you really can't get involved in those kinds of things right now, can you?

KNIGHT: I think that Cheaney should be the Player of the Year. I think that he has been an outstanding player. There are things that he has been able to do in the game of basketball, both here and throughout our league, that nobody has been able to do. He's been at the forefront of our being a pretty good basketball team over the last three years, not just this year. He would be the most deserving recipient there would be of that award. You go beyond the basketball a little bit, and you've got a kid in Calbert Cheaney that should be what every kid is all about. If every kid could be Calbert Cheaney, the problems for our youth would be reduced and almost nonexistent. I've had a lot of great players. I don't know that Cheaney is the best player that's played here. I didn't think he was in yesterday's game, but he's as good as any. He's just been a wonderful, wonderful kid to have as a part of Indiana basketball.

FISCHER: You can almost say that about this year's entire senior class, can't you?

KNIGHT: Well, the whole team. I like the team, I like the kids, I like what they try to do, I like where they have come to from where they were. I like the toughness about them that I hope just continues through as long as we can keep it going. I thought there was a real toughness in the game with Purdue. We made some errors and mistakes, but I don't think that not being mentally tough in situations where it was required was one of our shortcomings.

FISCHER: Coach, doesn't that please you as much as anything looking back at where these kids started out, to where they are now, as far as their mental frame of mind is concerned?

KNIGHT: Yes. There's no question about that, Don. I think that's been a really important move for them to make. It's been instrumental in whatever success we've been able to enjoy to this point. Without having developed a mental toughness that was different than what we had two years ago, we wouldn't come close to being the kind of team we are now.

FISCHER: You also cast the leadership role on these four seniors last year at the end of the campaign. If you could, evaluate them to this point in this season, as far as leaders are concerned.

KNIGHT: They showed last year in the NCAA Tournament that they were very capable. Cheaney, as much as anybody, is responsible for that. He has really come to the forefront in terms of what he wants to do as a leader and what he tries to do with other people from the standpoint of his position as the player on our team.

FISCHER: Can you rank him, at this point, with all the leaders you have had?

KNIGHT: He's as good a combination of leader and player as we have ever had.

FISCHER: Coach, we have some questions sent in letters by listeners. This is from Terre Haute. There seem to be more unfamiliar referees in the Big Ten this year. I thought Big Ten referees worked Big Ten games only, but you see them in other conference games as well. What are the rules?

KNIGHT: We used to have some rules but I don't think we have any anymore. We used to try to limit the number of games that a guy worked during the week to four. Now these guys work five and six games a week, and sometimes they come in here the morning of an afternoon game when I think they should be required to be here the night before. We've had a lot of changes in our officiating, basically to bring new officials that are considered to be really fine officials into the Big Ten. I think we've done some really good things in that regard.

FISCHER: You had one official that did not make the game yesterday because he was weathered out, flying on the day of the ballgame.

KNIGHT: We were very fortunate in getting a really good official, Jerry Petro from Franklin, who actually probably has a bigger schedule with the Big Eight than he does with the Big Ten, although he has worked a lot of Big Ten games. Having him in the game was very important to the administration of the ballgame, and he did a pretty good job in the game.

FISCHER: This next question is from Ligonier. On the 11th before the talk show, they played Dick Vitale's "Talking Roundball." He said that the NCAA needs a five-year rule where freshmen athletes sit out their first year and then become eligible to play four years. Would you agree with something like that?

KNIGHT: No, not at all. I think that's a rule that is put in primarily for kids who probably should not be able to qualify for higher education anyhow. I think that the five-year rule, with a kid sitting out a redshirt year, is sufficient. I don't think it's necessary for all freshmen coming to college to sit out the first year. No, I'd be very much opposed to that.

FISCHER: Our next questioner says that on the January 18th radio show, I mentioned that the team was traveling that night before per Big Ten regulations. What are the rules regarding team travel on game day and the day before?

KNIGHT: There is a requirement in the Big Ten that you be there the night before an afternoon game. I don't think there is a requirement that you be there the night before a night game, however.

FISCHER: Here's the second part of that question. After the Michigan game, a few weeks back, the first Michigan game, you said that you didn't agree with Don when he called it a "great win." You noted that there were only three or four great wins in your tenure at IU I can tell you right now that Coach said "three." Please explain which games you thought were great wins.

Listener, I will answer this for Coach Knight. Those were the three NCAA Championship games.

This was Indiana's second game in 48 hours and third game in seven days. And they were shorthanded due to the loss of Alan Henderson. Meanwhile, the Hoosier's high ranking in the national polls made them a target in every arena they played. Ohio State fans sensed a chance for a high-profile kill today.

This type of schedule is common during the NCAA Tournament, and Bob takes the approach that the team should play through the short preparation time. The short rest should not be a factor to the players.

Knight begins by talking about the Purdue game and then gives his study of the Ohio State Buckeyes.

The things that we tried to emphasize after the Illinois game on Wednesday were good starts in the first half and second half. As we discussed, going into the Purdue game, we had not gotten off to a really good second-half start and had not gotten off to a good first-half start for some time. In the Illinois game we did have a very good start to the first half. I felt that in the Purdue game we got the thing going fairly well in the first half. Actually, we developed as much as a 15-point lead.

I think our overall play and the direction we took after the start of the first half and the start of the second half were pretty good. It took a little while for things to settle down and work themselves out, and then in each case we seemed to move in both halves so that we were able to gain control of the ballgame. We were then able to wind up the game playing it very conservatively and putting them in a very difficult position to have any chance to come back.

We rebounded sufficiently to not have it become a big deficit for us. I think we did enough on the boards to neutralize Purdue, which is a good rebounding team. The board play didn't become such an overwhelming factor that the game was either won or lost on the boards.

We've had some players shoot 20 free throws before, and Greg could thank Purdue for four of them with technical fouls. Over the course of the game, he took 28 free throws which might be the most that we've ever had a player take, at least since I've been at Indiana. There are a couple of things involved in that. One is, at the end of the game as I mentioned a moment ago, the ball was in Greg's hands a lot. They are trying to get the ball back, and we handled it well enough to get it back so they had to resort to some fouls. Greg, with the ball in his hands a lot, was a target for fouling. He's obviously the wrong guy to foul. But more importantly, from our standpoint, during the course of the game, he did a lot of cutting and moving that put him in a position to draw fouls. He took the ball to the bucket hard and wound up shooting a lot of free throws in just working within the confines of what we wanted to do offensively.

Our physical preparation for this game tonight has not been very extensive, Don, because we just felt that after the Purdue game there just wasn't enough time left for us to try to come in and work on Monday and play on Tuesday. So all we've done is walk and talk about Ohio State, walk through things, set up what we want to do at both ends, and try to be as well rested as we possibly can be going into this game tonight.

We need to think of this game tonight first of all in its defensive context for us. We go from Purdue, which is basically an inside oriented team with a very, very good player in Robinson, and we had to take away the inside, first and foremost. Here, there is an inversion of sorts. We now play against a team that has a very good perimeter attack. They will have three people on the perimeter at all times during the game who are very quick, who are very good with the ball. You're not going to take the ball away from any of them. Penetration and shooting, penetration and dropping the ball off to inside people, is a very big part of their offense. Ohio State could say, "All right. When you get the ball, try to beat your man and create something when you do."

We've got to be solid defensively to the point where we don't have to help from our inside coming out and expose the inside part of our defense. Our perimeter defense has got to be good enough to contain people along the perimeter. We're not going to take the ball from these guards. They are just too clever and too good with the basketball. But what we have to do is maintain the kind of positioning that contains the penetration that creates so many things in their offense.

Then too, they have a strong inside game that complements what they do. Again, comparing these two teams, Purdue would use outside shooting to complement its inside game to keep everyone honest. This team uses its inside game in almost the reverse way, just to keep you honest. With their penetration, you can't go out or go all out with penetration because then, they are big enough and quick enough inside that you've got to get some help inside in several situations. Defensively, I obviously have no idea what they will try to do against us. When we played them the first time, they basically played straight man to man against us which is their basic defense and their best defense. But when we played against Penn State, we played against a matchup zone defense that gave us some problems because of our lack of real quick movement against it. Ohio State has played at times, and did a little against us the first time, in that same defensive setup. I imagine, at least early in the game, there will be times when we see it. Depending upon how we react to it and what we do against it will be the determining factor in how much of it is played.

Ohio State presses occasionally, has pressed some teams more than others. What they choose to do in that context as far as we are concerned I wouldn't know. Basically they've got as many as three or four different defensive setups we need to go against. It's going to be important for us to think well, to react well to what's done, and to execute things that are a basic part of our offensive scheme.

The thing that you are really pleased about Pat Graham coming back is that he is a very competitive kid. He is going to play as hard as he can and give you everything that he's got when he plays. He gave us nine minutes against Purdue. As he gets more and more into things from a basketball standpoint, he will be a difficult guy to play against because he can drive, he can shoot, and he cuts well. He probably adds more to us at this point as an offensive player than he does as a defensive player. That still becomes an important addition to us, and we have to try to make the most of that.

GAME SUMMARY

OVERTIME

OHIO STATE 81   INDIANA 77

The winning streak came to an end at 13 for Bob Knight's Hoosiers with the Ohio State Buckeyes pulling out a wild overtime triumph in Columbus. The Hoosiers once again faced a team's best effort, but this time they could not make the most of the opportunities they had to pull it out.

Some of the sparkle this team played with earlier in the season was not present in Columbus that night. On the other hand, Ohio State was primed for the Hoosiers, and the Buckeye fans stormed the floor after the game as if their team won a championship game.

It was cold that night and I left the arena after the press conference. I was surprised that many Buckeye fans were still gathered in the parking lot outside Ohio Stadium and shouting cheers an hour after the game was over.

Poor free throw shooting, which occurred in the only other defeats this year, cropped up in this game as well. And, as it was in the previous two losses, the team's effort was not at the level that Knight felt the team should be putting forth. Perhaps having only one day's rest in between games played a role, but Bob Knight would not use that as an excuse. Knight said after the ballgame that Ohio State simply made fewer mistakes than Indiana, especially when the game was on the line.

For the contest, Greg Graham supplied the primary scoring punch, hitting for

21 points, while freshman Brian Evans added 13. It was also the second straight game that scoring leader Calbert Cheaney was less than his best, with just 12 points. He did pull down 9 rebounds. The Hoosiers failed to score a field goal in the final eight minutes of regulation, and while sizzling from the field in the first half with 57 percent shooting, they hit just 40 percent in the last half.

The story was the same in rebounding, with IU outrebounding the Bucks 21 to 8 in the first half, and then being outrebounded 21 to 17 in the second half. The players seemed to me to be fatigued in the second half and could not capitalize on opportunities.

Another indicator of this was that Indiana had one of its poorest games in turnovers in Big Ten play, with 18 turnovers compared to Ohio State's 13.

This was the first road game that Indiana played without Alan Henderson, and perhaps that was a factor as well. But Indiana was outscored 35-28 in the second half, and went 0-6 in three-point shooting. In the first half, the Hoosiers matched the Buckeyes in every aspect of the game.

The Hoosiers were 13-1 in the Big Ten and 24-3 for the season.

INDIANA

No.	Player	Total FG		3-point				Rebounds									
		FG	FGA	FG	FGA	FT	FTA	Off	Def	Tot	PF	TP	A	TO	Blk	S	Min
22	Bailey, Damon	5	8	0	1	1	2	1	4	5	2	11	4	2	0	0	34
40	Cheaney, Calbert	5	12	0	2	2	2	4	5	9	0	12	0	3	0	1	43
24	Nover, Matt	4	8	0	0	1	4	3	3	6	5	9	0	3	0	0	32
20	Graham, Greg	8	14	2	5	3	5	2	2	4	2	21	4	6	1	0	42
21	Reynolds, Chris	2	3	0	0	4	6	3	2	5	2	8	4	3	0	0	36
34	Evans, Brian	4	11	1	5	4	4	1	4	5	4	13	4	1	0	0	27
30	Leary, Todd	1	2	0	1	1	1	0	2	2	1	3	1	0	0	1	9
33	Graham, Pat	0	2	0	0	0	1	0	0	0	0	0	0	0	0	0	1
25	Knight, Pat	0	0	0	0	0	0	0	0	0	0	0	0	0	0	0	1
	Team							1	1	2							
	TOTALS	29	60	3	14	16	25	15	23	38	16	77	17	18	1	2	225

Total FG%　1st Half .567(17/30)　2nd half .375(9/24)　OT .500(3/6)　Game .483(29/60)　Deadball
3-Pt. FG%　1st Half .500(3/6)　2nd half .000(0/6)　OT .000(0/2)　Game .214(3/14)　Rebounds　8
FT%　1st Half .667(6/9)　2nd half .625(10/16)　OT .000(0/0)　Game .640(16/25)

OHIO STATE

No.	Player	Total FG		3-point				Rebounds									
		FG	FGA	FG	FGA	FT	FTA	Off	Def	Tot	PF	TP	A	TO	Blk	S	Min
34	Funderburke, Lawrence	4	12	0	0	4	9	3	4	7	1	12	1	3	1	0	35
15	Skelton, Jamie	8	17	4	8	2	3	0	3	3	4	22	3	0	0	2	34
41	Watson, Antonio	2	2	0	0	0	0	0	2	2	4	4	0	2	1	0	16
3	Simpson, Greg	4	8	0	3	4	4	0	1	1	3	12	9	2	0	2	41
23	Anderson, Derek	7	8	2	2	4	4	1	2	3	5	20	3	2	0	3	33
40	Dudley, Rickey	0	0	0	0	0	0	0	0	0	0	0	0	0	0	0	6
20	Davis, Alex	3	8	2	4	0	0	2	1	3	3	8	1	0	0	0	22
33	Macon, Charles	1	5	0	0	1	2	2	3	5	3	3	0	3	1	1	26
42	Ratliff, Jimmy	0	0	0	0	0	0	0	0	0	0	0	0	0	0	0	5
31	Brandewie, Tom	0	1	0	0	0	0	0	2	2	1	0	0	0	0	0	7
	Team							1	2	3					1		
	TOTALS	29	61	8	17	15	22	9	20	29	24	81	17	13	3	8	225

Total FG%　1st Half .462(12/26)　2nd half .538(14/26)　OT .333(3/9)　Game .475(29/61)　Deadball
3-Pt. FG%　1st Half .250(2/8)　2nd half .667(4/6)　OT .667(2/3)　Game .471(8/17)　Rebounds　4
FT%　1st Half .833(10/12)　2nd half .429(3/7)　OT .667(2/3)　Game

Officials　　　　Eric harmon, Ed Hightower, Tom Rucker
Tecnical Fouls
Attendance　　13276

Score by
Periods	1	2	OT	OT	Final
Indiana	43	28	6		77
Ohio State	36	35	10		81

Knight opens the show with an analysis of the loss to Ohio State. As you read his comments, you realize that this was a game that Indiana lost because of errors. Knight would not accept any excuses related to lack of rest or the loss of Alan Henderson.

After the difficulty Minnesota caused the Hoosiers earlier in the season at Assembly Hall, it didn't take much to get Knight and his team focused on the re-match game at Minnesota. The Golden Gophers were contenders in Big Ten play, and even Minnesota Governor, Arne Carlson, got in the act with a few pre-game potshots at the Hoosiers.

Coach Knight has talked various times during his radio shows about the big game. This game today is certainly one of the biggest of the season for the Hoosiers.

We got off to a really poor start in Columbus. We didn't handle the ball very well against the press, and I think that over the course of the year, the press has really been an ally for us. When teams have chosen to press us, it has almost invariably been an asset to us offensively because we've scored an awful lot of points against the press.

We threw the ball away a lot. Greg Graham had 6 turnovers in the first 12 minutes of the ballgame, and yet we still survived that to have a chance to go up by as much as 16. I think 14 was the biggest lead we actually had. We missed the one-and-one with a 14-point lead. Things kind of settled down for us then.

Ohio State got into a better shooting rhythm in the second half. They shot pretty well, but we still were able to take a 7 point halftime lead and hold it right down to near four minutes. We had several opportunities to increase that lead to 10 and weren't able to take advantage of the opportunities that we had. What we found ourselves with then was an accumulation of mental and physical errors at the end of the ballgame that made it necessary for us to make a free throw to win the game. The game should have never been in that position, yet it was. We missed the free throw; we missed a tip in. Those are the obvious things that happened in the game.

Other things are not quite as obvious. We didn't keep the ball away from their best shooter at the end of regulation time. We made a foul on a hurried three-point shot that turned an Indiana possession into 2 Ohio State points. We lost track of a shooter again, at a critical point in their offense, with a tie score.

So the game was, for us, more than anything else an accumulation of errors that put it all into one play, one chance for us to win the game, and we didn't capitalize on the chance. I think that Chris Reynolds made an absolutely great play at the end of the game (picking up a foul) to give us a chance to win. Had we had the same kind of play at other points in the ballgame, in terms of his alertness, his seeing the play, his paying attention to what could be done, in the way the floor developed, it would have really made that play unnecessary.

It was just not a good game for us from the standpoint of our alertness and our concentration. I think that we've had stretches like that over the course of the year, but I really believe in this ballgame, right from the early passing against the half-court trap, right on down to losing the man at the end, that this lack of concentration crept into our play throughout the ballgame.

Minnesota will be a very good team today. They are a strange team because they are two different teams. They play a lot better at home than they play on the road. I thought they played pretty well against us in Bloomington, and I think they still made some mistakes in that game that enabled us to get back in it and win the ballgame. At home, for whatever the reason, they are just a different team.

They start out with most of the ingredients necessary to be a really good basketball team. They may not have the kind of outside shooting on the front line that you might like to have. They don't have somebody that can shoot the ball like Evans, for example, but they make up for that with depth, size, and strength. They can really beat you on the boards and can post a lot and can get to the free throw line a lot. We're going to have to be very alert to that.

Their outside shooting comes basically from McDonald and from Leonard, and both of them are very good outside shooters. They play the perimeter and their shooting helps a great deal with the post play because we've got to go out with both of them. It's a big team. McDonald is listed at 6-2, maybe, but he's a big kid, a very strong kid, big arms, pretty big bodied kid. Leonard is a bigger-bodied kid yet. It's not a slow team. I mean it's a good, physical team. I would have felt that Minnesota would have been able to beat Michigan here. Michigan really was not in any danger of losing that ballgame in the last five minutes, which was kind of surprising to me because of the kind of personnel they have.

We're going to have to be able offensively to spread the floor, to be able to drive. I think we have a little advantage in quickness. We're going to have to take advantage of that. Starting with today, we're going to be playing Pat Graham a lot. He's here. We're going to use him. I think I probably made a mistake in the game in Columbus, in not using him a lot more than I did. There's an intensity about Pat's play and there's an intensity in Pat as far as practice is concerned. I'm not sure that I've ever been around a kid that just genuinely enjoys playing basketball more than Pat Graham does. Consequently, I think that's the kind of shot that this team needs. I think we need somebody who has that kind of enthusiasm and shows that kind of enthusiasm playing, and Pat is going to just play from here on for us.

I wouldn't mind at all playing this game up here at a half-court tempo, but I don't think that will be the case. I think this game will be played at a faster tempo. We'll just see how the tempo goes and whether we can play at the tempo. I think that Minnesota will try to play at a very fast tempo. I think they'll try to get the ball down the floor and into the post just as quickly as they can.

We'll go with Pat and Greg Graham at the guards and Evans, Nover and Cheaney inside.

GAME SUMMARY

Indiana 86   Minnesota 75

If there was any question about Bob Knight's basketball team having the character and toughness to win a championship, those doubts were removed with the victory over Minnesota. IU was facing its third game without Alan Henderson and was coming off what could have been a confidence shattering loss to Ohio State on Tuesday. But this IU squad has learned to embrace the challenge, and it took Minnesota's best shot and gave it right back to them.

The buildup the Gophers gave this Big Ten rematch was incredible, and their coach and players made it known that this meeting, after the 4-point loss in Bloomington, was going to be a basketball war.

The Gophers gained an early advantage late in the first half when starters Brian Evans and Calbert Cheaney both got in foul trouble. Then a lineup that included Pat Knight, Todd Leary, and Damon Bailey during the final 7 minutes of the first half, brought the score to a tie at the break. The Hoosiers then exploded on a 21 to 4 run to start the second half, and the game was under control from that point on.

This, again, was a complete team victory with contributions from every player on the roster. Greg Graham led the team in scoring for the third straight game with 19 points, while Damon Bailey and Matt Nover each added 17. Cheaney had 15, and Pat Graham had 9 in his first start. Nover led the rebounding with 9, Bailey handed out 5 assists, and Cheaney picked up 4 steals. IU shot 57 percent while holding the Gophers to 44 percent, and each squad had just 11 turnovers.

For the Hoosiers, the record now stands 25-3, with a Big Ten mark of 14-1, with three games to go.

INDIANA

No.	Player		Total FG FG	Total FG FGA	3-point FG	3-point FGA	FT	FTA	Rebounds Off	Rebounds Def	Rebounds Tot	PF	TP	A	TO	Blk	S	Min
34	Evans, Brian	f	1	3	0	1	0	0	0	4	4	3	2	1	0	0	0	16
40	Cheaney, Calbert	f	5	9	2	3	3	4	0	5	5	3	15	2	3	0	4	32
24	Nover, Matt	c	5	6	0	0	7	8	2	7	9	2	17	0	1	1	0	39
20	Graham, Greg	g	6	9	2	3	5	6	0	2	2	2	19	4	2	0	0	37
33	Graham, Pat	g	4	7	1	2	0	0	0	1	1	3	9	3	2	0	0	27
22	Bailey, Damon		4	8	2	3	7	8	2	2	4	3	17	6	2	0	0	28
25	Knight, Pat		0	1	0	0	1	2	0	1	1	1	1	1	0	0	0	9
30	Leary, Todd		2	4	1	2	1	1	0	0	0	0	6	0	0	0	0	8
21	Reynolds, Chris		0	0	0	0	0	0	0	0	0	1	0	2	1	0	0	4
	Team								1	1	2							
	TOTALS		27	47	8	14	24	29	5	23	28	18	86	19	11	1	4	200

Total FG% 1st Half .500   2nd half .640   Game .574   Deadball
3-Pt. FG% 1st Half .714   2nd half .429   Game .571   Rebounds 1
FT% 1st Half .857   2nd half .800   Game .828

MINNESOTA

No.	Player		Total FG FG	Total FG FGA	3-point FG	3-point FGA	FT	FTA	Rebounds Off	Rebounds Def	Rebounds Tot	PF	TP	A	TO	Blk	S	Min
4	Tubbs, Nate	f	4	10	1	2	0	0	2	4	6	2	9	3	1	0	1	32
34	Carter, Randy	f	6	10	0	0	3	4	7	4	11	4	15	0	3	0	0	25
51	Kolander, Chad	c	0	1	0	0	3	8	3	3	6	4	3	1	0	1	1	17
21	Lenard, Voshon	g	7	15	5	9	3	3	0	2	2	4	22	2	0	0	3	33
10	McDonald, Arriel	g	5	16	2	6	4	4	1	0	1	3	16	4	1	0	2	36
32	Walton, Jayson		2	5	0	0	0	0	0	3	3	3	4	1	2	0	1	15
53	Nzigamasabo, Ernest		2	3	0	0	0	0	1	2	3	2	4	0	0	1	0	17
25	Jackson, Dana		0	0	0	0	0	0	0	1	1	1	0	1	1	0	0	16
3	Wolf, Ryan		0	0	0	0	0	0	0	0	0	2	0	1	2	0	0	6
33	Baker, Kevin		1	1	0	0	0	0	0	0	0	0	2	0	0	0	0	1
11	Crittenden, Hosea		0	0	0	0	0	0	0	0	0	0	0	0	0	0	0	1
30	Roe, Robert		0	0	0	0	0	0	0	0	0	0	0	0	0	0	0	1
	Team								1	0	1				1			
	TOTALS		27	61	8	17	13	19	15	19	34	25	75	13	11	2	8	200

Total FG% 1st Half .452   2nd half .433   Game .443   Deadball
3-Pt. FG% 1st Half .600   2nd half .417   Game .471   Rebounds 2
FT% 1st Half .727   2nd half .625   Game .684

Officials   Phil Bava, Randy Drury, Tom Clark
Technical Fouls
Attendance   16,638

Score by Periods	1	2	OT	OT	Final
Indiana	39	47			86
Minnesota	39	36			75

BOB KNIGHT TALK SHOW
March 1, 1993

The Minnesota game was a big win for the Hoosiers, and once again you see a lighter side of Knight. He talks about the short preparation time for the Ohio State game, but concludes, again, that Indiana should have won the contest. Knight expects to be late for the show and asks assistant coach Dan Dakich to sit in for the beginning of the show.

FISCHER: As you know by now, the Hoosiers won over Minnesota on Saturday knocking off the Golden Gophers, 86 to 75, in Minneapolis. Indiana picked up its 25th win against three defeats and is now 14-1 in the Big Ten.

Here at the very outset of tonight's program, Coach Knight will be here in a minute, Dan Dakich, one of the assistant coaches has joined us.

Dan, I know you guys had to be quite happy coming from Minneapolis on Saturday with that victory under your belt.

DAKICH   We really were, Don. You know it started out as a very tough game. Don, we have a visitor who just came in for the show.

FISCHER: Who's that?

KNIGHT: What's the deal, Fischo?

FISCHER: Coach, I just simply asked Danny to talk a little bit about the Minnesota ballgame and likewise Ohio State, the two ballgames since last week's show, and just your feelings on the way your ball club performed.

KNIGHT: When, Don?

FISCHER: The last two ballgames, on Tuesday and then on Saturday.

KNIGHT: The last two we played?

FISCHER: Yeah. (Laughter)

KNIGHT: Good and bad.

FISCHER: One of the things that I think was interesting going into the Ohio State game was the real problem from an emotional and mental standpoint. We just played a very intense ballgame against Purdue, lost Alan Henderson two days prior to that, and then played Ohio State on Tuesday night. Can you talk a little bit about that? Was it a difficult time for the coaching staff and for the players?

KNIGHT: One of the things that makes basketball a lot different in approach than football is that you have a pretty established routine in football. The game is over on Saturday. Kids get treated for injuries, and one thing and another, on Sunday. Then Monday, Tuesday, Wednesday, Thursday, and Friday are all fairly the same, and you play again on Saturday.

The big thing that separates basketball in terms of preparation is that you don't have anything like that. We had Thursday, Friday, and Saturday, both coaches and players, to get ready for the Purdue game. We took Thursday off. That was reduced to Saturday because Alan Henderson was hurt on Friday. Yet we put into the minds of the players the things that Purdue does offensively and defensively and what we had to do and so forth.

For the Ohio State game, we just had that one day. We played a good and a tough game against Purdue on Sunday, and then had to come right back again and play on Tuesday night. That was a tough thing for us, but that's one of those things that you've got to be able to do. There are a lot of inequities in the basketball schedule in the league. You get the league schedule, and it's all Saturday games, and then television steps in and Saturday games are moved to Sunday and Wednesday games are moved to Tuesday or Thursday. You can wind up with Wednesday-Saturday or Sunday-Tuesday games where both teams might not have the same kind of preparation, as was the case when we played at Ohio State. They had a Saturday to Tuesday, and we had a Sunday to Tuesday.

But, again, over a period of time, that would probably even itself out for you, where you would probably be about the same as anyone else would be over a three or four year period. When it does happen to you, it's a difficult thing.

I think the most difficult game of that nature that we've ever had was in 1984, when we beat North Carolina in the first game of the Regionals at Atlanta. If you will recall, we didn't get done until about 11:30 that night, and we ended up coming back at noon playing when I thought just given a couple more hours, a 4:00 game instead of a 12:00 noon game, would have made a really, really big difference for us.

FISCHER: Coach, your feeling on the way your ball club played at Ohio State.

KNIGHT: Can you hear me all right?

FISCHER: You're echoing a little bit.

KNIGHT: Well, I'm at the refrigerator. I'm getting myself a peach pop here. (Rattling and clattering.) You go ahead and talk for a minute.

FISCHER: Well, I will tell the fans that even though ratings are not at the top of your list to talk about, ratings did come out today. Both the CNN-*USA Today* and the AP polls rank Indiana number two. North Carolina has taken over the number one position.
Coach, are we ready?

KNIGHT: No, I can't find the peach pop.

FISCHER: Did somebody steal it?

KNIGHT: Well, I don't know. I'm kind of mixing a little diet here with some Hawaiian Guava fruit juice. How does that sound?

FISCHER: Just fine, Coach, as long as you are drinking it.

KNIGHT: What we had, Don, were two games, from our standpoint. One was very disappointing and the other one anything but disappointing. Disappointing in the Ohio State game, not in the outcome of the game, but in several of the things we did in the game.

We really started out very poorly against the press, a half-court trap. It's the only time this year, I think, that we haven't turned the press into our advantage. We did somewhat later in the game, but the press hurt us in the first half. We maintained a pretty good position, I thought, throughout most of the ballgame. Ohio State came back a time or two, and we were able to get a little spread to what we were doing. Then at the end, we made some less than good plays. I would have hoped that our play at the end would have been such that we would have made really good plays, that we would have made plays that enabled us to hang on and win the ballgame. But we just didn't, and to Ohio State's credit, they did make some pretty good plays. They made some plays that really enabled them to win the ballgame.

FISCHER: Coach, talk about Minnesota on Saturday, a ballgame that you felt was going to be a very difficult contest.

KNIGHT: Hello. HELLO. Don? I've got a call here from Fuzzy Zoeller, and he wants me to ask you just exactly what you have against golf.

FISCHER: What I have against golf? I have nothing against it. In fact I love the game.

KNIGHT: Well, Fuzzy, he says that he likes it, but I'll tell you one thing he can't do, and that's play it. Yes. Don? Fuzzy wants to know if when you swing, do you inhale or exhale?

FISCHER: I don't know. I've never thought about it.

KNIGHT: He doesn't know. That's the same answer Fuzzy gives, Fischo. Are you guys still out there at the restaurant? OK. Thanks for calling. Well, I'm just telling them what Pfau told me to tell them. Pfau told me to tell them not to give away any of the secrets he gave the team at practice tonight. OK, Fuzz, thanks a lot. Goodbye.

This has got to be kind of an interesting show, Fischo, because nobody knows what's going to happen. My wife comes in and talks, Dakich talks, Fuzzy Zoeller talks. Who knows what's next?

FISCHER: That's true. Coach, give us a quick thought on Minnesota.

KNIGHT: We won.

FISCHER: (Laughter) We'll be back after this two minute time out.
Fischer often takes a commercial break when the show gets out of control and he uses the time to try to settle down Coach Knight. Tonight it did not work.

FISCHER: Coach, just a brief comment, if you would, about the Minnesota ballgame and Indiana's 86-75 win.

KNIGHT: (Phone rings) Hello? Yeah. Hey, Don? They had a meeting. Fuzzy and Pfau and this jerk they have that owns the airplane. They had this meeting, and they fired me. You have to do the show by yourself. I'm going home.

FISCHER: I don't think we want to do that, Mr. Pfau and Mr. Zoeller. I think we want the Coach to be a part of the show for the time being.

KNIGHT: Going back to the Minnesota game, we were all really disappointed at the results of our game in Columbus. Going up to Minnesota, I thought, was a very tough trip for us. Minnesota is a deep, strong physical team. They've got good guard play. We were very fortunate to have been able to win the ballgame here. So Don, that we came up with a win there, we had to be really pleased with the way we played. I think that Pat Graham came back and played well, very pleased that the guys came off the bench the last 8 minutes and played as they did. That really enabled us to get to a point at the half where we had a chance to come out and play well in the second half instead of playing from behind.

FISCHER: One of the real keys in that ballgame, as you have already stated, was the play of Pat Graham, going 27 minutes for the first time. Actually, the first time this year he's played that many minutes.

KNIGHT: Well, he played quite a bit in the Florida State game, the game where he got hurt. But I doubt if he played quite that much. Pat came in, did a really good job at the start of the ballgame. Everybody got a piece of that ballgame. Don, everybody played pretty well.

FISCHER: Looking back, there are a lot of ballgames where everybody played pretty well this year. Certainly the Michigan ballgame also comes to mind.

KNIGHT: It was really important, too, from the standpoint of all of our kids playing, that the Governor of Minnesota got to see each of our players. I know he's a great fan, and he certainly would not want to go to the game without getting to see all of our team play. I was really pleased that he did have that opportunity. I just think that the most envious guy in the world, or at least who I know well, should be Evan Bayh, our Governor. You know he just works his tail off every day handling the things that come up in the State of Indiana, and I think he's really done an excellent job.

Yet you look at the Governor of Minnesota. People up there probably do not even pay attention to who they are going to vote for because there are no problems in Minnesota. All the Governor up there has to do is work on officiating for Big Ten basketball. I would think that if Evan could take a break like that once in awhile, it would be really good for him, but he just doesn't do it. He's busy trying to work on behalf of the people of the State of Indiana. I'm not sure there could be a better job in America than being the Governor of Minnesota.

FISCHER: Let's take some calls this evening. Our first call is from Indianapolis. What encouraged you to become a basketball coach?

KNIGHT: Probably the fact that I wasn't good enough to be a player.

FISCHER: Did anybody kind of push you into that area?

KNIGHT: When I was a kid growing up, my high school football and basketball coaches and a couple of other coaches really took an interest in me and spent a lot of time with me. They took me a lot of places.

I played three sports in high school, football, basketball, and baseball. It just kind of seemed the thing to do. I'm not sure it was the smartest thing to do.

I've really tried to keep my players, as much as I can, out of coaching. I've tried to get them channeled into other areas that I think are going to be lifetime occupations for them rather than coaching. But certainly, as it has turned out, having the opportunity to be here at Indiana, coaching has been a very, very good choice for me.

FISCHER: From Indianapolis, Coach. What characteristics do you look for in high school players as potential IU players?

KNIGHT: There are really three basic things that you would like to have. You'd like to have a kid that first of all is going to work as a student so you are not going to have problems there. Then, you'd like to have a kid that has some combination of quickness and strength. Then we'd like to have a kid that can shoot the ball.

FISCHER: This from Indianapolis. I've seen most of the games in person this year. The Minnesota game was one of the first I've seen on television. I was amazed at how much defensive holding you could see on the replays. Was Minnesota doing what you've seen other teams do, or were they just a more physical ball club?

KNIGHT: This has really bothered me as we've gone through the season. What we've had is a tremendous increase in the hand checking, particularly as far as Calbert Cheaney is concerned. It's at that point where I really felt that our officiating as a whole in the Big Ten this year has declined immensely. I was looking at three games earlier today on tape, just one of which involved us. I just see too many mistakes that are the absolute, short vision of officials. There are mistakes that go against us, or that go against the opponent or go against one of the two teams, when someone else plays.

I think we get hurt more than anybody does because cutting is so much a part of our offense. Cheaney is the heart of it, and when he gets held or grabbed, our whole offense is thrown out of kilter.

FISCHER: Also from Indianapolis. You seemed to move Calbert Cheaney on top in the second half of the Minnesota game, and that seemed to open things up in the middle. Have you done that in the first half of ballgames this year?

KNIGHT: We've done it from time to time, but one of the basic reasons we moved Cheaney is just what we've been talking about, to get him someplace where it was more difficult to hold him than it was along the base line.

FISCHER: This is from Richmond. You usually have Chris Reynolds handle the ball when there is three quarter-court pressing and trapping against your team. In the Ohio State game, it was Greg Graham, and he had a number of turnovers. Could you expound on that?

KNIGHT: The turnovers that Greg had, basically, and I just looked at that film again this morning, were really just poor mistakes on his part. He just did not do a good job handling the basketball. He's a much better ball handler than that. It's impossible to have one person handle the ball against half-court trap. The ball has to go from side to side and then in the middle. There's no way that one person can get the ball in position for you to do something with it. It's much easier to utilize a one man attack against full-court press than it is against half-court.

FISCHER: Again from Indianapolis. Damon Bailey seems to be doing much better coming off the bench than he does when he starts. In your opinion, is this the effect of "bench motivation," or does he just do better watching the game develop before he comes in?

KNIGHT: I think that Damon has played very well when he has started ballgames. Because he played well in this game against Minnesota, and did so coming off the bench, people are a little bit too quick to say that Bailey plays better coming in off the bench.

FISCHER: This is from Joe Falcon of Indianapolis, Coach. He says that the Ohio State timer had a hair trigger when we were holding the ball, but it didn't seem to react very fast when Ohio State had the ball and had a chance to win.

KNIGHT: I didn't think that the timing was handled very well at all for the Ohio State game. I hate to say that, but I've watched it on replays enough to just feel that it just was not very well administered.

FISCHER: He also asks who regulates the timers. Is it the Big Ten or is it the participating school?

KNIGHT: The home team.

FISCHER: Our next caller is from Elkhart, Indiana. During a game, are you equally concerned with exploiting weaknesses of the other team or seeing how your players match up to their opponents?

KNIGHT: I am most concerned about tight shorts.

FISCHER: I think Fuzzy and Ned are right. You're fired. The next question is from Indianapolis. Do you maintain any contact with Lou Watson, and if so, how is he doing?

KNIGHT: I just talked to Lou two days ago and he was doing well. He really follows the team. Lou was just a great supporter and a great friend while we were here together. He's retired now, lives down in Florida. He had the tragedy of his wife passing away earlier this year, but he has planned to come back and spend six or seven months in Bloomington, beginning in the spring so we'll get in a lot of fishing and golf when Lou gets back.

FISCHER: From Unionville, Coach. Is Alan Henderson's injury a torn ligament, a strain, or something else?

KNIGHT: It's a variety of different things, and we are working hard on the rehabilitation of the knee during practice today.

FISCHER: This from Jasper, Coach. At Ohio State, the crowd was warned against throwing debris on the floor and when it happened the second time, no technical foul was called. Why not? The crowd has been warned that a "T" would be called if it happened a second time.

KNIGHT: I think that's something that you would have to write to the Big Ten office to get an answer to.

FISCHER: From Fort Wayne. If Calbert Cheaney breaks the record on Thursday night as Indiana's all-time career scorer and the Big Ten's as well, will you stop the game and present him with the ball?

KNIGHT: If that were to happen, I think we would give Calbert the ball after the game is over. If it's really in the heat of a game, it is kind of a disservice to do something like that. You've got a game going, the opponent has his rhythm and timing going, and I think that it's just a little bit unfair to do that at any time in the course of a contested ballgame. If that were to happen, I think we would see that Calbert is honored for his accomplishment when the game has been completed.

FISCHER: This is from Bloomington. The play at Ohio State involving Chris Reynolds drawing a foul at the end of the game, was that a play that you set up in the huddle, or was it simply an alert play on Chris' part?

KNIGHT: Well, we wanted to set up a screening situation where we had a chance to get the ball as far down the floor as we possibly could with the hope getting a shot. I've seen replays on two games, just in the last week, one involving Auburn and Kentucky, and another involving Arizona and Syracuse where with a second and a half to go, Syracuse was able to get a shot from base line to the other end of the floor that won a game, and Auburn was able to get a shot that just barely missed winning the game. So that was essentially what we were trying to do, and I think the fact that Chris got to the free throw line to give us an opportunity to win the game was far more the result of Chris' quick thinking and his recognizing opportunity out there than anything else.

FISCHER: This is from Madison, Indiana. How did Pat Graham manage to stay in shape throughout this season when he had a broken foot?

KNIGHT: He did a lot of work on the bicycle and worked with various devices that we have here, trying to maintain a physical conditioning and enabling him to play.

FISCHER: From Richmond, Indiana. Regarding Calbert Cheaney's play in the last three ballgames, Coach, is he just a tired player at this point in the season, or is he struggling with his shot right now?

KNIGHT: I think there is a combination of a lot of things right now. Calbert is worn down a little bit. I think he is tired. I think that people are really putting a lot more into playing against Calbert. You've got to keep in mind in these last three games we have scored fairly well. We've scored 93. The 71 in regulation time against Ohio State was by far our low, and then 86 against Minnesota. At least in the Purdue and Minnesota games we were scoring in such a way that even though Calbert didn't have quite the production he has had in other games in terms of total points, the total point total for Indiana was pretty good.

KNIGHT: Don, let me say just this to you before we close. It was another really enjoyable Monday night with you, made so for old Coach Knight because of the efforts and the play of our players Saturday afternoon at Minnesota. I simply close by saying that we have not had many "guttier" performances for many games in all the time that I've been here where the kids put more on the line and gave more of themselves than they did in the game against Minnesota.

The game against Northwestern had a storybook setting. Several milestones were converging on this one game. Indiana had a chance to clinch a tie for the Big Ten Championship with a win. Calbert Cheaney was only a few points away from becoming Indiana's all time leading scorer and a few more points from breaking the all-time Big Ten scoring mark held by Glenn Rice of Michigan.

To add to the excitement, Knight invited actor Nick Nolte to visit the IU team for a week to prepare for a basketball movie he was starring in, "Blue Chips." Nolte's presence added Hollywood glitz to the game and the show that was about to play out in Bloomington.

Nolte's presence had the added effect of keeping everyone loose, including Bob Knight. Nolte took some of the spotlight off Chaney and the Big Ten Championship that was about to be.

I was at the practices that Nolte and his producer attended. Nolte studied every thing Knight did, on and off the court, in order to develop his role for the movie. During the game, Nolte had his own camera crew filming Knight and the crowd and the players on the bench.

Knight, an accomplished showman in his own right, produced his own show for Nolte, giving him a view of Hollywood in Indiana. Coach Knight demonstrated how to fire up a team before a game for Nolte, and gave one of his most emotional pre-game talks of the season to his players. The players and assistant coaches were smiling and also shaking their heads when they walked out of the locker room after Knight's speech. They were still talking about it on the basketball court as they warmed up for the game.

Knight begins by talking more about the Minnesota game and then about the preparation for tonight's contest.

When I talked about the Minnesota game being a "gutty" performance, I think there are a lot of things that go into it. We're coming off a loss, and none of us were particularly pleased with our performance at Ohio State, players, coaches, anybody. It was a game that we felt was really very, very important to us in the overall scheme of things in the Big Ten. We've kind of got our backs to the wall, if we go up and lose at Minnesota. It is then a dead heat again between Indiana and Michigan, and Illinois is still very much in the picture at that time.

Being able to go up there and play well and have a chance to win was going to be a tough thing for us to do. Then by being able to win, as we did, I thought that our players did a great job against a very physical team, a team that for all intents and purposes is much better on paper physically than our own team is. It's a team that would really be a very, very tough team on the boards, one that could, if anything, maybe just beat us through its strength and its depth on the backboard.

I thought we were able to counteract their inside strength with some pretty timely shooting on occasion. We were able to have some movement, do some things through the course of our offense that put us in position to score some points. Being able to score 85 or 86 points, whatever it was, I thought was important to us. Offense becomes a key to us now. We got some really good help from Pat Graham, but everybody in the ballgame helped as well.

"Gutty" because we were in a little bit of foul trouble in the beginning. Both Evans and Cheaney had two fouls very early in the ballgame. We played the last seven or eight minutes of the half without Cheaney in the ballgame. I think that Graham's foot is going to be sore, and Pat seems to have played through it real well. He seems to have been very much alert and ready to play, ready to do the things that we have to have done.

Our guys in the game at that time actually wiped out a 6-point deficit and made it a tie ballgame at the break. It's a lot easier for us in those circumstances to go out the second half, playing from scratch, than it is to have to overcome an 8-point lead or a 10-point lead, or whatever it might be. We just did not have to do that in this ballgame because of the job that our players did. The ones in the ballgame at the end of the first half.

I think this was one of two significant parts of the game. When we started the second half with the kind of offensive movement and the sort of shot development that we had, that also became very good for us.

Northwestern, on the other hand, has been a team, over the years that has always knocked on the door and has had a tough time getting into the house. They have had some problems with injuries and some defections that have kept them from being as good as they might have been. Yet they are a team that in every game we have played against them has had some very good moments. They've been a team that tries to take advantage of what we do defensively. They back cut a lot, they try to get the ball cutting to the basket. Our defense has got to do a much better job defending that kind of movement here tonight than we did when we played up at Evanston earlier in the year.

Dewey Williams from Indianapolis has taken Howell's place, and Williams is a good shooter, has a very nice touch out at 15 or 17 feet. Rankin, I think, remains one of two keys to what Northwestern does offensively because he's a very good post man.

The second key, from a scoring standpoint, is Neloms. Neloms has had some very big games for them over the course of his time at Northwestern. The scoring of Rankin and Neloms is supplemented by Baldwin's ability to penetrate and hit the shot during penetration. Baldwin has been a very, very good guard at Northwestern. He is alert, opportunistic on the defensive end, and a very, very good player on the offensive end with his penetration and ability to go either way.

Fischer then asks about having a chance to clinch a tie for the Big Ten Championship.

From a conference standpoint, the first thing we are after is to insure ourselves of a first place finish. Having the opportunity to do that is, like I said a little while ago about playing against Minnesota, having the opportunity to win, and then being able to go on and in fact win the ballgame.

Here tonight, this becomes maybe the 13th time or 14th time that we have had a chance to get a piece of the conference championship during the season. As I said, that's always our objective, and I am certainly pleased that we have an opportunity to do that tonight.

I know that Don Fischer is concerned about the lineup, and I want Don to know that we'll have a good lineup tonight.

GAME SUMMARY

INDIANA 98   NORTHWESTERN 69

Indiana's victory over the Northwestern Wildcats assured the Hoosiers of a tie for the Big Ten Championship and an opportunity to win it outright in Wednesday night's ballgame with Michigan State. The victory over Northwestern was an 98-69 triumph, and the big star of that ballgame was Calbert Cheaney who scored 35 points.

With this performance, Calbert became Indiana's all time career scoring leader and the Big Ten's all time career scoring leader; in fact, he needed just 10 to pass the Big Ten record held by Glenn Rice of Michigan and just 6 to pass Steve Alford as the all-time leading Indiana scorer. Calbert had an outstanding ballgame

Indiana was helped as well by Greg Graham who had 19 points. Pat Graham had 11. Pat continues to play well in his role in the last two ballgames as a starter, after being out for two months with the foot injury that he suffered in the third game of the season against Florida State.

IU hit 12 unanswered points to break it open at the start of the second half. The contest was never in question. The Hoosiers hit a phenomenal 18 of 23 shots, 78 percent, in that final 20 minutes. For the ballgame, IU ended with 60 percent from the field. Northwestern was held to 46 percent in the contest. Indiana was also able to out rebound the Wildcats 37 to 28. IU had only 11 turnovers in the ballgame, while forcing Northwestern to 15.

The Hoosiers are now 26-3 on the season, and they have clinched no less than a tie for the Big Ten Championship with the win over Northwestern. They are ranked number one in the country, and have six days off to prepare for their next ballgame at home with Michigan State to close out the home portion of this year's campaign.

NORTHWESTERN

No.	Player		Total FG		3-point		FT	FTA	Rebounds			PF	TP	A	TO	Blk	S	Min
			FG	FGA	FG	FGA	FT	FTA	Off	Def	Tot	PF	TP	A	TO	Blk	S	Min
4	Neloms, Cedric	f	8	13	2	3	5	5	2	3	5	4	23	2	4	0	0	26
44	Williams, Dewey	f	2	5	0	0	0	0	0	2	2	2	4	0	1	2	1	17
55	rankin, Kevin	c	5	13	0	0	0	0	1	2	3	3	10	2	4	0	0	29
23	Baldwin, Pat	g	3	6	0	1	2	2	0	4	4	3	8	6	1	0	0	33
30	Kirkpatrick, Kip	g	4	5	0	0	2	2	1	2	3	4	10	4	0	0	2	31
3	Purdy, Matt		1	2	1	2	0	0	0	1	1	1	3	3	1	0	0	11
40	Howell, Charles		2	6	0	0	0	0	1	0	1	1	4	0	0	0	0	9
24	Lee, Dion		0	5	0	2	0	1	1	5	6	1	0	1	2	0	1	19
34	Rayford, T.J.		2	3	0	0	0	2	1	0	1	2	4	0	0	0	0	14
22	Simpson, Eric		0	0	0	0	0	0	0	0	0	1	0	0	1	0	1	4
33	Yonke, Bret		1	2	1	1	0	0	0	1	1	0	3	0	1	0	0	5
10	Ling, tony		0	0	0	0	0	0	0	0	0	0	0	0	0	0	0	1
12	Kreamer, Tommy		0	0	0	0	0	0	0	0	0	0	0	0	0	0	0	1
	Team								1	0	1							
	TOTALS		28	60	4	9	9	12	8	20	28	22	69	18	15	2	5	200

Total FG% 1st Half .517(15/29)   2nd half .419(13/31)   Game .467(28/60)   Deadball
3-Pt. FG% 1st Half .250(1/4)   2nd half .600(3/5)   Game .444(4/9)   Rebounds ___1
FT% 1st Half .571(4/7)   2nd half 1.00(5/5)   Game .750(9/12)

INDIANA

No.	Player		Total FG		3-point		FT	FTA	Rebounds			PF	TP	A	TO	Blk	S	Min
			FG	FGA	FG	FGA	FT	FTA	Off	Def	Tot	PF	TP	A	TO	Blk	S	Min
33	Graham, Pat	f	5	9	0	2	1	2	0	3	3	2	11	1	1	0	2	23
40	Cheaney, Calbert	f	14	19	3	4	4	6	5	1	6	3	35	1	3	2	1	34
24	Nover, Matt	c	3	4	0	0	2	3	1	4	5	1	8	3	0	0	0	29
20	Graham, Greg	g	5	10	4	6	5	6	1	3	4	0	19	6	0	0	1	30
22	Bailey, Damon	g	3	6	1	3	2	4	1	6	7	2	9	7	4	0	0	29
30	Leary, Todd		2	5	1	3	2	2	0	0	0	1	7	0	0	0	0	9
21	Reynolds, Chris		2	2	0	0	2	5	0	1	1	1	6	4	0	0	2	20
34	Evans, Brian		0	2	0	1	1	2	1	5	6	2	1	0	1	0	0	18
25	Knight, Pat		1	1	0	0	0	0	0	1	1	1	2	2	2	0	1	8
	Team								2	2	4							
	TOTALS		35	58	9	19	19	30	11	26	37	13	98	24	11	2	7	200

Total FG% 1st Half .486(17/35)   2nd half .783(18/23)   Game .603(35/58)   Deadball
3-Pt. FG% 1st Half .385(5/13)   2nd half .667(4/6)   Game .474(9/19)   Rebounds ___3
FT% 1st Half .545(6/11)   2nd half .684(13/19)   Game .633(19/30)

Officials   Ed Hightower, Tom O'Neill, Ted Valintine
Technical Fouls
Attendance   16,704

Score by Periods	1	2	OT	OT	Final
Northwestern	35	34			69
Indiana	45	53			98

BOB KNIGHT TALK SHOW
March 8, 1993

FISCHER: Coach, I know this has been kind of an interesting week for you since you have but one ballgame since we last talked. That's been somewhat unique because you did have five ballgames in 14 days at one point.

KNIGHT: Correct, Don.

FISCHER: Coach, can you talk a little bit about that Wildcat win on Thursday night of last week?

KNIGHT: Good for us.

FISCHER: How good was it?

KNIGHT: Real good.

FISCHER: (Laughter) Any more elaboration on that particular game whatsoever?

KNIGHT: I thought that the one thing we wanted to do was have a really good evening for Calbert to set that scoring record. Now any time a kid sets an individual record, particularly here, I think it's the result of an extremely good team effort. I think that was definitely the case with Calbert's scoring record. We wanted it to be a night that everybody could enjoy and everybody could remember, and I think it turned out to be that kind of a night.

FISCHER: Coach, it was interesting that you gave the ball to Ed Hightower to present it to Calbert during one of those time out periods.

KNIGHT: Well, Eddie has been an official in the league as long as Calbert has played. He's a very good official and a very good person along with it. I think that Eddie appreciated the opportunity to do that. After all, the referee is in charge of the game, the game ball is his, and for it to be given to Calbert, what could be more appropriate than the referee giving him the ball?

FISCHER: Coach, one final note on that ballgame. It did give you no less than a tie for the Big Ten Championship. I know that that's a goal that your ball club, of course, shoots for every season.

KNIGHT: Every time that we go into a season, our major objective is to have a chance to win the Big Ten Championship. We get into a position to be able to win it, we are obviously pleased, but even more so when we have a chance to finish first.

FISCHER: Let's go to this call from Indianapolis, Coach. Do you think Quinn Buckner taking the coaching job with the Dallas Mavericks was a good move for him?

KNIGHT: Don, I think it was a good move for him. I think that he'll do well with the job.

FISCHER: Again from Indianapolis. What is the progress of Alan Henderson's rehabilitation?

KNIGHT: He's coming along really well at this time.

FISCHER: This is from Carmel, Coach. The caller would like to know about Nick Nolte's presence at Indiana and what he's really like.

KNIGHT: Good guy. Good guy. He needs a haircut, and he has to have a better wardrobe than he has right now if he's going to be a coach in the movies. Bad clothes, but a really good guy. Really good guy. Very impressive guy.

He has two very impressive two guys with him. Billy Cross is the brains behind the movie industry. Bill Freiken is a great, great director, a really good person and outstanding director. A very good guy. He overrates "French Connection" however.

FISCHER: This is from Indianapolis, Coach. The managers at Indiana seem to get index cards from the scorers' bench and give them to the assistant coaches. What kind of information is on those cards, and what are you tracking?

KNIGHT: They're Bingo cards. We have a little Bingo game at the north end of Assembly Hall.

FISCHER: All right. (Laughter) We have the studio in stitches.

KNIGHT: On the call about the scorers' table. We get the numbers of the opponent's players that are substituted and in the game at that time, If we have any matchup changes to make, we make them then rather than on the floor when we might see that Smith is in for Jones and we haven't talked about that change in the lineup. So that's what the caller is seeing.

Let me go back to Nick Nolte being down here. It is truly interesting listening to how he prepares for the various roles that he has had. The questions are interesting that we have all asked, both of Nick and of Billy Freiken, relative to the things that Bill has directed and those roles that Nick has played in various films. Nick is a very thorough, extremely thorough person in his preparation. He is a great lesson for preparation.

We had Nick and Bill this afternoon talk to our players and answer questions. Of course the players have seen Nick in a lot of films, and they have seen some of Bill's films, "French Connection", and several others. They answered a lot of questions about people they see and how films are put together. It was a very, very interesting thing for our players. Nick is one of the very top people in the acting profession and Bill has certainly long been recognized as one of the best directors in Hollywood.

Giving our players a chance to spend time with the two of them was really good. Then Nick has a man that has worked with him for 20 years and has been in an awful lot of things on his own as an actor, Billy Cross, who was the third person in the party that has been with us for this past week. Bill does a lot of the help with Nick in his preparation for roles and will be in this film, "Blue Chips," in which Nick will be playing a college coach. Bill Freiken will be directing it, and Billy Cross will play the role of Nick's assistant in that film.

FISCHER: Coach, I think I saw in the Bloomington paper that you and the four seniors will have an opportunity to perform in that movie. Is that correct?

KNIGHT: Well, that depends on whether or not that interferes with my fishing schedule in July.

FISCHER: This is from Plainfield, Indiana, Coach. With Alan Henderson out, are there any plans or would a certain kind of . . . .

KNIGHT: No. No. No.

FISCHER: All right. This is from . . .

KNIGHT: Go ahead and finish the question, but the answer is "NO."

FISCHER: He wanted to know if any type of ball club would present any kind of a situation where you might be interested in using a zone defense.

KNIGHT: That's already been answered.

FISCHER: From Greenfield. Why isn't Todd Leary getting more playing time with the statistics he has been posting?

KNIGHT: I think Todd has played quite a bit. I think Todd has made a major contribution to our squad this year.

FISCHER: From Speedway, Indiana. Without Henderson's absence, would Pat Graham have come back to play as soon as he has?

KNIGHT: We actually should have brought Pat Graham back to play in the Illinois game. We brought him back one game later than we probably should have. The answer to that is definitely "yes."

FISCHER: This is from Indianapolis. I seem to recollect that you and Bill Foster did shake hands at the end of your ballgame, did you not?

KNIGHT: We certainly did.

FISCHER: That's what I thought. I don't know where the caller got the idea that you hadn't. This question is from . . .

KNIGHT: Why would that be such a big deal? I get a little bit tired of "you don't shake hands the right way" or "you don't do this or that." What, in fact, is there about shaking hands before the game or after the game. It certainly isn't going to bother me if somebody doesn't want to shake hands with me. People who pick something apart that is a totally meaningless thing that has no ulterior motive and no negative connotation to it at all, wears a little bit thin on me over the years.

FISCHER: I agree with that. This is from Indianapolis. Was there any play that stands out in your mind . . . .

KNIGHT: Let's get some better questions. Those are the kind of questions you ought to send to some other school in the conference.

FISCHER: This is from Indianapolis, Coach. Was there any play that stands out in your mind as being critical or a turning point in a game this particular season?

KNIGHT: Well, I think that no single play ever determines the outcome of a game. It may determine the outcome of the game because of the score at the end of the ballgame like a shot made or a shot missed. But there have been so many plays prior to that that have allowed the game to develop as it has, that no single play can ever be singled out as the turning point. There are periods in the game, the start of the game, the start of the second half, a particular period at the end of the half, that have been very important in the outcome of the game, but not singular plays.

FISCHER: This is from Indianapolis, Coach. Why didn't the Michigan players get called for unsportsmanlike conduct when they made smart comments on the floor to other players and to the officials?

KNIGHT: You would have to ask the officials of the games that. I have no way of knowing what was said or anything else.

FISCHER: This is from Indianapolis. What is the best team you faced so far this season?

KNIGHT: There have been a lot of good teams that we have played against. For example, a team that has not had a great record over the course of the season but played very well against us was Ohio State.

FISCHER: This is from French Lick, Coach. You visited the Southridge Sectional over the weekend. Were you looking at any one particular player?

KNIGHT: No.

FISCHER: This is from Danville, Indiana. A lot of people were calling for Gene Keady's firing after Purdue's loss to Northwestern. Do you think wins and losses are the only criteria for keeping coaches, and do you think a coach's union will help coaches?

KNIGHT: There won't ever be a coach's union. That's the same thing that we were talking about a moment ago, relative to hand shakes. I didn't hear about anybody that called for anyone's firing. Coach Keady has done an outstanding job with his team over the years and will continue to do that for as long as he's at Purdue.

FISCHER: This is from Bainbridge. The caller says that on your TV talk show, you talked about some surgery you had recently. Are you feeling well? *(Note: Knight said on an Indianapolis talk show that he had a "testicular tuck.")*

KNIGHT: What surgery was that?

FISCHER: I don't know. I assume this guy heard you on some other show because I didn't know anything about it. Apparently you haven't had surgery.

KNIGHT: It might have been surgery to repair my memory, but I forgot.

FISCHER: This is from . . .

KNIGHT: That went over Fischer's head.

FISCHER: Concerning scholarships.

KNIGHT: Did you hear that, Fischer? I had surgery to repair my memory, but I forgot.

FISCHER: I heard you, but I didn't think it was that funny. This is from Rushville. Concerning scholarships, Kelsey Mucker is headed for IU on what he understands is a three-sport scholarship.

KNIGHT: There are no three-sport scholarships because of the way things are set up in the Big Ten. Kelsey will be attending Indiana on a football scholarship and will have the opportunity to play either basketball or baseball in addition to playing football.

FISCHER: All right. This is from Indianapolis, Coach. How many different structured offenses does Indiana run?

KNIGHT: We use different alignments. We put our players in different positions on the floor and do different things from different alignments, but basically the principles of our offense, regardless of the alignments, are all constant, from one alignment to the other.

FISCHER: Our next caller is from Richmond. Is the game film that you review the same as the TV coverage film that is aired?

KNIGHT: It's a little better. It's a wider angle and a little bit more inclusive than the TV shots, but the TV shot is actually pretty good. We do all of our scouting using TV tapes, but the game tape is shot from way up in the top of Assembly Hall.

FISCHER: This is from Indianapolis. Did you and your staff have any idea of the potential of Calbert Cheaney when he was recruited, and what were the indicators?

KNIGHT: We recruited him because we thought he was going to be a very good basketball player. He could shoot the ball, he could move with the ball. There are a lot of things that he could do with the ball. He wasn't nearly as aggressive as he has become, nor did he play as hard as he has played here.

FISCHER: This is from Oakland City, Coach. One Big Ten coach said that Greg Graham is the best defensive player in the Big Ten. Would you tend to agree?

KNIGHT: No, I don't think so. I don't think Greg Graham is the best defensive player on the Indiana team.

FISCHER: Who would that be, Coach?

KNIGHT: Well, who asked that question?

FISCHER: A guy from Oakland City.

KNIGHT: Well, who asked the question about who the best defensive player would be?

FISCHER: I did.

KNIGHT: I don't have any interest in your questions.

FISCHER: This is from Evansville. When IU is on defense, what are the execution keys fans should look for?

KNIGHT: Well, are we able to maintain fairly good position on the man with the ball, or does he get past our guards? Does he get past us and penetrate? When the ball goes inside, do we get in a good help position? Are there baskets made on back cuts or baskets made on cuts away from the ball where we have guys getting beat when they are not playing the basketball? What kind of a job have we done on taking away or cutting down the second-effort shots?

FISCHER: This is from Bloomington. When Ewe Blab was at IU, you commented that you were trying to teach him a good hook shot. The hook shot doesn't appear to be used much anymore. Why would that be?

KNIGHT: It will be when Todd Lindeman plays.

FISCHER: This is from Indianapolis, Coach. What are your thoughts on the Michigan State ball club you face on Wednesday?

KNIGHT: Michigan State has been an interesting team. It probably has not been real interesting for Heathcote in a number of ways, but interesting to watch from an outsider's point of view. They have played extremely well against a lot of good basketball teams—most recently, against Michigan, a game in which, at Ann Arbor, they had a chance to win at the buzzer.

They are a strong team. Peplowski and Miller, 270 and 275. A very good shooter and offensive player in Respert. Weshinskey is a good offensive player and Snow is a good defender with an excellent ability to drive the ball.

FISCHER: This is from Greensburg. Concerning Calbert Cheaney's new scoring record, will points scored during NCAA Tourney play count in that record?

KNIGHT: Yes, they will.

FISCHER: This from Indianapolis. Do you think Northwestern will be more of a contender in the Big Ten next year?

KNIGHT: Well, when I think about what's going to happen in the future, the thing I'm most concerned about is whether I'll catch any fish in July and August.

FISCHER: This is from Indianapolis. Do you think that a team with an 8 and 10 record in the Big Ten should be able to be invited to the NCAA Tournament?

KNIGHT: It all depends on what its record prior to the Big Ten has been. The problem with making rules on conference records is this. If you say a team has to have an above 500 record in conference play to get there, all right? So many of the tournaments that exist at the end of the season in so many leagues enable a team with a relatively average or mediocre record to wind up winning the tournament and the bid to the NCAA. So there is an avenue for that team to get to the NCAA. But not an avenue for a good team in a very good conference like ours that might not have a 500 season within the conference.

I think it would be much fairer to make a ruling like that against conference teams.

FISCHER: All right. That's all the time we have for this segment tonight, Coach. I appreciate your being with us. Any final thoughts?

KNIGHT: Yes. I do have. It's really enjoyable to be with you again, Don. I appreciate the opportunity to do so. We have already cast you as the broadcaster in "Blue Chips." You'll be broadcasting Western University's games, and also, Don, Bill Freiken has done a great thing with the game. He's going to have interpreters in four different languages explain the game to the press.

A BIG TEN CHAMPIONSHIP FOR SENIOR NIGHT

"OUR FIRST
OBJECTIVE IS
ALWAYS TO
WIN THE
BIG TEN
CHAMPIONSHIP."

**Michigan State
Wisconsin**

Indiana vs. Michigan State
March 10, 1993
Bloomington
Pre-game Show

The last home game of the season is senior night at Indiana. This is a very special evening for the players and many of the 16,000 fans will stay after the game to pay tribute to the players who are graduating. Calbert Cheaney, Greg Graham, Matt Nover and Chris Reynolds have the honors tonight. After the game, Coach Knight says a few words about each senior and then the seniors have the microphone and a chance to thank family, coaches, teammates and IU fans.

To add to the excitement of senior night, a victory over Michigan State will wrap up the Big Ten Championship for Indiana, and give the Hoosiers a good shot at the top seed in the NCAA's and the number one ranking in the regular season college basketball polls. So the entire team has an opportunity to present a cherished gift to the seniors on this last night before a home crowd and a Hollywood ending for their coach.

I have included Don Fischer's questions in this Pre-game Show since they serve to pull together the season for Indiana and Coach Knight.

FISCHER: This is the last regular season home ballgame for this Indiana basketball team this year. Could we talk about last week's ballgame with Northwestern and the fact that you played just one ballgame in a week's time which has been most unusual for this club in the last three or four weeks?

KNIGHT: First of all, having the time to rest and having days to use as either practice days or non-practice days has been a really good thing for us. Obviously, we will know tonight how good it has been. I think this is a team that needed some rest, it needed some break days, and we were able to get that here after the Minnesota game and going into this game here tonight with Michigan State.

We took off the day immediately following the Minnesota game, which was Sunday, and then our practices were very limited going into the Northwestern game. Then we took off two days, actually a 48 hour period, with just a day's break from when we finished practice, about 3:30 Saturday, until Monday, at the same time when we started preparing for tonight's game. That came after a Friday away from basketball after the Northwestern game. I think from the standpoint of rest and where we should be in terms of freedom from both mental and physical fatigue, we're about as good right now as I think we possibly could be. Whether that will be enough for the ballgame tonight, we'll find out.

FISCHER: Coach, you clinched a tie for the Big Ten Championship after your game against Northwestern last Thursday night. That had to be pleasing for not only you and the staff but for the ball players as well.

KNIGHT: Don, you've been with us since I've been here, and our first objective is always to win the Big Ten Championship. When we are in a position and have the opportunity to compete for the Championship, then it becomes a very interesting season for us. When we actually get to a point where we are assured of finishing in first place, then we are obviously very pleased with that.

An interesting thing over the years, 22 seasons, is the number of teams that have finished ahead of us in the Big Ten. An example is these last three years, now that we've added Penn State to the number, there would have been 28 opportunities for teams to finish ahead of us in the last three years. Only one has done that. Only one out of 28 has finished in front of us in league standing. That's something that we try to keep track of on a yearly basis. Eleven seasons, nobody has finished in front of us, and there are four or five other times probably that only one team has finished in front of us. So we take the whole thing together and add up the number of years times nine, which is the number of chances teams have to finish in front of us each year, and now with Penn State, ten chances. Then there's the relatively small number in terms of percentages, where teams have finished in front of us, and that might be the best mark of our teams during the entire time that I've been here.

A mark, obviously that you have never thought of before nor anyone else in the news media.

FISCHER: Bob, tonight you take on a Michigan State ball club that I guess could be considered the hard luck basketball team of the Big Ten this year. Here's a team that has lost ten ballgames, eight of those have been in overtime or by four points or less. Talk a little bit about this Michigan State ball club.

KNIGHT: Michigan State, first of all, can play two different teams, Don. It's a team that can play big or it's a team that can play small, depending upon what they're looking for. Miller and Peplowski give them two very strong people in the ballgame. That could be a real problem for us tonight. It could be a problem for them trying to defend us with bigger, stronger, but slower people. Whether it becomes strength's advantage or quickness' advantage, we'll have to see.

Respert gives them an outstanding perimeter scorer. I use the word "scorer" rather than "shooter" because he drives the ball well, he gets in on the break, he scores about every way you can. Then Weshinskey is a very, very good shooter from outside. Snow is a good defensive player. They've got good people coming in off the bench. Stephens is a player that I think is very much improved. He's had a pretty good senior year, and, as you said, they've been a hard luck team as far as scores are concerned.

They've lost a couple of times in overtime. They've lost by two here or three there, and they are really probably a half dozen plays away from being eleven and five instead of being six and ten.

FISCHER: Coach, what about their defensive play? Apparently, it's been pretty strong. At least from a field goal percentage standpoint, they lead the Big Ten in keeping the opponents down to around 40 percent.

KNIGHT: They have played a defense that has made it difficult to get to the basket, where the highest percentage shots are. They have done a very good job of blocking out, which cuts down on second effort or third effort shots. When they keep an opponent from going to the bucket and the rebounding follow up shot, then they have taken away some of the better shot opportunities that the other team has.

FISCHER: Bob, it's always a very special evening, especially for the four seniors on your basketball team, this being their final, regular basketball game here at Assembly Hall. Just some thoughts about these senior kids that you have as a part of your program this year.

KNIGHT: Obviously they have been very, very good for us, both on the floor and off the floor. This has been a great run with these players, particularly these last three years. Their freshman year was one of understanding and getting acclimated to what the Big Ten was all about. When you look at the record that they have compiled over these last three years, with the exception of the Ohio State team in '60, '61, and '62, and our Indiana team in '74, '75, and '76, it very well may be as good a three year record as anybody has ever compiled in the Big Ten.

So as we say goodbye on the home floor to these four seniors tonight, we do so realizing that they leave, individually and collectively, a lot of tremendous contributions to Indiana basketball and a lot of great memories to all of us as fans.

GAME SUMMARY

INDIANA 99   MICHIGAN STATE 68

Calbert Cheaney, Matt Nover, Greg Graham, and Chris Reynolds set the stage for memorable senior night by scoring 66 of Indiana's 99 points in a near perfect game against Michigan State. In the process, they give Indiana University another outright Big Ten Championship. This was an emotional, standing-room-only crowd at Assembly Hall, and IU's four seniors played exceptionally well for the occasion. Greg Graham fired a career high equaling 32 points. Calbert Cheaney had 17, Matt Nover had 15, and Chris Reynolds added 6, with 4 assists.

They each took their turn at the microphone at post-game ceremonies, thanking their family, teammates, and the fans for their support throughout their college careers.

Indiana conducted a first half clinic, drilling 66 percent of their shots, including seven of 12 three-pointers, to open a 26-point lead against the Big Ten's best defense. Then, the Hoosiers coasted the rest of the way in wrapping up the school's 19th conference title and 11th under Bob Knight.

For the game, Indiana hit 61 percent while holding Michigan State to 47 percent. From three-point range, Indiana hit ten of 19 three-point attempts, Michigan State only 1 of 6 in that area, and Indiana also conquered the free throw stripe with 19 attempts and connecting on 17. Michigan State did win the rebounding category with 35 boards to IU's 24. Indiana had only 6 turnovers in the entire game compared to 15 for Michigan State.

The victory closed out the home schedule for the Hoosiers, leaving just Sunday's road trip to Wisconsin, leading into NCAA postseason tournament play. The Hoosiers can become only the second team in conference history to record a 17-1 league record with a victory over the Badgers on Sunday.

Nick Nolte is still in Bloomington studying Coach Knight and Knight continues to show the successful actor and his directors a dramatic and exciting real-life production of what college basketball can be to players, coaches and fans.

With Knight's unique sense of timing and showmanship and with the game decided, he pulled the seniors out, one at a time over the last few minutes of play to thunderous standing ovations. Then with emotion in Assembly Hall already at an unbelievable high, and with just five seconds remaining in the game, Knight put Alan Henderson in the game for a token appearance. Henderson brought the house down as he stepped to the scorers table. Knight provided his own script for a perfect end to the season in Bloomington.

Almost all of the 16,000 in attendance stayed to see Jim Delaney, the Big Ten Commissioner, present the Championship trophy to the seniors and then to hear Knight's and the seniors' comments.

Thirty minutes after the game ended, Assembly Hall was still full and the fans were cheering for the seniors as loudly as they did during the game. I was sitting at the end of the press table, near the visitor's locker room. I happened to see the Michigan State players began to leave their locker room and head for their bus. When they saw the huge turnout for the ceremony, and Knight making his comments, many stayed to see the post game events.

Nick Nolte came to Bloomington to prepare for his own movie, "Blue Chips." He saw a unique display of showmanship and drama as Knight orchestrated the past two home games and this grand finale for the seniors.

MICHIGAN STATE

No.	Player	Total FG		3-point		FT	FTA	Rebounds			PF	TP	A	TO	Blk	S	Min
		FG	FGA	FG	FGA	FT	FTA	Off	Def	Tot	PF	TP	A	TO	Blk	S	Min
31	Stephens, Dwayne f	1	5	0	2	0	0	1	2	3	2	2	5	0	0	0	29
34	Miller, Anthony f	2	5	0	0	0	0	4	2	6	1	4	0	1	0	1	22
54	Peplowski, Mike c	7	12	0	0	1	2	4	9	13	3	15	1	4	1	0	30
13	Snow, Eric g	3	6	0	0	2	2	0	0	0	5	8	2	2	0	1	18
24	Respert, Shawn g	7	13	0	2	0	0	1	2	3	2	14	0	4	0	0	32
3	Weshinskey, Kris	5	11	1	2	2	2	2	0	2	1	13	6	3	0	0	25
23	Beathea, Damon	1	3	0	0	0	0	0	0	0	0	2	0	0	0	0	7
40	Brooks, Quinton	3	6	0	0	2	2	3	2	5	3	8	0	1	1	0	23
25	Zulauf, Jon	1	3	0	0	0	0	0	1	1	0	2	0	0	0	0	7
22	Nicodemus, Steve	0	0	0	0	0	1	0	1	1	1	0	2	0	0	1	4
4	Hart, David	0	0	0	0	0	0	0	0	0	0	0	0	0	0	0	3
	Team							0	1	1							
	TOTALS	30	64	1	6	7	9	15	20	35	18	68	16	15	2	3	200

Total FG% 1st Half .375(12/32) 2nd half .563(18/32) Game .469(30/64) Deadball
3-Pt. FG% 1st Half .000(0/2)   2nd half .250(1/4)   Game .167(1/6)   Rebounds 1
FT% 1st Half 1.00(6/6)   2nd half .333(1/3)   Game .778(7/9)

INDIANA

No.	Player	Total FG		3-point		FT	FTA	Rebounds			PF	TP	A	TO	Blk	S	Min
		FG	FGA	FG	FGA	FT	FTA	Off	Def	Tot	PF	TP	A	TO	Blk	S	Min
34	Evans, Brian f	1	3	0	2	0	0	0	2	2	3	2	1	0	0	1	14
40	Cheaney, Calbert f	7	13	1	1	2	2	2	2	4	0	17	4	2	1	0	34
24	Nover, Matt c	5	6	0	0	5	6	0	5	5	2	15	2	1	0	0	32
20	Graham, Greg g	11	16	4	6	6	7	1	2	3	1	32	3	1	2	0	37
21	Reynolds, Chris g	2	2	0	0	2	2	0	1	1	2	6	4	1	0	1	16
33	Graham, Pat	4	7	3	5	0	0	0	2	2	2	11	3	0	0	0	22
22	Bailey, Damon	2	6	1	3	2	2	1	3	4	1	7	3	1	1	0	26
30	Leary, Todd	4	5	1	2	0	0	0	1	1	2	9	2	0	0	1	12
25	Knight, Pat	0	1	0	0	0	0	0	0	0	1	0	1	0	0	1	6
44	Henderson, Alan	0	0	0	0	0	0	0	0	0	0	0	0	0	0	0	1
	Team							0	2	2							
	TOTALS	36	59	10	19	17	19	4	20	24	14	99	23	6	4	5	200

Total FG% 1st Half .656(21/32) 2nd half .556(15/27) Game .610(36/59) Deadball
3-Pt. FG% 1st Half .583(7/12)   2nd half .429(3/7)   Game .526(10/19) Rebounds 1
FT% 1st Half .778(7/9)   2nd half 1.00(10/10) Game .895(17/19)

Officials Jody Silvester, Gene Monje, Sam Lickliter
Technical Fouls
Attendance 16,863

Score by Periods	1	2	OT	OT	Final
Michigan State	30	38			68
Indiana	56	43			99

Indiana played its last regular season game against Wisconsin in Madison. The Hoosiers had the Big Ten Championship and a number one ranking going into the game. The Hoosiers are looking forward to learning their bracket in the NCAA, however Knight has always stressed finishing strong before the NCAA. He likes to carry the emotion of the last games of the regular season into the tournament, and he has the team focused on the game today.

Knight starts with a review of the Michigan State game and senior night and then turns to the Wisconsin team he faces today.

The thing that we are always trying to do, going into any season, is to have a chance going into the last couple of games, the last game, the last two weeks, whatever it might be, to have our team in a position where it is a contender for the Big Ten Championship. Sometimes the most rewarding situations are those when you win the championship on the last day. It comes down to you being able to beat somebody to win the championship, and it's also, perhaps, the most frustrating situation, as was the ending to our season a year ago. Yet, a lot of times I feel the most satisfying end to a season is one where you have already won the championship, where you have been able, as we have a few times, to win the championship with games to play.

If someone was to ask me which I prefer, I think I would obviously say let's win it as soon as we can. If we can win it after 12 games, let's win it after 12 games. Because of the emphasis we put on the championship and the emphasis we have always placed on the Big Ten Title, we have to be very careful about what happens in the game or two games that follow those situations where the championship has been clinched with games left to play. That's what we are confronted with here at Wisconsin today. Yet, I believe of all the situations, I would sooner have this one than any.

We started the season, Don, and I think the consensus of coaches, with the exclusion of myself, talked about how this was the toughest they had ever seen the Big Ten. Well, I never did agree with that and don't agree with it now. A lot of times coaches make comments like that to protect themselves a little bit as the year wears on. "Well, how did you expect us to do any better than this? This is the greatest league known to man this year!" So, anyhow, with a team like

Michigan in it, a team as talented, as big, and as deep as Michigan is, to win the championship outright, I think, was a really significant accomplishment for our players. One I think they were very pleased with and one we certainly were pleased with.

We had some adversity to overcome during the course of the season. We had some spells where we were tired. The idea of playing with nine and practicing with ten throughout the entire course of the year was tough on the players. Pat Graham getting hurt just at a point where he was starting to really play well after a year's absence was a very tough thing for the players to handle, and that took an outstanding player away from us for most of the season. Then just as Pat's ready to come back, Henderson goes down, and our leading rebounder is taken out of play. Rebounding is a very, very important thing to this team because it's not something we overwhelm anybody with. We get into that position where, going back to the Ohio State game, we are in the driver's seat with a three-game lead, and we lose there and win at Minnesota. A big point in winning the championship this year was the Minnesota game. Then I thought we played very, very well against Northwestern and Michigan State in wrapping it up.

I was really pleased with the concentration that we had, the effort that we had on the part of all players, and particularly those four seniors that have meant so much to us during the past four seasons. They've done a great job. We started out rather shakily in the Big Ten and didn't make much of a dent in the NCAA the first year that they were here, which in some cases would be understandable, one of those eternally young teams that populates the Big Ten. We wanted more than we got that first year. We expected more, and I think our players grew from that experience. Here we are with this one last game in the regular season and then on into the Tournament with what I think has been for the players an outstanding set of accomplishments over the course of this year: the NIT Preseason Championship, the Big Ten outright title, the holiday tournaments that we have won, the Co-Championship that they had a couple of years ago, and the Final Four appearance that they had last year. And still there are some opportunities to do some things down the road. As a coach, I have to be really pleased with, proud of and very happy for these players and what they have accomplished.

Looking to Wisconsin, they were in a position where they could have either been set to go into the NCAA Tournament or certainly could have been playing for that opportunity today. They took themselves out of it with losses to Penn State, here in Madison, and Northwestern at Evanston. So I would imagine that whatever happens in this game today, Wisconsin will have a chance to go on and play in the NIT.

They will be a team that I think will have to be reckoned with in the NIT. I think they have two players who are very, very tough to play against, maybe the two players hardest to play against on any one team in the conference, except for Michigan, in Webster and Finley. Finley is an outstanding scorer. He can score in every way possible. He reminds me a lot of Mike Woodson, and is probably quicker than Mike was. He has shown himself, almost without exception over this season, to have a real consistency in his ability to score. Webster is very, very quick and good with the ball, an excellent passer, and sets up things. Webster is able to get kids that perhaps, are not in the same talent level as he and Finley, opportunities to be able to score and to contribute to this team. That's what basketball is all about. It's a team that, as we told our players, in terms of size, strength, quickness, speed, any basketball parameter that you want to use, is certainly our equal physically. It will be a very interesting game from our standpoint, seeing just what we are able to do mentally, coming back from a very emotional evening against Michigan State.

I thought that of all the really nice evenings or afternoons that have been a part of Indiana basketball over the years, Don, that none was any nicer than last Wednesday night after the Michigan State game. Our four players, in speaking to the crowd and thanking the fans for their support during the four years each played here with us, showed exactly what a college athletic program is capable of doing with regard to the development of a student athlete. They just all reflected extremely well on themselves and the quality of the education that they have received while attending Indiana University. It was an evening, a rarity actually, where seniors are being honored, and, at the same time, they are playing for the league championship at home, following on the heels of Calbert's achievement in setting the all time Big Ten scoring record as well as the Indiana record. So it was just a great evening, and one that I think we all will remember and cherish for a long time.

Fischer asked Knight how he would approach this final game.

We had an interesting situation in 1989, a couple of players really banged up, and a couple more that were just tired. We had a two game lead going into that last game at Iowa City. We had a two game lead over Illinois. I think we had won 15 games and Illinois had won 13 going into the last game. I chose to rest our players, and I think that proved to be a really good thing. I felt we played very well out in Tucson and maybe, I don't know, that was a funny seeding thing by the NCAA. We had lost to Illinois twice, and we had Illinois, in the next to the last game at home, the third game from the end, down by 14 points with six or seven minutes left to play, and we just got tired and the game got away from us and they won and went on to be a first seed in the NCAA Tournament as the second place finisher in the Big Ten.

I felt that we were in the best position possible because of what we did. Yet, on that team, we had 12 or 13 players. Here, we really don't have, with Henderson out, we don't have a real complement of big players to stay with the ballgame, to make the game competitive. We have a lot of guys playing that are pretty well rested. I would think, Don that we would play this game, depending upon how the game goes, fairly close to how we would play any game over the course of the season. I can see where there would be some things that would arise that might cause us to deviate from that plan a little bit. Basically going into the game, we will start the ballgame with Greg Graham, Chris Reynolds, Bailey, Cheaney, and Nover. We'll go from there and we will certainly substitute and play and get people playing time. But I'm not so sure that will be any different from what we've been doing.

GAME SUMMARY

INDIANA 87   WISCONSIN 80

No matter what happens in postseason play, this Indiana basketball team will be able to look back at a brilliant regular season that ended with a victory over Wisconsin on the road in Madison. The Hoosiers were near perfect in the first half, then hung on for the triumph that might have eluded many teams when there was little to play for except pride.

In the first half, Indiana hit a sizzling 62 percent but cooled to 46 percent in the second half. Still, they connected on 55 percent of their shots for the ballgame, while holding Wisconsin to 48 percent. In that first 20 minutes, Indiana had built a 22-point lead. In the second half the Badgers came back and made a game of it for a time, but Indiana really never lost control.

For the game, Indiana hit 55 percent compared to Wisconsin's 48 percent. The Hoosiers also hit 47 percent from three-point range and 76 percent from the free throw line. Indiana again outrebounded the Badgers with 32 boards to Wisconsin's 30. Both teams gave the ball up 9 times.

Greg Graham led IU with 27 points on his continued hot shooting streak, Calbert Cheaney added 22 points, Matt Nover had 16 points and 10 rebounds, while Damon Bailey added 13 points and 5 assists.

This year's 17-1 record equals the 1953 Hoosier mark. The only other two teams with better records were the unbeaten 1975 and 1976 squads that were 18 and 0. Indiana University is the only school to have ever won that number of games in league play.

As the Hoosiers head for postseason play, their overall mark is 28 and 3. They are the top seed in the Midwest Regional to start tournament action, and the number one ranked team in the country at the end of regular season play in both the AP and the CNN-USA Today coaches' poll.

INDIANA

No.	Player	Total FG FG	FGA	3-point FG	FGA	FT	FTA	Rebounds Off	Def	Tot	PF	TP	A	TO	Blk	S	Min
22	Bailey, Damon f	5	9	2	3	1	1	1	4	5	2	13	5	1	1	1	30
40	Cheaney, Calbert f	9	15	1	3	3	3	0	4	4	1	22	4	3	0	2	40
24	Nover, Matt c	6	7	0	0	4	5	2	8	10	2	16	1	0	1	0	36
20	Graham, Greg g	10	16	4	6	3	5	2	1	3	1	27	2	0	0	0	37
21	Reynolds, Chris g	0	3	0	0	3	5	1	5	6	1	3	5	3	1	2	33
33	Graham, Pat	0	2	0	1	0	0	0	0	0	2	0	0	2	0	0	5
34	Evans, Brian	1	3	0	2	0	0	1	2	3	2	2	0	0	1	0	8
30	Leary, Todd	1	3	0	0	0	0	0	0	0	0	2	2	0	1	0	10
25	Knight, Pat	0	0	0	0	2	2	0	1	1	0	2	0	0	0	0	1
	Team							0	0	0							
	TOTALS	32	58	7	15	16	21	7	25	32	11	87	19	9	4	5	200

Total FG%	1st Half .618(21/34)	2nd half .458(11/24)	Game .552(32/58)	Deadball
3-Pt. FG%	1st Half .500(6/12)	2nd half .333(1/3)	Game .467(7/15)	Rebounds 3
FT%	1st Half .833(5/6)	2nd half .733(11/15)	Game .762(16/21)	

WISCONSIN

No.	Player	Total FG FG	FGA	3-point FG	FGA	FT	FTA	Rebounds Off	Def	Tot	PF	TP	A	TO	Blk	S	Min
24	Finley, Michael f	9	21	1	6	4	4	2	2	4	2	23	3	2	0	0	38
33	Ely, Louis f	4	6	0	0	1	1	0	5	5	4	9	0	1	2	1	22
41	Harrell, Damon c	0	4	0	0	2	2	0	1	1	1	2	0	0	0	0	16
11	Webster, Tracy g	6	11	3	4	0	0	0	3	3	3	15	9	1	0	1	38
15	Kilbride, Andy g	7	11	6	9	3	3	2	2	4	2	23	2	2	0	0	31
4	Kelley, Brian	0	1	0	0	0	0	1	4	5	3	0	2	1	0	0	14
3	Johnsen, Jason	0	2	0	2	0	0	0	1	1	1	0	0	1	0	0	9
43	Petersen, Jeff	3	6	0	0	0	2	1	0	1	3	6	0	0	1	1	19
10	Carl, Adam	0	0	0	0	0	0	0	0	0	0	0	0	0	0	0	2
22	McDuffie, Otto	0	0	0	0	0	0	0	0	0	0	0	0	1	0	0	2
52	Johnson, Grant	1	1	0	0	0	0	0	0	0	1	2	0	0	2	0	9
	Team							2	4	6							
	TOTALS	30	63	10	21	10	12	8	22	30	20	80	16	9	5	3	200

Total FG%	1st Half .367(11/30)	2nd half .576(19/33)	Game .476(30/63)	Deadball
3-Pt. FG%	1st Half .455(5/11)	2nd half .500(5/10)	Game .476(10/21)	Rebounds 1
FT%	1st Half .667(4/6)	2nd half 1.00(6/6)	Game .833(10/12)	

Officials   Tom Rucker, Phil Bova, Eric Harmon
Technical Fouls
Attendance   11,500

Score by Periods	1	2	OT	OT	Final
Indiana	53	34			87
Wisconsin	31	49			80

Bob Knight Talk Show
March 15, 1993

FISCHER: Hello again, everybody. This is Don Fischer welcoming you again to the Bob Knight Talk Show.

As you might be able to hear in the background, the coach is on a bicycle tonight. We're not sure just what he's working out for. Coach, your team wrapped up its regular season yesterday with their 28th win of the season against just three defeats for 1992-93. They wrapped up a 17-1 campaign in the Big Ten, winning the Championship with one game to go, and are only the second team in history to end with a 17-1 record. They are one of only four teams, all from Indiana University, who are at 17-1 or 18-0, the conference. This team has one of the best records ever turned in by Big Ten Conference teams, and those all belong to the Hoosiers. So, a very, very positive season it has been, one of tremendous entertainment for all Indiana basketball fans.

As we indicated, yesterday's final was 87 to 80, with a victory over Wisconsin, and the Hoosiers certainly had to feel good about their performance, especially considering how many ball clubs here in the last couple of weeks have gotten beat at this late stage of the campaign.

Coach, are you with us? (Whirl, whirl, whirl, of stationary bicycle in motion.)

KNIGHT: Yeah, Yeah!

FISCHER: Coach, can you talk a little bit about your ballgame yesterday with the Wisconsin Badgers?

KNIGHT: Big game!!

FISCHER: Can I ask you a question about what you're working out for? Just to get ready for the show?

KNIGHT: No. Fishing, Don!

FISCHER: How much fishing will you do on an exercise bicycle?

KNIGHT: It gets me in shape to walk, cast.

FISCHER: (Laughter) Well, let me just ask you to talk just a moment about this season and your feeling on your ball club's performance.

KNIGHT: I think it was a singularly unique season for our team. We got a start with winning the Preseason NIT, which was a really nice thing for us, having a chance to win a national tournament at the beginning of the season, where 16 different conferences were represented by teams in that tournament. Other than the NCAA, it's really one of the only two major national tournaments that you can play in. One is the Postseason NIT. Of course, this one is the Preseason NIT, something that we were really pleased to have a chance to go to.

We then went on to play a pretty decent regular preseason to the Big Ten. You will recall that we had a couple of poor free-throw shooting games against Kansas and Kentucky, but you know, I don't know what that may or may not have meant for us down the road. We had, particularly in the Kentucky game, a lot of poor play defensively that cost us the ballgame. It would be easy to look on the outside of the thing and attribute all that to just free throws. But that just wasn't the case there, Don.

Then, when we got into conference play, I'm not sure that we really could have done much more than we did in conference play. We had a real big week when we went to Ohio State and were beaten in overtime there, after having had a couple of chances maybe to win the ballgame. We really had a tough situation going up to Minnesota to play, and I think that probably was the biggest game in the conference season for us, our being able to win up there.

We came back, then, with Henderson being injured, another thing that these kids had to overcome, I'm not sure that people really understand the importance that Alan is to our team and the things that he is able to do. What we think he gives to us starts with the board play, the defensive play, and Alan probably makes far more big plays defensively than anybody that we have. Yet, he does a lot of good things offensively, so the kids have had to overcome his being gone and make up for that in a variety of ways. Winning 17 games in the Big Ten was something that we really, with all the good teams that we have had, Don, we've only had two teams ever do that. We have finished first place in the Big Ten eight different times winning 15 or fewer games. This is only the third time that we have ever had a team win over 15 games in the Big Ten. So, obviously, we were very, very pleased with that.

I think another singular thing for our team is to finish the regular season ranked number one in the country. I think that's a really nice thing for them. You know, when you consider the national championship is played for in tournament fashion, there's an awfully lot, obviously, still to be played for. Yet, I think that's a very nice thing for these players to have accomplished being the number one ranked team at the end of the regular season.

As we close out the regular season now, Don, and get ready for the tournament play, I think you wind up by just mentioning from a coaching standpoint the game that we played yesterday at Madison. I think it was a game that a lot of teams could have and would have lost. Our team played about as well as we've played at any time this year in the first half of the ball game yesterday, and then things sailed away for us in the second half. But even with that, we were able, after losing 16 points of our lead, to come back and get 7 or 8 of it back.

At no time that I have coached have I been any more pleased with the overall accomplishments and the effectiveness, the efficiency, the productivity of a team during the regular season than I was this year.

FISCHER: Coach, let's just talk for a moment about the NCAA Tournament. Five Big Ten teams have been selected for the field. Of course, Indiana was selected the number one seed in the Midwest, and you'll be playing Wright State on Friday night in the second ballgame that evening, and 10:00, apparently is the scheduled tip off time. Just a thought about five teams going from the Big Ten, first of all, then your first round opponent.

KNIGHT: Well, I think, Don, that the Big Ten has probably historically, at least since open selection has been the format for the tournament, has averaged slightly more than five teams per year, wouldn't you think?

FISCHER: Right. I think six has been the norm.

KNIGHT: So this year, we are right at that or slightly under that. I think that that will always be pretty much the case in this league. I've answered the question.

FISCHER: (Laughter) Coach, . . .

KNIGHT: It's time for you to pick it up and, you know, come in with another question.

FISCHER: Let me just jump in there then. This is from Greencastle. Talk a little bit about Wright State, your first round opponent, and what do you know about them?

KNIGHT: Well, I think Wright State is a very good basketball team, a very talented team, and a big team. Any of you fans that think that because you've got a number one team seeded playing a 16th seeded team that there is a tremendous difference between the two, let me dispel that thought for you very quickly. Wright State's got a 7-foot center who is a tremendously improved player, perhaps the most improved player in the country over a year ago. In a forward named Edwards and a guard named Woods, they have two players that could be impact players, very good players on any team in the Big Ten. Then those three are backed up by a kid that's an awfully good three-point shooter for them, a kid from England, a kid that has a little injury problem but nevertheless has been a really good athlete for them, named Herriman. The three-point shooter is a kid from here in Indiana, named Andy Holderman, who has shot over 170 threes in the course of their season and made over 80 for 47 percent. He's an outstanding free throw shooter as well.

Their five man starting lineup is one, I think, that would stack up very well against several of the teams that we have been playing in the last two months in the league, Don. It's not a Michigan, but neither is anybody else. As far as the rest of us are concerned in the Big Ten, this is a team that has at least the same, maybe even more size than several of the teams, the same kind of quickness, two outstanding players in Woods and Edwards, and a kid, like what Pat Graham was for us before getting hurt, in Holderman who can knock down three's. It's a team that I think will give us all we can handle. It is not going to be a game that will be decided anywhere but probably down the wire. I think it is a team that could play anywhere through this tournament, Don, seeded in any position, and give an excellent account of itself.

FISCHER: Coach, our next questioner is Joe Falcon of Indianapolis. He would like to know what your practice schedule will be prior to the tournament this week, and do you change anything to what you do prior to the regular season coming to a close?

KNIGHT: Well, we really won't, Don. We did some things, as an example, this afternoon in practice, over the course of about 50 to 60 minutes, working on defensive positioning and defensive recognition. I didn't think that we maintained our level of defensive play in the second half of yesterday's game from the first half. I thought that the first half we were a pretty good defensive team, and particularly in the second ten minutes of the first half. Then I felt that our intensity slipped in the second half, our awareness slipped, our anticipation slipped. If intensity slips, then everything slips. You can have a team playing very intently and it makes some mistakes because of overzealousness. Maybe it tried to make a steal it shouldn't or tried to deflect a pass it can't get to. That kind of team will give up a bucket here and there, but just by virtue of the aggressive nature with which it is playing, it's going to do a lot of pretty good things as well.

What we had was a team that kind of lost its intensity, and in losing its intensity, we weren't nearly as good a team defensively because we were kind of sitting back on our heels. We weren't really ready to go out after anything, and we reacted after Wisconsin had already acted too many times in the second half. Consequently, we wound up giving up some fairly easy baskets in the second half. I don't think that anything is better for a team in its confidence, its thrust, its momentum, than to get a couple of baskets that they didn't work really hard to get, and we enabled Wisconsin to do that a little in yesterday's ballgame. So we spent a lot of time today trying just to discuss and go through, at half speed, our positioning on defense established through recognition and anticipation.

Tomorrow, we will begin to work on what we do offensively. Wright State plays a variety of defenses, probably none of which we haven't played against during the course of the season, but we will try to get our people aware of just what they will be confronted with from a defensive standpoint in the ballgame.

And that's pretty much what we will be doing the next three days in practice. They won't be long practices. We are at a point in the season where we want to cut down a lot on practice time. I would imagine that we will be working every afternoon for about an hour.

FISCHER: All right. This question is from Huntington, Coach. How are teams assigned to the NCAA Regional locations, and why does a team like Michigan go to the Western Regional? Shouldn't the Western Regional be played by Western teams?

KNIGHT: Well, it was at one time, but now with the seeding, you have to understand how these teams are seeded now. There are four different seeds at each number, one through 16. So when they seed the first four teams, then to try to establish a balance, each of those four teams is assigned a different regional. And seeding makes all the difference, as opposed to geographical assignments. Seeding will then send teams from one section of the country to another. That's been going on, now, for probably 15 years.

FISCHER: This is from Elkhart, Coach. A local newspaper here says that Ross Hales has been interviewed as a potential basketball player at IU for next year. Is there any truth to that?

KNIGHT: Well, I don't discuss recruiting, but suffice it to say that our recruiting for next year was completed back in October.

FISCHER: This is from Rensselaer, Indiana. He asks, do you see anyone in the Big Ten today who has skills reminiscent of Jerry Lucas' basketball skills?

KNIGHT: Jerry Lucas is the best player, to my way of thinking, that's ever played in the Big Ten. No, there is nobody in the Big Ten today even remotely close to being able to do what Lucas was able to do as a player, as a rebounder, as an inside scorer.

FISCHER: Coach, our next questioner is from Greencastle, Indiana. He wants to know about Alan Henderson's situation as far as post season play.

KNIGHT: Well, we really don't know yet. That's going to be up in the air every day this week, just to see how far Alan progresses day-by-day.

FISCHER: This is from Indianapolis. Please give your thoughts on the NCAA Regionals regarding the strength of each.

KNIGHT: I haven't even studied it, Don. I couldn't tell you about any Regional but ours. I really don't have any concern about anybody's Regional but ours.

FISCHER: All right. This is from Indianapolis. Why do you think the three-second violation in the lane is not called very much any more.

KNIGHT: Well, I really think that most teams have pretty good movement. That's something that we really look at when we study game films of any particular game, most recently Wisconsin. Quite frankly, it is not a call that comes to light very often. I just don't think there are a lot of three-second violations being committed in the Big Ten or in games we play. I think most teams have good mobility and they work at movement.

FISCHER: This is from Crown Point. How are college football and basketball team classifications made as far as Division I, II, or III? Is that classification based on the enrollment size of the school?

KNIGHT: No, that has nothing to do with the size of the enrollment. It is simply determined by the number of varsity sports that are played, supported by the Athletic Department, have varsity status and not club status, as well as the record that teams are able to compile in these sports. I think it may have a little bit to do with the funding of varsity sports and certainly the number of scholarships that are given. There are different numbers of scholarships given at the Division I and the Division II levels, and the Division III level of athletic competition in the NCAA, Don, is entirely determined, as far as financial assistance with individual athletes, on a need basis.

FISCHER: Coach, that's all the time we have for phone calls this evening. I just want to reiterate from the staff of University Broadcasting Company . . .

KNIGHT: How are we done so early?

FISCHER: (Laughter) Well, with commercials and everything, we are going to be right up to the bottom line.

KNIGHT: Well, let me tell you, Don, that I have, as always, really enjoyed being with you. I hope that people have enjoyed our attempts, somewhat lame on occasion, at humor. We've tried to answer questions honestly, over the course of the 15 shows that we've done this year, Don. I want to thank the fans for paying attention to what we are doing and for being involved with Indiana basketball. Now, everyone have a nice seven month hiatus, and Don and I will be back with you again in December.

FISCHER: All right, Coach. Thank you very much for being with us. Again, on behalf of University Broadcasting, our thanks to you for an outstanding season and some outstanding shows as well.

KNIGHT: SOME outstanding shows? Is that an inference that some haven't been outstanding?

FISCHER: That's just terminology, Coach. They've all been Class A.

KNIGHT: Well, I kind of had to fish for that.

FISCHER: (Laughter)

KNIGHT: To coin a little bit of a pun. What I think we'll do though, Fischo, is that I think we are going to devise a show simply called, "Fishing with Fischer," or it may be "Fishing for Fischer," or "Fishing without Fischer."

FISCHER: That may be the best alternative yet.

Good night everybody from all of us at University Broadcasting Company.

NCAA TOURNAMENT

"VICTORY FAVORS THE TEAM MAKING THE FEWEST MISTAKES!"

Wright State
Xavier
Louisville
Kansas

The NCAA Tournament is the grand stage of college basketball. Bob Knight has a gunslinger's edge in tournament play and a record that has won the respect and admiration of his peers. He has had 25 teams invited to the tournament. Five of his teams have made it to the Final Four, and three of those teams won the NCAA Championship.

Indiana, with a 28-3 record, and a Big Ten Championship, begins NCAA play as the number one seed in the Midwest bracket. Indiana will go against 16 seed Wright State which had a 20-9 season. Knight begins by talking about the season and the different parts of the season. Then he summarizes the difference in winning a conference championship and the NCAA Tournament, a tournament that he has won three times, 1976, 1981 and 1987.

As they often do, Indiana fans have made an emotional investment in this basketball team, and in another of many firsts for Bob Knight, 25,000 people turn out for the 30 minute shoot around the day before the game. At the end of the practice session, Knight showed his appreciation by having his players, coaches and assistants spell out "thanks" by lying on the Hoosier Dome court. Bob Knight himself served as the exclamation point.

Coach Knight wraps up the pre-game show talking about the Wright State team he plays tonight. As he has done all year, Coach Knight emphasizes their strengths and considers Murray State a real threat.

I mentioned to our players tonight that we had our season divided up into three parts so far. The first, the NIT, was quick and also good preparation for the rest of the season. To be able to play and have a chance to win the Preseason NIT, which we did, was very important for us. Probably next to the NCAA Tournament itself, the Preseason NIT is the best thing that a team can win over the course of a year with the exception of its own conference.

Then, after the Preseason NIT, we played our December schedule to get us ready to compete for the Big Ten Championship. We had a couple of slippages in the December schedule where we didn't play particularly well. Not just the Kansas and Kentucky games, which we lost, because we had some very good play in both of those games, but in other poor spots in December. Basically, I thought we had a pretty good non-conference season, but we had some spotty play.

Then when we got into conference play, we probably had as little really spotty play, symbolizing lack of concentration as maybe any team we have had. This team is pretty consistent in its approach, its effort, and the way it played throughout the entire conference season.

We really were never in a position in the conference season, with the possible exception of Minnesota at home, where we had to make up some drastic difference. I guess in the first half of the Michigan game we had a little of that, but basically in the second half of all the games that we played, we were always in a position to have a chance to win the ballgame. We followed the Preseason NIT and the non-conference with a real successful run in the Big Ten Championship.

Now here we are in the last phase of our season. Following what we do in conference play, we hope to have an opportunity to play in the NCAA Tournament, and again this year we have that opportunity. In talking to the players earlier today, I asked them this question, "What's the difference between winning a conference championship and winning a tournament championship?" And very quickly the players say that you can't lose in a tournament. That's it in a nutshell.

In a conference season, there have only been two teams in the 18 game schedule of the Big Ten that have not lost. Only one other team, this year's team of ours, to go with those two 18 and 0 teams in '75 and '76, has won more than 16 Big Ten games. Yet we did lose a game and we still won the conference championship.

Now there are really only three words that need be used to totally explain the NCAA Tournament: "Win or out!" That's where we are tonight, and that's where everybody is that's in the tournament, and that's regardless of what you have done. Like last year, we had a good four game run in the Tournament, winning both first round games and then winning our Regional in Albuquerque and yet, in our fifth game against a really good Duke team, it was "win" or "out" again, and we were out of it at that point and did not advance to the final game. So we start that whole route again here tonight.

My guess is that nobody on the Tournament Committee saw Wright State play. Wright State was given a 16th seed on the basis of computer ratings, of schedules, teams, games, wins, losses, all kinds of things, and I have known a lot of computer ratings to go a little bit cockeyed when people get involved. We don't have computers playing against each other. We have people, and the people on both sides of the scorers' table determine what's going to happen, what the outcome of any game will be.

In looking at Wright State, you see a team that has excellent size, a 7-foot, 260 pound center that has improved enormously. I would hope that our own Todd Lindeman can show that kind of improvement that Nahar has shown for Wright State. They have a very legitimate NBA first round draft choice in Edwards, a 6-8 forward that would be very similar in terms of how he plays for this team to how

Robinson plays for the Purdue team. A guard, Woods, who did not play last year, and people who have watched Wright State the last couple of years feel that Woods makes a tremendous difference. He is the kind of a guard that you don't take the ball away from. He is good with the ball, he has good judgment, he gets other people in position to score, and then gives them the ball. In addition to those three players, they have another four or five kids that fit in well and do their jobs, and with good size too, I might add. That's what has made them a very good basketball team.

Somebody has to be a first seed, so based on our record and who we've played, Don, we become a first seed. I am sure there are other teams, a lot of other teams on given nights, which would be able to play very well against us, if not beat us. Somebody has to be the 16th seed. I would imagine that there would have been a lot of 14, 15, and 16th seeded teams that would be capable of beating a lot of other teams on those given nights or on any night, as far as that's concerned. So seeding is always a thing that I have never paid any attention to. I'm not sure, after all of the things that we're dealing with in this game, that there's a lot to be said for getting a first seed.

In looking to this game today, first of all, let's talk about our defense. We've got to do a good job containing Woods and Edwards. We've got to keep Nahar away from areas where he's very effective as a scorer. Offensively, they are a team that likes to press, so we've got to be able to handle that. Their defense, then, becomes a part of their offense. We've got to make the press a very big part of our offense, as we have tried to do all year long. They change defenses a lot, and we've got to be able to handle the changing of the defenses from zone to man to man to whatever they decide to use.

I think everyone who follows Indiana basketball knows how much I appreciate the turnout for practice yesterday. Not only is it the case with me, but everybody affiliated with Indiana basketball, the kind of statewide support and national support that our team has had is very much appreciated. Nowhere is that support greater or more in evidence than in the central Indiana area. Certainly the display of affection for our team last night from the fans was something that all of us will always remember and always be appreciative of having been able to share in such a wonderful moment.

GAME SUMMARY

INDIANA 97 WRIGHT STATE 54

Indiana opened NCAA Tournament play with an easy victory over the Wright State Raiders. The Hoosiers dominated from the onset, taking Wright State completely out of its offense by playing tenacious defense, opening a 45 to 29 half-

time lead. The second half was even worse, as Indiana scored 52 points to Wright State's 25.

For the game, the Hoosiers hit 57percent from the field, and the second half shooting was over 61 percent. They canned eight of 17 three-point field goals, while Wright State managed only three of 16. The Hoosiers went to the free throw line 20 times and connected on 15, while Wright State hit seven of eight. The turnovers were almost equal, the Hoosiers with13 and Wright State turned it over 14 times.

Indiana had four players in double figures, led by Calbert Cheaney with 29, 17 for Matt Nover, 12 for Pat Graham, and 10 for Brian Evans. The Hoosier's leading rebounder was Cheaney with eight, and Damon Bailey led the squad in assists with nine.

Alan Henderson played 8 minutes and had 4 points on 2 for 6 shooting. He also had 3 rebounds.

Over 36,000 fans saw this opening game in the Hoosier Dome, but maybe just as impressive was the previous night's practice session in which the Hoosiers drew over 25,000 fans for that 30 minute shoot around.

WRIGHT STATE

No.	Player		Total FG FG	FGA	3-point FG	FGA	FT	FTA	Rebounds Off	Def	Tot	PF	TP	A	TO	Blk	S	Min
	Herriman	f	3	7	0	2	0	0			2	3	6	0	2	0	2	30
	Edwards	f	6	23	1	4	5	6			8	4	18	1	3	0	1	33
	Nahar	c	4	8	0	0	1	1			6	3	9	0	2	0	0	30
	Woods	g	6	15	1	3	1	1			0	0	14	5	3	0	1	34
	Holderman	g	0	4	0	4	0	0			2	2	0	0	0	0	2	24
	McGuire		1	2	0	1	0	0			0	3	2	4	0	0	0	16
	Unverferth		0	0	0	0	0	0			3	1	0	1	1	0	1	11
	O'Neal		0	2	0	0	0	0			2	2	0	1	0	0	0	5
	Wills		1	1	1	1	0	0			0	0	3	0	1	0	0	3
	Skeoch		1	2	0	0	0	0			3	0	2	0	1	0	0	5
	Ramey		0	4	0	1	0	0			0	0	0	0	0	0	0	5
	Smith		0	1	0	0	0	0			0	0	0	1	0	0	0	3
	Blair		0	1	0	0	0	0			0	0	0	0	0	0	0	1
	Team								0	0	4							
	TOTALS		22	70	3	16	7	8	0	0	30	18	54	12	14	0	7	200

Total FG%	1st Half _____	2nd half _____	Game .314(22/70)	Deadball
3-Pt. FG%	1st Half _____	2nd half _____	Game .188(3/16)	Rebounds ____
FT%	1st Half _____	2nd half _____	Game .875(7/8)	

INDIANA

No.	Player		Total FG FG	FGA	3-point FG	FGA	FT	FTA	Rebounds Off	Def	Tot	PF	TP	A	TO	Blk	S	Min
	Bailey, Damon	f	2	6	0	2	0	0			4	3	4	9	2	0	3	25
	Cheaney, Calbert	f	12	17	1	3	4	6			8	2	29	0	1	0	1	21
	Nover, Matt	c	7	10	0	0	3	5			5	2	17	0	3	1	1	31
	Graham, Greg	g	2	8	1	4	4	4			5	2	9	1	1	0	0	30
	Reynolds, Chris	g	0	2	0	0	0	0			6	0	0	4	1	0	0	16
	Leary, Todd		3	3	2	2	0	0			2	0	8	2	2	0	0	11
	Graham, Pat		3	5	2	2	4	4			4	1	12	2	2	0	2	26
	Evans, Brian		4	6	2	4	0	1			9	1	10	3	0	1	1	27
	Henderson, Alan		2	6	0	0	0	0			3	0	4	0	1	0	0	8
	Knight, Pat		2	2	0	0	0	0			0	0	4	1	0	0	0	5
	Team								0	0	4							
	TOTALS		37	65	8	17	15	20	0	0	50	11	97	22	13	2	8	200

Total FG%	1st Half _____	2nd half _____	Game .569(37/65)	Deadball
3-Pt. FG%	1st Half _____	2nd half _____	Game .470(8/17)	Rebounds ____
FT%	1st Half _____	2nd half _____	Game .750(15/20)	

Officials _____

Technical Fouls _____

Attendance 36,003 _____

Score by Periods	1	2	OT	OT	Final
Wright State	29	25			54
Indiana	45	52			97

Indiana moves to the second round of the NCAA Midwest Regional to play Xavier, a 23-6 team, coached by Pete Gillen, that has been outstanding all season long.

Knight begins with a summary of the Wright State game and then talks about the tempo that he is looking for in the game today.

We went into the Wright State game, obviously, with a degree of apprehension. We didn't know a great deal about Wright State. When we watched them play on tape, they did some things very well. They scored a lot of points over the course of the year. They averaged a little over 90 points a game.

Edwards, the 6-8 forward, was thought of as a potential first round draft choice. They had a big kid in Nahar, a 7-foot center, very much improved player, a player they had done a good job working with over the course of a year. So we weren't sure just where we were going to be in the ballgame. You never are. We had to be pleased with the results we had over the course of the game. We had only one real slippage spot in the game, and that was the beginning of the second half. Then we got that turned around quickly and went from there to take the game out of reach.

We were in good position through the latter part of the first half, which was a very positive thing for us due to the fact that Cheaney was in foul trouble through that last 10 or 11 minutes of the first half. He had two fouls, and we took him out of the ballgame and played the remainder of the first half with Calbert on the bench. We got good balanced scoring from everybody that was in the ballgame and pretty good defense as well.

What pleased me then was that Wright State scored 25 against us in the second half and got 6 of those in the first minute or so of play, so really over the last 18 minutes, we were able to keep their scoring to a total of 19 points. Our defensive effort was good. We were able to do the things I think we do best. We got the ball up the floor quickly. We took advantage of openings and moved the ball and passed the ball for good offensive opportunities. So, all in all, it was an effort that we were pleased with, and it was a game played in such a way that we were pleased with our play.

Brian Evans did a good job defensively. Edwards was averaging almost 26 points a game. He got two of his six baskets very early in the ballgame, and got another couple, I think, very early in the second half. During the time that Brian was on him, he had a very tough time scoring. We thought that Brian moved well with him, did a good job on him, and Brian has not played as well as a starter as we would like to see him play. He is certainly going to have to play better next year. He has come in well a lot of times off the bench and played. We'll change that a little bit and see what he does as a starter here this afternoon.

We are trying to matchup as well as we can against Xavier's big men. The Xavier coaches have done an outstanding job with their team over the past several years, seven or eight years. Xavier and Evansville have been far and away at the top in that league. They have battled back and forth almost every year. On occasions, such as this year, both of them have gone to the NCAA Tournament. In other years, one or the other has gone, and the other has gone to the NIT. Pete Gillen and Jimmy Crews both have done outstanding jobs with their teams.

This team is very typical of Xavier teams that I have watched in the past. They are quick and play very hard at both ends of the floor. They are a very aggressive team, a team that controls a lot of its offense with the use of the dribble, the penetrating dribble. They've got four kids that play around the perimeter and three inside players which gives them good depth. They have a good player coming inside in Sikes and a good player outside in Walker, complementing their three starters. Outside, the two big kids, Williams and Grant, did an outstanding job against New Orleans. The two big players, in fact, were the key to the ballgame with New Orleans. The Xavier kids dominated the two big players from New Orleans that had pretty much dominated in their season all along.

They do a good job mixing up defenses. They press, play zone, man to man. They are trying to throw enough things at you to keep you off balance. Yet, in doing that, there are things that we have to be able to take advantage of. Any time a team presses, they also provide you with some opportunities to score. If we take advantage of them, then that becomes an offensive plus for us. If we don't, then it obviously becomes their plus.

I don't know what the tempo will be. I don't have any tempo in mind for this game. I want us to have patience at half-court offense. To get good shots, we've got to make their perimeter players play defense both inside and outside. We've got to be able to try to score against their press. So in one respect, we've got to be able to play at a fast, hard tempo; in another respect, we've got to be able to play just as hard but with a tempo that centers on patience.

We have had a small bench this year, four guys. Now we are all the way up to six guys on the bench, with Henderson playing some against Wright State. In all that time when we had just four players on the bench, each of them, many different times, made very significant contributions to our play, and many times in the first half of games where, had they not been able to do so, we would have been in a difficult position at halftime. They prevented that from occurring and then usually went on then to play well in the second half of the game. Our bench has been very important to us.

We'll go with Graham (Greg), Bailey, Cheaney, Evans, and Nover. We will be doing a lot of maneuvering, depending on what they are doing, and how the game is going, and what it is we are trying to accomplish.

GAME SUMMARY

INDIANA 73   XAVIER 70

The Hoosiers' second game in NCAA Tournament play was a complete change from their opening game with Wright State. The Hoosiers had their hands full with the very fine Xavier team that had gone 23-6 entering the contest. Pete Gillen's Musketeers were well coached and stocked with a solid inside and outside game. They gave Indiana all it could handle in this second round Midwest matchup.

The Hoosiers broke to an early lead, then built it to a 13-point advantage just before halftime. The Musketeers roared back to cut the lead to four at the 20 minute break, 35 to 31. The second half was more of the same with Indiana leading throughout but never able to shake the pesky Musketeers.

Indiana hit 48 percent from the field for the contest, while Xavier hit 42 percent; Indiana connected on just 3 of 10 from three-point range, while the Musketeers hit on 7 of 17. From the free throw line, however, Indiana outscored Xavier 18 to 9, while the Musketeers out rebounded the Hoosiers 39 to 32. The turnovers were almost even. Xavier had 9, and the Hoosiers had 7.

IU had four players in double figures. Again, Calbert Cheaney led the way with 23 points, and Greg Graham was right behind with 19. Damon Bailey had 11 points, and Pat Graham had 10. The rebounds were evenly split for Indiana with eight each for Calbert Cheaney and Matt Nover.

Indiana advanced to the NCAA third round at St. Louis.

Xavier

No.	Player		FG	FGA	FG	FGA	FT	FTA	Off	Def	Tot	PF	TP	A	TO	Blk	S	Min
			Total FG		3-point				Rebounds									
25	Hawkins, Michael	f	6	12	4	8	0	0	1	0	1	4	16	2	2	0	0	33
44	Williams, Aaron	f	6	13	0	0	5	8	3	7	10	4	17	2	1	1	2	36
33	Grant, Brian	c	5	13	0	0	1	2	8	8	16	1	11	2	1	3	2	36
12	Gentry, Steve	g	1	5	0	0	0	0	1	4	5	5	2	2	0	0	0	29
22	Gladden, Jamie	g	6	16	3	9	3	4	0	1	1	2	18	3	4	0	1	37
5	Poynter, Mark		1	1	0	0	0	0	0	0	0	0	2	0	0	0	0	1
21	Mack, Chris		0	0	0	0	0	0	0	0	0	1	0	0	0	0	0	1
34	Walker, Tyrice		2	4	0	0	0	0	1	2	3	4	4	0	1	0	0	19
50	Edwards, Erik		0	0	0	0	0	0	0	1	1	1	0	0	0	0	0	1
54	Sykes, Larry		0	0	0	0	0	0	0	0	0	1	0	0	0	0	0	7
	Team								1	1	2							
	TOTALS		27	64	7	17	9	14	15	24	39	23	70	11	9	4	5	200

Total FG% 1st Half .355(11/31) 2nd half .485(16/33) Game .422(27/64) Deadball
3-Pt. FG% 1st Half .375(3/8) 2nd half .444(4/9) Game .412(7/17) Rebounds 3
FT% 1st Half .667(6/9) 2nd half .600(3/5) Game .643(9/14)

Indiana

No.	Player		FG	FGA	FG	FGA	FT	FTA	Off	Def	Tot	PF	TP	A	TO	Blk	S	Min
			Total FG		3-point				Rebounds									
34	Evans, Brian	f	0	2	0	1	0	0	0	4	4	1	0	1	0	0	0	15
40	Cheaney, Calbert	f	8	17	0	1	7	9	1	7	8	1	23	1	2	2	0	39
24	Nover, Matt	c	3	5	0	0	0	0	2	6	8	4	6	0	0	1	0	30
20	Graham, Greg	g	7	9	2	3	3	3	2	0	2	3	19	3	4	2	2	33
22	Bailey, Damon	g	2	8	0	2	7	10	0	1	1	1	11	3	1	0	1	28
21	Reynolds, Chris		1	3	0	0	0	3	0	2	2	0	2	4	0	0	2	19
30	Leary, Todd		1	3	0	2	0	0	0	0	0	0	2	0	0	0	0	10
33	Graham, Pat		4	5	1	1	1	1	0	2	2	2	10	2	0	0	0	19
44	Henderson, Alan		0	2	0	0	0	0	2	0	2	1	0	0	0	0	0	7
	Team								1	2	3							
	TOTALS		26	54	3	10	18	26	8	24	32	13	73	14	7	5	5	200

Total FG% 1st Half .467(14/30) 2nd half .500(12/24) Game .481(26/54) Deadball
3-Pt. FG% 1st Half .429(3/7) 2nd half .000(0/3) Game .300(3/10) Rebounds 4
FT% 1st Half .571(4/7) 2nd half .737(14/19) Game .692(18/26)

Officials Larry Lembo, Tom Lopes, Charli Range
Technical Fouls
Attendance

Score by Periods	1	2	OT	OT	Final
Xavier	31	39			70
Indiana	35	38			73

┌───┐
│   │
│   **Indiana vs. Louisville**   │
│   March 25, 1993   │
│   NCAA Midwest Regional   │
│   St. Louis   │
│   Pre-game Show   │
│   │
└───┘

Indiana went to St. Louis to play the Louisville Cardinals, which had a 22-8 record. Knight gave a detailed study of the Xavier game that Indiana sometimes struggled with. With frightening accuracy, Knight again predicted how the game would be played with his team in the pre-game walk through. One of the keys for Indiana was being able to put Xavier in a position where it was committing a lot of fouls at the end of the game.

Coach Knight then turned to the matchup with Louisville. He winds up the show where he began the season, talking about mental toughness and how his team has developed in that critical area.

The Xavier game was a 40 minute game, but I don't know what else that that game could have been. Xavier's a very tough minded team, very well put together. A well coached team with good, tough kids playing. It had to be the kind of game that was going to be a tough one for us.

We had two chances to do something with the game from the standpoint of getting control of it. It looked like we were on our way to being able to do so, both in the first half and in the second half. We had just given up 19 points in the first 16 minutes of the ballgame, and then in the last 4 minutes of the first half, we gave up 12 points. That's all to Xavier's credit, getting back into things at that point, outscoring us something like 12 to 2, right in there, 13 to 2 at that moment. Then in the second half, almost the same thing happened. We worked and worked and gradually got ahead by 9 and then had to come back and make some very good plays at the end. It was a hard earned game for us and one that we were very pleased with.

We got some spread to what we were doing on offense, and we exerted perhaps a little bit more patience in the second half than we did in the first half. Again, we were also playing from ahead, too. I think there was only one point in the entire ballgame, maybe at 15-14, where we were behind in that game. As we got down into the last seven or eight minutes, we were able to take advantage of the clock and the lead.

Louisville's eight losses, with the kind of talent they have, is very deceiving. I don't think it has the talent to lose eight times, and I think that's a reflection of early season games that were lost. I really feel, as I've watched this team play in our preparation for them, that they have gotten better and better as the season has moved along. Had they been able to start the season here in the last two or three weeks, their record would not have involved eight losses, I'll assure you.

They are a very big, athletic team and will pose problems for us because of that. We've got to be able to play on the offensive end with really good patience, and yet play with quickness. We've got to be able to move the ball, move our people. We've got to be able to react well to defensive pressure and defensive play. I would think particularly important would be how well we can react to the switching that Louisville does. They usually like to do a lot of switching and there have been times when we have reacted very well to that. So we'll just see what that brings tonight.

On our defensive end, we just can't let them be able to maneuver the ball at will. Xavier had far too much freedom at its offensive end against us than we would want them to have. Certainly then, we can't allow that and play well defensively. Xavier rebounded well against us. Louisville is a better rebounding team.

If I were Louisville, and now I'm thinking about what I would do if I had Louisville's players against our team, I would really emphasize pounding the offensive board. We're going to be playing against two very quick, very agile 6-6 kids, Morton and Miner, along with Roziers who really has a lot of good foot work and a lot of good foot speed in and around the basket. All of that makes them really good offensive rebounders.

I think that they will see what they can do against us with the press. If they have success with it, they will stay with it, and if they don't, they'll get out of it. I think they would like to be able to press and create offense from their press, from forcing turnovers, yet I think there will be no question about the fact that they'll likely get the ball down the floor quickly, and that will push our transition game.

We're going to try to do the same thing. At one point we had taken some stuff off the TV tape from our game with Xavier for today's game. Xavier's a team that likes to run and pressure, and at one point, on break points, open floor points, conversion points, we had 15 and Xavier had 3. Our running game there, against a team that really likes to run, actually was a real positive or a real plus for us.

Fischer then asked Knight if the team was becoming a more mature basketball team, a mentally tough basketball team.

I think they've done a great job. They've gone through two really tough injuries to two excellent players in Pat Graham and Alan Henderson. They came off the first injury and won a tournament, the final game in New York, right on the heels of that first injury. Actually, Pat was about as responsible as anybody for us getting into the championship game in the Preseason NIT.

Then with Alan's injury, they followed that up by winning the Big Ten Championship.

In a couple of situations, as you look at "we're playing so and so at such and such and these circumstances," you say, "Well this is an important game, and that this team has got to be able to win it." We were able to win it.

I think all of these things really emphasize, point out, and illustrate the maturation of our players into a team that, I think, over the course of a year has been a tough team to play against. That's what we've hoped for and we got it. I think that wherever we go in the tournament, whatever happens in the tournament, that maturation and that toughness helped us to get to this third game in the tournament. If we are able to go beyond this, it will be a key factor as well.

GAME SUMMARY

INDIANA 82   LOUISVILLE 69

This third round game in the NCAA Tournament's Midwest Regional matched the Hoosiers against a team much like Michigan and Minnesota in physical talent. Louisville had big, strong, quick athletes, and its athletic ability had carried it to a 21-8 season entering the game, including the Metro Conference Championship.

Bob Knight was hoping his team could get off to a quick start, and it did, hitting 74 percent in the first half. Despite Indiana's hot shooting hand, the Hoosiers held only a seven point lead at the break, 50 to 43. The Cardinals hung with Indiana throughout most of the second half but with eight and one half minutes remaining in the contest, Calbert Cheaney took control and scored 9 of Indiana's next 11 points to put IU in the driver's seat for the remainder of the ballgame.

Cheaney's incredible night included 10 of 12 field goals, two of three from three-point range, and 10 of 12 free throws for a game high total of 32 points. Calbert tied Matt Nover for high in rebounds with 8, and he tied Brian Evans for high in assists with 4.

The Hoosiers as a team hit 62 percent in this ballgame, while pulling down 30 rebounds, equaling the rebound total of Louisville. The Cardinals were held to 41 percent shooting from the field, 32 percent from three-point range, and 69 percent from the free throw line. Indiana turned the ball over 13 times, while the Cardinals gave it up just 10. Other individual statistics included Greg Graham adding 22 points, and Matt Nover had 15 with 8 rebounds.

The Hoosiers earned the right to meet Kansas in the Midwest Regional Title ballgame.

LOUISVILLE

No.	Player		Total FG		3-point		FT	FTA	Rebounds			PF	TP	A	TO	Blk	S	Min
			FG	FGA	FG	FGA	FT	FTA	Off	Def	Tot	PF	TP	A	TO	Blk	S	Min
	Smith	f	3	4	0	0	2	4			6	2	8	6	2	0	2	29
	Morton	f	4	14	1	4	3	4			3	5	12	3	3	0	1	29
	Rozier	c	8	14	0	1	0	0			10	2	16	2	2	0	0	34
	Legree	g	1	5	0	2	0	0			3	3	2	4	2	0	1	27
	Minor	g	5	8	5	7	0	0			6	4	15	0	1	0	0	36
	Brewer		4	16	2	10	3	4			0	4	13	1	0	0	0	27
	Webb		0	0	0	0	0	0			0	0	0	0	0	0	0	11
	Rogers		1	2	0	1	1	1			1	0	3	1	0	0	0	6
	Kaiser		0	0	0	0	0	0			0	0	0	0	0	0	0	1
	Team								0	0	1							
	TOTALS		26	63	8	25	9	13	0	0	30	20	69	17	10	0	4	200

Total FG%	1st Half _____	2nd half _____	Game .413(26/63)	Deadball	
3-Pt. FG%	1st Half _____	2nd half _____	Game .320(8/25)	Rebounds ____	
FT%	1st Half _____	2nd half _____	Game .629(9/13)		

INDIANA

No.	Player		Total FG		3-point		FT	FTA	Rebounds			PF	TP	A	TO	Blk	S	Min
			FG	FGA	FG	FGA	FT	FTA	Off	Def	Tot	PF	TP	A	TO	Blk	S	Min
34	Evans, Brian	f	0	0	0	0	0	1			3	1	0	4	1	0	1	16
40	Cheaney, Calbert	f	10	12	2	3	10	12			8	2	32	4	2	1	1	34
24	Nover, Matt	c	7	9	0	0	1	1			8	2	15	1	2	0	0	40
20	Graham, Greg	g	7	11	1	4	7	7			1	2	22	3	3	1	3	35
22	Bailey, Damon	g	2	7	2	4	0	0			1	1	6	2	1	0	0	29
33	Graham, Pat		1	3	1	2	0	1			3	0	3	3	1	0	0	19
44	Henderson, Alan		0	1	0	0	0	1			3	0	0	1	1	1	1	11
30	Leary, Todd		1	2	1	1	0	1			0	0	3	1	0	0	0	10
25	Knight, Pat		0	0	0	0	0	0			0	0	0	0	1	0	0	3
21	Reynolds, Chris		0	0	0	0	1	2			2	1	1	0	1	0	0	3
	Team								0	0	1							
	TOTALS		28	45	7	14	19	25	0	0	30	9	82	19	13	3	6	200

Total FG%	1st Half _____	2nd half _____	Game .622(28/45)	Deadball	
3-Pt. FG%	1st Half _____	2nd half _____	Game .500(7/14)	Rebounds ____	
FT%	1st Half _____	2nd half _____	Game .760(19/25)		

Officials _____

Technical Fouls _____

Attendance 17,883

Score by Periods	1	2	OT	OT	Final
Louisville	43	26			69
Indiana	50	32			82

Indiana advances to the title game against Kansas, a ball club that went 28-6 in their season. Indiana played Kansas in December. It was a game that Kansas won and a game in which Knight was not pleased with his team's effort.

Knight begins by reviewing Thursday's contest with Louisville, an 82-69 win, and talks about how his team performed and then talks about Kansas. At the end, he talks about Brian Evans who injured his thumb to make the third serious injury to confront the Indiana team this season.

The Louisville game got off to a game where I thought both teams were pretty good offensively. I don't think that you could say that the defense dominated or shined for either team. Yet that may be unfair because, as I said, they both played very well offensively. I would not have thought that we would have scored 50 points in the first half. Had I been told Louisville was going to have 43 at the half, I would have thought, well, we are going to have to hustle the second half if we want to get back into the ballgame.

The halftime score was a little bit surprising. Then it settled down a little bit more in the second half to the kind of game that was maybe a little bit better for us than the first half game was. Yet, the first four or five minutes of the second half was not very good for either team. I didn't think we played very well, and I didn't think they played very well during that time. We were fortunate that they didn't come out and jump all over us, the way we kind of hammered and egged it around at our end of the floor offensively. Then after the first time out from about the 15 minute mark on, I thought that the play picked up from the standpoint of both teams. For about the last 10 or 12 minutes, I thought that we played well.

Everybody from the bench had something to do with the game, and I don't think anything's been better. Maybe we've never had a better season than this. After games that have been good games for us, that have seen us win something, a tournament, the Big Ten, important games along the way to the conference, or here in the NCAA Tournament, we've had everybody on the team feel as thought he has had a part, not just in the preparation but a part in the actual play of a ballgame perhaps more so than in any year that I've been in coaching.

I don't think this Kansas team has changed as much as they have developed. I think they're probably about as good right now, or playing as well as they have played all year. I don't think that when we played them in December that they were as good as they can be. I don't think we were as good as we can be.

It was a game that I didn't think we played particularly well throughout the course of the game. When it came right down to it, we actually were in the game right to the end and did have a little bit of a lead with a couple of minutes to play and couldn't capitalize on it.

I think if we were to play now as we did then, we wouldn't have much of a chance in the ballgame. I think we have to play a lot better than we did in that December game because I think they are a better team and will play better. It could go right down to the wire and be anybody's ballgame, then you can be surprised sometimes at what happens in games.

I just feel that our team has really risen to a lot of challenges over the course of the year, in individual game situations and because of injuries. At times when it didn't look like we were going to be able to get things done the way we did. So it's been a great team to work with. I am sure that there's nothing that those kids want more than to play as well as they can play this afternoon. If we can get to that point, then I think that we will be satisfied with whatever happens.

I think that I would like for us to be able to first of all, defensively, be alert, be attuned to what's happening. We told them four things, offensively. We've got to be able to have good spacing; we've got to keep our offense above the base line; we've got to make good screens and we have to set up the cuts.

A lot is being made in the papers about how much these two teams play alike, but I think that the teams have similar goals. I think execution would be a goal that both teams have. I would think that shot selection is a goal that both teams have. I think that being tough to play against at the defensive end is a goal that both teams would have. I think that what I have said already surpasses immensely in depth anything that you would find in the newspapers.

Brian Evans has a bad thumb, it's broken. We'll probably have to put it in a cast when we get done. He's got a broken thumb, but he's able to play. It's on his right hand.

We will start Graham, Graham, Bailey, Nover, and Cheaney.

GAME SUMMARY

KANSAS 83   INDIANA 77

Kansas unmasked Indiana's weaknesses in beating the Hoosiers in the Midwest Regional Championship. The win allowed the Jayhawks to advance to the Final Four.

The Hoosiers never seemed to develop momentum in this ballgame because of Kansas' unrelenting defense and their effort to get easy baskets in the low post. The Hoosiers simply couldn't matchup inside.

Jayhawk's coach Roy Williams used wave after wave of Kansas substitutes to wear the Hoosiers down and the fatigue showed on the Indiana players as the game went on. Coach Knight played Henderson for only three minutes during the game.

Indiana hit just 46 percent from the field for the game, while Kansas hit 60 percent, including a 68 percent shooting percentage in the second half. Indiana struggled from the three-point range with 5 of 15. Kansas hit just 4 of 10. But in the free throw department, the Jayhawks out shot Indiana 17 of 20, while Indiana connected on just 12 of 16. The rebound totals surprisingly showed Indiana with 36 and Kansas with 27. Both teams turned the ball over 15 times.

The Hoosiers were led by Greg Graham with 23 points and Calbert Cheaney with 22. The only other player in double figures was Brian Evans with ten, even though he was playing with a bum thumb. Cheaney also led IU with 9 rebounds, while Matt Nover and Damon Bailey each had 7 boards. Bailey also led the Hoosiers with 4 assists.

So Indiana's season came to a close. Its final record was 31-4, the second highest number of wins in Indiana University history.

This particular team's three year total of 87 victories is the highest number of wins in any three year span.

For the season, the Hoosiers shot. 522 from the field, and .425 from three-point range. Indiana had a .717 perfromance from the line, and averaged 36.6 boards per game compared to 33.7 for their rivals. The team had 620 assists with only 450 turnovers, a 1.4 to 1.0 ratio, while their opponents had 468 assists and 541 turnovers.

Every IU player had an important role on this team. Calbert Cheaney was the leading scorer with a 22.4 point average. Greg Graham led the team in steals and three-point shooting and was .514 from that range. Matt Nover had a team high field goal accuracy of .628, marking his inside play. Todd Leary shot .889 from the line. Henderson led the team with 8.1 boards and 1.4 blocks per game, even though he played sparingly the last few games. Bailey led with 144 assists, and Reynolds had a team-leading assist ratio of 2.6 to 1.0 with 102 assists and only 39 turnovers.

Patrick Knight and Brian Evans offered valuable relief throughout the season to this team that was short of players. Late in the season, Evans contributed significant scoring. The emotional boost Pat Graham gave his team was just as important his excellent play.

The players developed a collective mental toughness that overcame the injuries and adversity they faced. Their intensity pulled them through a challenging schedule.

KANSAS

No.	Player		Total FG FG	FGA	3-point FG	FGA	FT	FTA	Rebounds Off	Def	Tot	PF	TP	A	TO	Blk	S	Min
32	Hancock, Darrin	f	3	4	0	0	6	6	1	3	4	2	12	1	1	1	1	20
34	Scott, Richard	f	7	10	0	0	2	4	1	1	2	1	16	0	2	0	0	26
51	Pauley, Eric	c	6	12	0	0	1	1	2	2	4	2	13	3	3	2	1	25
23	Walters, Rex	g	4	8	1	4	3	4	0	2	2	2	12	8	5	0	0	29
30	Jordan, Adonis	g	4	7	2	3	1	1	0	4	4	2	11	4	1	0	2	37
20	Woodberry, Steve		2	3	1	2	4	4	1	1	2	4	9	4	2	0	3	26
10	Rayford, Calvin		1	1	0	0	0	0	0	0	0	0	2	2	0	0	1	3
12	Richey, Patrick		0	0	0	0	0	0	1	1	2	1	0	1	1	0	0	14
00	Ostertag, Greg		3	5	0	0	0	0	0	6	6	1	6	0	0	2	0	15
33	Gurley, Greg		1	1	0	0	0	0	0	1	1	0	2	0	0	0	0	4
21	Pearson, Sean		0	1	0	1	0	0	0	0	0	1	0	0	0	0	0	1
	Team								0	0	0							
	TOTALS		31	52	4	10	17	20	6	21	27	16	83	23	15	5	8	200

Total FG%   1st Half .533   2nd half .682   Game .596   Deadball
3-Pt. FG%   1st Half .333   2nd half .500   Game .400   Rebounds   0
FT%   1st Half .800   2nd half .867   Game .850

INDIANA

No.	Player		Total FG FG	FGA	3-point FG	FGA	FT	FTA	Rebounds Off	Def	Tot	PF	TP	A	TO	Blk	S	Min
33	Graham, Pat	f	0	3	0	1	0	0	0	0	0	1	0	1	2	0	0	11
40	Cheaney, Calbert	f	10	19	0	2	2	2	5	4	9	3	22	1	1	0	0	40
24	Nover, Matt	c	3	5	0	0	3	4	1	6	7	2	9	2	0	0	1	39
20	Graham, Greg	g	8	14	3	4	4	5	2	1	3	4	23	2	5	0	1	33
22	Bailey, Damon	g	3	7	0	1	1	2	4	3	7	4	7	4	4	0	0	27
44	Henderson, Alan		0	1	0	0	0	0	0	0	0	0	0	0	0	0	0	3
30	Leary, Todd		2	7	0	4	2	3	0	0	0	2	6	1	1	0	0	12
25	Knight, Pat		0	0	0	0	0	0	0	0	0	0	0	0	0	0	0	3
21	Reynolds, Chris		0	1	0	1	0	0	0	0	0	1	0	1	1	0	0	5
34	Evans, Brian		4	9	2	2	0	0	4	3	7	3	10	1	1	0	3	27
	Team								2	1	3							
	TOTALS		30	66	5	15	12	16	18	18	36	20	77	13	15	0	5	200

Total FG%   1st Half .444   2nd half.462   Game .455   Deadball
3-Pt. FG%   1st Half .500   2nd half.222   Game .333   Rebounds   1
FT%   1st Half .700   2nd half.833   Game .750

Officials   Paparo, Donato, Patillo
Technical Fouls
Attendance   17,883

Score by Periods	1	2	OT	OT	Final
Kansas	38	45			83
Indiana	34	43			77

SECTION VIII

SEASON RECAP

"A SINGULARLY UNIQUE SEASON."

SEASON TOTALS

Player	GS	Total FG			3-point			Free Throw			Pts	Avg
		FG	FGA	FG%	FG	FGA	FG%	FT	FTA	FT%		
Cheaney, Calbert	35	303	552	.549	47	110	.427	132	166	.795	785	22.4
Graham, Greg	32	180	327	.550	57	111	.514	160	194	.825	577	16.5
Henderson, Alan	25	130	267	.487	1	6	.167	72	113	.637	333	11.1
Nover, Matt	35	147	234	.628	0	0	.000	92	160	.575	386	11.0
Bailey, Damon	24	117	255	.459	38	91	.418	83	114	.728	355	10.1
Graham, Pat	3	31	61	.508	9	21	.429	13	18	.722	84	6.5
Evans, Brian	4	62	146	.425	23	65	.354	37	54	.685	184	5.3
Leary, Todd	4	57	122	.467	22	57	.386	32	36	.889	168	4.8
Reynolds, Chris	13	35	64	.547	0	2	.000	43	71	.606	113	3.2
Others	0	0	4	.000	0	1	.000	11	12	.917	11	1.4
Knight, Pat	0	14	30	.467	0	0	.000	4	9	.444	32	1.0
IU	35	1076	2062	.522	197	464	.425	679	947	.717	3028	86.5
Opponent Totals	35	951	2176	.437	192	533	.360	412	588	.701	2506	71.6

Player	G	Rebounds				PF	D	Ast	TO	Blk	Stl	Min
		Off	Def	Tot	Avg							
Cheaney, Calbert	35	75	148	223	6.4	76	1	84	85	10	33	1181
Graham, Greg	35	39	73	112	3.2	71	1	102	66	8	47	1116
Henderson, Alan	30	90	153	243	8.1	74	1	27	45	43	35	737
Nover, Matt	35	72	135	207	5.9	88	3	26	69	24	11	1013
Bailey, Damon	35	38	79	117	3.3	79	0	144	58	7	20	932
Graham, Pat	13	2	15	17	1.3	16	0	18	15	0	7	205
Evans, Brian	35	32	106	138	3.9	50	0	46	27	5	18	615
Leary, Todd	35	5	29	34	1.0	30	0	43	23	1	12	424
Reynolds, Chris	35	12	57	69	2.0	55	1	102	39	1	29	640
Others	8	0	3	3	0.4	8	0	1	6	0	3	41
Knight, Pat	32	1	16	17	0.5	10	0	27	17	0	3	196
Team Rebounds				101								
IU	35	366	814	1281	36.6	557	7	620	450	99	218	7100
Team rebounds				116								
Opponent Totals	35	382	680	1178	33.7	783	37	468	541	89	198	---

PER GAME AVERAGES

Player	Total FG FG	FGA	3-point FG	FGA	Total FT FT	FTA	Pts	Reb	Ast	TO	Blk	Stl	Min
Cheaney, Calbert	8.7	15.8	1.3	3.1	3.8	4.7	22.4	6.4	2.4	2.4	0.3	0.9	33.7
Graham, Greg	5.1	9.3	1.6	3.2	4.6	5.5	16.5	3.2	2.9	1.9	0.2	1.3	31.9
Henderson, Alan	4.3	8.9	0.0	0.2	2.4	3.8	11.1	8.1	0.9	1.5	1.4	1.2	24.6
Nover, Matt	4.2	6.7	0.0	0.0	2.6	4.6	11.0	5.9	0.7	2.0	0.7	0.3	28.9
Bailey, Damon	3.3	7.3	1.1	2.6	2.4	3.3	10.1	3.3	4.1	1.7	0.2	0.6	26.6
Graham, Pat	2.4	4.7	0.7	1.6	1.0	1.4	6.5	1.3	1.4	1.2	0.0	0.5	15.8
Evans, Brian	1.8	4.2	0.7	1.9	1.1	1.5	5.3	3.9	1.3	0.8	0.1	0.5	17.6
Leary, Todd	1.6	3.5	0.6	1.6	0.9	1.0	4.8	1.0	1.2	0.7	0.0	0.3	12.1
Reynolds, Chris	1.0	1.8	0.0	0.1	1.2	2.0	3.2	2.0	2.9	1.1	0.0	0.8	18.3
Others	0.0	0.5	0.0	0.1	1.4	1.5	1.4	0.4	0.1	0.8	0.0	0.4	5.1
Knight, Pat	0.4	0.9	0.0	0.0	0.1	0.3	1.0	0.5	0.8	0.5	0.0	0.1	6.1
IU	30.7	58.9	5.6	13.3	19.4	27.1	86.5	36.6	17.7	12.9	2.8	6.2	202.9
Team rebounds													
Opponent Totals	27.2	62.2	5.5	15.2	11.8	16.8	71.6	33.7	13.4	15.5	2.5	5.7	—

GENERAL INFORMATION

Score by Period	1	2	OT	OT	Total	Deadball Rebounds
IU	1492	1498	27	11	3028	118
Opponent	1126	1345	28	7	2506	78

Overall Team Record	31-4	Cumulative Attendance	585,965	Avg Attendance	16,742
Big Ten	17-1	Home	245,814	Home	16,388
Preseason NIT	4-0	Away	127,973	Away	12,797
Indiana Classic	2-0	Neutral	213,178	Neutral	21,418
Hoosier Classic	2-0				

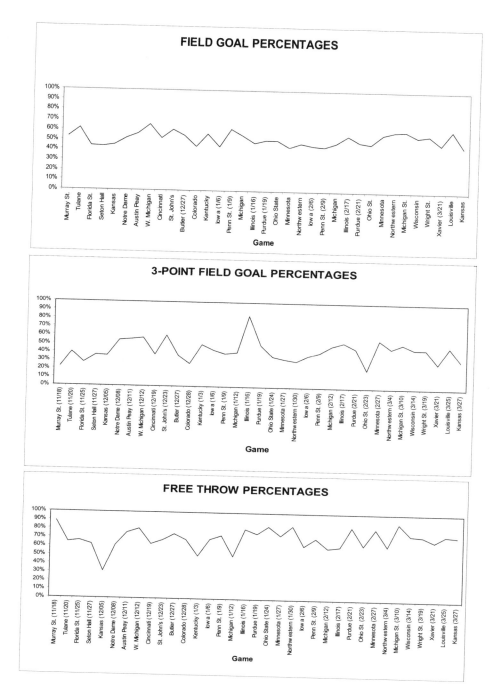

INDIANA AGAINST RANKED OPPONENTS

DATE	TEAM	OPPONENTS RANK	IU RANK	W/L	SCORE
Nov					
20	Tulane	17	4	W	103–80
25	vs. Florida State	7	4	W (OT)	81–78
27	vs. Seton Hall	6	4	W	78–74
Dec					
5	vs. Kansas	3	2	L	69–74
19	Cincinnati	19	4	W	79–64
Jan					
3	vs. Kentucky	3	4	L	78–81
6	Iowa	8	5	W	75–67
12	vs. Michigan	2	6	W	76–75
19	vs. Purdue	13	2	W	75–65
24	Ohio State	24	2	W	96–69
Feb					
6	vs. Iowa	9	1	W	73–66
14	Michigan	4	1	W	93–92
21	Purdue	14	1	W	93–78
Mar					
21	Xavier	22	1	W	73–70
25	vs. Louisville	15	1	W	82–69
27	vs. Kansas	9	1	L	77–83

AFTER INDIANA BASKETBALL

"THE MOST IMPORTANT THING...."

AFTER INDIANA BASKETBALL

Bob Knight's basketball programs have one of the highest graduation rates in the country. Attending classes and receiving a degree are stressed to his players and they respond or leave the program.

This basketball team had a combined grade point average of 2.95 during the fall semester, which was higher than the average for Indiana University that semester.

As you read through this book, you realize how demanding a college basketball season is on coaches, players and staff. It is a tribute to the players that they make grades and receive degrees while playing through four years of 35 game schedules.

Player	Degree	Pro Basketball	Current Profession
Damon Bailey	B.A. Education	CBA	Owns a small business
Calbert Cheaney	B.A. in Arts and Science	NBA	NBA Golden State Warriors
Brian Evans	B.A. Sports Mgt.	NBA	European basketball
Greg Graham	B.A. Health, Physical Ed. and Recreation	NBA	NCAA staff
Pat Graham	B.A. Criminal Justice		Health and rehabilitation
Alan Henderson	B.A. Biology	NBA	NBA Atlanta Hawks
Pat Knight	B.A. Health, Physical Ed. and Recreation	CBA coach	Asst. Coach Texas Tech
Todd Leary	B.A. Sports Mgt.		Financial advisor, IU radio announcer
Todd Lindeman	B.A. Resource Mgt.	CBA	European basketball
Matt Nover	B.A. Business	Japan	European basketball
Chris Reynolds	B.A. Arts and Science, Law Degree		Assoc. Athletic Director, Indiana University

THE BOB KNIGHT RECORD

"BASKETBALL IS MY BUSINESS."

THE BOB KNIGHT RECORD

This narrative of the 1992–93 Indiana University basketball season is taken from 50 separate radio interviews with Coach Bob Knight that were originated as the 35-game season unfolded, game by game, week by week. It provides a behind-the-scenes view of a very good basketball team and an interesting time exposure of Bob Knight.

The focus of this book is the team and the players; however the reader will be drawn to Bob Knight, because this story is told in his own words. It is not filtered or interpreted.

Basketball is Bob Knight's business, and like this book, his record as a college coach speaks for itself. Listed are some of his remarkable coaching accomplishments.

Head Coach—Army	1965 to 1971	.671 record (102-50)
Head Coach—Indiana	1971 to 2000	.734 record (661-240)
Head Coach—Texas Tech	2001 to present	.672 record (45-22)
11 Big Ten Championships	During his 29 years at Indiana	
Olympic Gold Medal	1984 Olympics with amateur players	
25 NCAA Tournaments	24 while at Indiana, 1 with Texas Tech	
3 NCAA Championships	1976, 1981 and 1987	
5 Final Four appearances	1973, 1976, 1981, 1987, and 1992	
14 NBA first-round picks	A long record of developing players	
17 All-Americans	While coaching at Indiana	
4 time Coach of the Year	1975, 1976, 1987 and 1989	
Basketball Hall of Fame	Coach Knight was inducted in 1991	
800 wins	Bob Knight was the youngest of four college coaches to reach 800 wins, and he is the only active coach at that level.	

(Sources: Indiana and Texas Tech Basketball Media Guides)

ABOUT THE AUTHOR

Art Angotti has been involved with Indiana University athletics much of his life. His father, Arthur Angotti, Sr., was a scout for Indiana University from 1945 to 1973, and IU coaches would often stay at the Angotti home in Gary while recruiting high school athletes in the area.

Art Angotti made his own mark in athletics by winning the Indiana High School State Championship in the mile run in 1962. He attended Indiana University on a track scholarship and was a letterman and held indoor records in the 1,000 meter run. He later received the Clevenger Award from the Indiana University Athletic Department.

Upon graduation from Indiana in 1966, Mr. Angotti was commissioned as a Second Lieutenant in the United States Army. In 1967, while serving in Vietnam as an armored cavalry platoon leader, he was wounded in a rocket attack and lost much of his vision and hearing. He was awarded the Purple Heart and several other decorations while serving in the Armed Services.

Angotti returned to Indiana University in1968 and received an MBA degree. He began a career in venture capital that started in Philadelphia and later brought him to Indianapolis, where he now lives. He was a founder and Director of several significant companies, including Indianapolis Cablevision, Indianapolis Cellular Telephone Company, Heritage Management, Artistic Media Partners and Syndicate Systems Inc. He formed and managed four successful venture capital funds. Mr. Angotti was awarded the Distinguished Entrepreneur Award from the Indiana University School of Business.

From 1977 to 1981 he was Associate Professor of Finance at Butler University. He also served on the Washington Township Board of Education in Indianapolis for eight years, serving as its president for two terms.

Mr. Angotti assumed the radio broadcast contract for Indiana University in 1992 on behalf of Artistic Media Partners, because the prior holder of the contract did not want to continue to carry IU sports. He immediately contracted with Coach Knight for the exclusive rights to his pre-game and weekly radio broadcasts. Because he had difficulty hearing the Knight broadcasts, he taped and transcribed the shows so that he could follow the programming.

He and his wife of 35 years, Barbara Weirmiller Angotti, live in Indianapolis. They have two children, Arthur III, is Sr. Vice President of Artistic Media. Laura is a costume and clothing designer and is a graduate student at UCLA.

Art Angotti is the founder and CEO of Artistic Media Partners, a broadcasting company that operates 14 radio stations in Indiana including the flagship stations for the Indiana, Notre Dame and Purdue University sports radio networks.

ARTISTIC MEDIA PARTNERS RADIO STATIONS

BLOOMINGTON, INDIANA

WBWB FM
WHCC FM

SOUTH BEND, INDIANA

WNDV FM
WWLV FM
WZOW FM
WHLY AM
WDND AM
WNDV AM

LAFAYETTE, INDIANA

WAZY FM
WSHP FM
WLFF FM
WLAS AM

FORT WAYNE, INDIANA

WBTU FM
WSHI FM